T0286892

LIGHT FROM ABOVE

LIGHT FROM ABOVE

SACRED SCRIPTURES FOR THE 21ST CENTURY AND BEYOND

MARK AHAVEL
SECOND EDITION

TATE PUBLISHING
AND ENTERPRISES, LLC

Published by Tate Publishing & Enterprises, LLC
127 E. Trade Center Terrace | Mustang, Oklahoma 73064 USA
1.888.361.9473 | www.tatepublishing.com

Tate Publishing is committed to excellence in the publishing industry. The company reflects the philosophy established by the founders, based on Psalm 68:11,
"The Lord gave the word and great was the company of those who published it."

Published in the United States of America

ISBN: 978-1-62746-077-4
1. Religion / Comparative Religion
2. Religion / Biblical Criticism & Interpretation / General
14.03.12

Dedicated to peoples of faith everywhere who hear and hearken to the voice of the Global God.

Acknowledgements

First, I want to acknowledge the influence that all my Christian college and seminary professors have had on me, but there are too many to mention by name. There are also two nationally and internationally known Christian leaders whom I had the opportunity to personally meet both in the 1990s: the renowned apologist Dr. Ravi Zacharias and my leadership mentor Dr. John Maxwell. They both have had a real influence on my thinking through the many cassette tapes on their teachings which I had listened to.

In 2005, I consciously expanded my spiritual horizon to get a more firm grasp on universal truths, and so had attended the local Baha'i House a few times. They had freely given me a Baha'i prayer book and a booklet *Thoughts on Peace and Prayers* which was the beginning point of my study of the Baha'i Faith in recent years. And I want to acknowledge and thank also Dr. Benjamin Coen for supplying me with two of the main sacred Baha'i Scriptures, namely *The Kitab-I-Aqdas* and *The Kitab-I-Iqan (The Book of Certitude)*, gifts from his own home library in 2008. Reading directly from the writings of Baha'ullah brought me directly to the source of the Baha'i beliefs, and therefore, more accurate knowledge, and likewise the similarities and differences the Baha'i beliefs have with Judaism, Christianity, and Islam.

During these years of broadening my religious studies and while on a quest for universals, I happened upon a Wayne Dyer PBS special on television called "Excuses Be Gone." I want to acknowledge him for his insight in so naturally and beautifully communicating the connection of the "Source, Creator, God, Tao" as basically all referring to the same Ultimate entity, just different words of communicating it. This harmonizing view of the Ultimate Power I found intriguing. It directly influenced my thinking and it has manifest into this book here and there.

Opening Verses

God, not merely the God of Jerusalem or Haifa, not merely the God of Mecca or Medina, not merely the God of Bam or Yazd, not merely the God of Allahabad or Amritsar, not merely the God of Benares or Gangotri, not merely the God of Lombini or Lhasa,, not merely the God of Gobekli-Tepe[1] or Istbanbul, and not merely the God of Rome or Rizvan, or any other sacred place on earth, but the global God... who through the ages has been enlightening millions of human souls around the world...

In this new millennium and early 21st century, greatly facilitated by global awareness through globalization, it is dawning on more and more people of these faith traditions, lay and ordained alike, that God cannot only be the God of specific places and spaces alone, but the God of the whole earth... the global God.

The global God has inspired prophet-sages and founding fathers and mothers of faith throughout the ages communicating truth, His eternalness, His sovereignty, thoughtfulness, righteousness, wisdom, mercy, compassion, grace, and love and other truths, leading humanity to worship God. His messages came through these prophet-sages who founded faiths in different continents and regions and in different human cultures.

Some prophets since ancient times have proclaimed God as the God of the whole earth. The prophet-sages, received and experienced

Divine messages which they attempted to purely convey through the imperfect medium of language and received by impure and imperfect peoples. The messages were embedded in cultures and received imperfectly through the cultural eyes, and within the limits of their geographical, historical, national, and political boundaries, none completely understood or purely received by any people because of each their own limitations of knowledge, experience, cultural boundaries, and impure natures.

People historically were so tied to their tribal loyalties and rooted to their ancestral lands and the ancestral lands of their founders' faiths, and each establishing their sacred sites, their holy places.

Despite all of the Divine messages being imperfectly understood, God placed such a sense of the sacred in humans from ancient times and in every age, deeply sensing the sacred of the visible and invisible realms, and sensing the Source.

Peoples of faith in many places heard the voice of the Divine through the human messengers. Greatly blessed are the names of these prophets upon the lips of all the faithful: Spitama Zarathrustra, Moses, Isaiah, Daniel, Gautama Buddha, Mahavira, Jesus Christ, Muhammad, Guru Nanak, the Bab (Ali Muhammad), Baha'ullah (Husayn Ali), and others. The faiths that some of these founders birthed into universal faiths, each in their own traditions, developed into living historic universal faiths, traditions that are still strong in the 21st century. Dawning on more and more souls in the 21st century is the awareness of and hearing the voice of the Divine through many faith traditions, while maintaining a footing within their own faith tradition.

Moreover, the truth has dawned that if God created all peoples, then God is for all peoples.

This truth should not negate truth of previous revelation of God covenanting with specific peoples on earth through whom God planned to bring His mercy and grace, light and love to all peoples around the world, as was prophesied, "and through you [Abram] all the families of the earth will be blessed."[2] This revelation of God's promise to Abram (and the Abrahamic covenant) has often historically been interpreted tangibly, focusing more on the physical descendency aspect of this covenant, but God's word is spiritual, and His desire has been that the Abrahamic blessings blossom out to all the tribes, peoples, families of the earth through the centuries. It is impossible that this seminal prophecy to be fulfilled by physical descendency and interpretation alone. It is to be understood spiritually which then requires faith If it is then by faith, let us stop focusing on race, but focus on God's grace. As each person accepts the truth of God's desire to bless all the families of the earth, this prophecy one-by-one slowly comes true. Your faith is a part of the living historic fabric of faith. The complete fulfillment of this prophecy is yet to come...

God desires to bless all His children. Whether you are a man or woman or a youth from whatever culture, ethnicity, or nationality of the earth, God desires to bless! Look first and foremost to the spiritual blessings, since tangible circumstances in this world of problems often does not reveal it. God's word has power through His promises and prophecy. Our faith is vital to effecting that power. Faith is facilitated and strengthened when looking to the word and promises of God. As a result, our actual faith is vital in the fulfilling of this most blessed prophecy and promise of God.

Faith is from the heart and soul which engages the mind. Because its from the invisible realm of heart and soul, science will never be able to fully unlock the mystery of faith, especially since faith is also directed to the invisible Source and Power of the whole universe. Within humanity, the eternity via the soul and the temporal, the earthly body, converge. This mystery has been contemplated by virtually all mystics, prophet-sages, and philosophers from ancient times to modern.

Faith, even faith in a global God, is for all kinds of minds (intellects). It is for those who have intellectual challenges to those who are very gifted intellectually and everyone in between. It is the mind, though, that doubts and can shut off faith in our soul by what it is *exposed to. Feeding the mind words that instill a good faith is good for the soul. Everyone, whatever kind of mind God has given them, should find something in these Scriptures to connect with and make it your own!.*

The voice of these Scriptures is a burgeoning human voice of millions whose souls, hearts, and minds in whom this truth of a global God resonates and in whom have become more conscious in the 21st century.

The power of these Scriptures, from the Source, the Sovereign God, goes out to all the earth like a loud trumpet, calling millions of souls to receive the blessed Scriptures In their minds and hearts.

O Precious soul who has searched and searched a religion with a universal outlook that speaks your heart-language, search these Scriptures also for truth, knowledge, wisdom, and life.

Search Scriptures for truth.

Search Scriptures for words that inspires and gives hope in this life and for the blessed eternal life to come.

Search these Scriptures to find seeds of true peace, that planted today, may bear fruit of peace for decades, even hundreds of years to come.

God, OM, the Source, the Eternal One, the All-Powerful and Sovereign of the universe, full of glory and majesty and holiness and integrity and perfect judgment, worthy of all praise, be praised, worshipped, thanked, loved and adored by all His human children now and forevermore! Amen.

CONTENTS

INTRODUCTION

The Scriptures of the great world's religions have withstood the test of time. Most of them were actually penned in ancient times.[3] Humanity has developed so much since then in thought, in social justice and human rights including equality, as well as in technology[4]. Humanity has "came of age," but most of the sacred Scriptures for the billions of peoples of faith on Earth are ancient. They have been the voice of faith for millions of human souls for as long as three millennia![5] This awareness was an impetus to the writing of this book. When viewed this way, it makes sense to have fresh Scriptures for the 21st century.

This is a great testament to these faiths which have endured through the centuries, and weathered the storms of great controversies and eventually earning the title "great faiths." Or, is it as much a testament to the religious nature of human beings and their tenaciously clinging to traditions brought into the modern age in which contemporary traditional believers are living on the fumes of past glory and triumph of their religions? This is stated only to provoke thought, not to reflect an attitude of arrogance, and to pave the way to expressing a rationale for this book below.

Peace is one of the main purposes of this book, global peace through religious faith, through an articulation of a fresh text which understands the differences and by God's Spirit can help to bridge the differences. In order to work toward peace, we must begin with a deep respect for peoples of all faith traditions and a respect for the foundations of these great faiths which have been laid in past ages: their prophets and Scriptures. We can affirm other Scriptures outside our own faith tradition in so far as we don't find a major incongruency with our own Scriptures. We also have the freedom to disagree with certain statements, premises, notions, assertions, interpretations, and teachings. We should also stretch our own understanding by study, careful study even of various Scriptures. Understanding is vitally important for all people working for peace. Finding and connecting people together through universals is one of the keys.

The better we understand other religions, the better we understand the people who adhere to them.

These Scriptures from beginning to end attempt to capture universals, never before perhaps expressed with such clarity, while maintaining a monotheistic perspective. It attempts to carry forward the thought, knowledge, wisdom, and faith from the great monotheistic Scriptures of the past, into the 21st century. God has already given much inspired Scriptures from ancient times. That wheel does not need to be reinvented, but carried forward in a fresh manner for this age. It does not attempt to meld all the faith traditions into one syncretic super-faith. Everyone should find some light, truth, wisdom, and peace in this book, whatever one's faith tradition. All are invited to read. The author has attempted to express the intended heart of these Scriptures to be a truth-gatherer6, a bridge-builder, and peace-maker among the billions of people on Earth yet consistently maintaining its monotheistic footing. This new Scripture attempts to capture, and culminate many of the truths from the great monotheistic traditions' Scriptures and other Scriptures and bring them into the present, articulating them in a fresh way for people in the

21st century. Because of the monotheistic moorings, the former Scriptures foundations are: the Torah and Bible (Judaism, Christianity), the Avesta (Zoroastrianism), the Quran (Islam), the Adi Granth (Sikhism), and the writings of Baha'ullah (Baha'i Faith). There are some incongruencies that the Quran and the Baha'i Scriptures have with the Bible, and in these cases, I side with the Bible in part because of their great light and spiritual strength through the testing of time, and because they are the Scriptures of my heritage.

While a study of the world's religions is not necessary to read or get the essence of this book, a person having a course in world religions would be better positioned to comprehend the breadth and depth of this text, particularly the Didactic section. The author references all the conscious sources used, but there is no doubt hundreds if not thousands of unconscious allusions or close parallels with passages in other of the world's sacred Scriptures.

In attempting to be a bridge of peace to humanity through sacred literature, it synthesizes and harmonizes, even, for example, Eastern concepts such as the Chinese phrase "yin and yang" in the creation narrative in an attempt to bridge East and West. But it is strongest in the truths and universality of the Abrahamic religions. These faiths have been ringing such a clear universal sound from ancient days of the first millennium BCE which has been remarkable. But it is not only the Middle Eastern monotheistic faiths that produced universal religions. The East too produced what they believed to be universal. Indian Emperor Asoka of the 3rd cent. BCE is a good example. After embracing Buddhism and believing it to be a universal religion worthy to be embraced by non-Indians, he sent Buddhist missionary-monks outside India throughout Southeast and East Asia (Hopfe and Woodward pg. 141).

THE RATIONALE FOR THIS BOOK

This book desires to express and expound upon many of the universally held truths even for people in the 21st century, to express them in fresh ways, blending new material along with reflections flowing out of past Scriptures. The Scriptures of past origins are well established and well accepted. Their adherents are not looking to replace them. Therefore, a rationale should be provided as to why a new Scripture. But the following rationale is more at the scholarly level. Those who are not scholarly, and desire to keep your pure "child-like" faith, I recommend you skip this section, and to go right to the first page of the text. The statements of rationale below will most likely not help your faith; it may even cause some confusion.

There were specific things stirring in the author's mind that produced seed-thoughts for writing a new Scripture. These are points of which the author was conscious, and may be called seed-thoughts that stirred in him leading him to eventually write this book. But because of His own traditional background, to write a new Scriptures seemed unthinkable, and he would have not begun to write a Scripture without the impetus of actual fresh insights that came to his mind ("fresh material") starting in 2004 (see Author's Story in the Postscripts). This next section details general and specific biblical and theological points that ultimately led the author to construct a sacred text for the twenty-first century.

The Bible was not only one of the greatest literary achievements of all time, but an unparalleled spiritual achievement of its kind, still held in high regard, but it was written in ancient times, reflects an older culture, held to some archaic notions, and its essence needs to be brought into the 21st century but the archaic things left behind. Two examples I give from the Torah/Pentateuch. The first is the view of God as a warrior-God (c.f. Ex. 15:3a) who fought for the ancient Israelites in their deliverance from bondage to Egypt. These passages were seminal in the forming of God's people Israel, but a "fighting God", after thousands of years of human beings killing each other, is no longer an acceptable image for God or His character. An example of archaic, in the literal sense, stemmed from the ancient people's lack of knowledge in the world of science. They apparently did not know what mold was when it was found growing on the walls of some of their homes. So it was called a "leprous plague" and the priest was to be called in to examine it (c.f. Lev. 14:33-48). It would be many centuries later before human beings would discover what mold it, a type of fungus. They had no bleach then to take care of mold. Today, we have this knowledge. Applying bleach is a solution remedy for such a problem. Calling the priest no longer seems necessary, but it has been embedded in the Torah which is viewed entirely as God's word by tradition. But God has given us the ability to understand these issues. We can capture the essence of the whole Torah and all the Prophets, but leave behind archaic understandings and practices which were based on the lack of knowledge.

The Bible and other sacred Scriptures have some divinely sanctioned violent verses which mandate violence. These verses have generally become embarrassing to modern sensitivities. Passages in the Bible, specifically the Torah/Pentateuch books of Leviticus and Deuteronomy, and the book of Joshua contain strong verses of sanctioning genocide: Deut. 3:6; 7:1-2; 9:3; Josh. 9:24, commanding the Israelites to kill the inhabitants of Canaan, even men, women, and children. These are descriptive historical texts which became a part of holy Scripture. But believers of sound mind after those early days of the Israelite conquest of Canaan do not interpret those passage *prescriptively*, but *descriptively*. In other words, God is not commanding the readers since that age to do the same, namely kill Canaanites. It was a command for that ancient historical context. That was a real time and a real place with special circumstances in which young Israel believed God was leading them on a military campaign to take the land of Canaan, based on God's promise of this land to them and their descendents, and it required mass killing of the peoples, they believed, so as not to be corrupted into false worship by their gods and cultic shrines. This context has not fit any context of peoples of faith ever since that time, but the account gets locked into sacred Scripture for all time and becomes embarrassing now for modern believers. To establish a text truly on peace, any verses that even hint of violence must be left out. In addition to the verses just cited above, there are two verses in Genesis, Gen. 38:7, 10 which says YHWH God killed two different individuals, both for a different reason. In vs. 7, God kills Er and in vs. 10, God kills Onan. The way these verses occur back-to-back and the harsh, even seemingly very unjust killing of Onan simply for deliberately not impregnating his widowed sister-in-law, strongly suggests a different voice behind this passage presenting God as a ruthless killer instead of a God of mercy and love. The passage does not seem to speak the voice of the Spirit of God but a human voice who had become a bit ruthless who witnessed enough killings in his life to have gotten a little bitter. But suggesting a human voice got worked into sacred Scripture presents a problem with divine inspiration of the whole of Scripture such as where Paul writes, "All Scripture is inspired by God..." (II Tim. 3:16) for which this author has no easy answer. Its also passages such as these that led not only Marcion but even modern students of the Bible to believe that there are two different portrayals of God, one in the Old Testament and one in the New Testament. Here is also one example from the book of Psalms, the hymnbook of the 2nd Temple period, that also contains a verse that seems to support careless violence. Ps. 137:8a, 9 reads, "O daughter of Babylon... happy [shall he be] who takes and dashes your little ones against the rock." A new text in the 21st cent. with a main goal of building a solid foundation of peace must leave such passages behind. Import the great faith and its universal principles but leave behind the polemics and passages which advocate violence which greatly impedes peace.

I assert that every former Scripture, especially when it has prophecies, has had a Self-Fulfilling Prophecy effect as the Scriptures were passed from generation to generation by its people. If they are good prophesies, such as Gen. 12:3, God desiring to bless all the families of the earth, it can be a good thing. But there may be some negative components that have created a self-fulfilling prophecy and carried forward for centuries, even over two thousand years. From my studies, I am convinced that one of the factors behind Jews being mistreated in most places of the world where they were dispersed to is that they attracted it by their mental view of an "Enemies-Around-Us" complex which was informed by their ancient Hebrew Scriptures. These Scriptures were passed on from generation to generation which perpetuated this complex for ages. It was lived out in real history, even carried forward all the way through the 20th century. The horrific Holocaust and modern Israel being surrounded by hostile Arab nations are modern manifestations of this "Enemies-Around-Us complex. This complex is by no means the whole reason, but a real factor. There are dozens of examples of biblical verse that contributed to the informing of this complex. For just one example, see Ps. 6:10. Unrighteous and ungodly people would join in with the "enemies" of Jews, mock them or mistreat them. But the righteous stand with the Jewish people. The reality of this complex should lead all people of biblical faith and all righteous persons to have compassion on Jews and all descendants of Israel. Moreover, peoples of the biblical faith, especially Christians, should realize how this complex actually ties into the all important doctrine of salvation. The "Enemies-around-us" complex became a driving force to salvation theology, the need for the coming of a delivering Messiah. This richness can now be appreciated. This complex opens the door to outsiders of this faith to potentially harbor ill-will although it is entirely inexcusable, inappropriate, unspiritual and God-dishonoring. Can these Scriptures be brought into our world without bringing all its elements? By default, all those "enemy" passages in the Hebrew Scriptures, which should be interpreted in their original historical context, becomes a part of the spirituality of this tradition. But a new Scripture could be written that desires to leave behind ancient hostile contexts that may have produced a negative spiritual aspect perpetuated by self- fulfilling prophecy and solidly plant a path of peace. The author has concluded that the "enemy-around-us" complex is an unhealthy spiritual aspect, while at the same time holding tension a high view of the biblical Scriptures that are the voice and light of God. Sacred Scriptures are generally embedded in cultural, historical, and social contexts reflecting these aspects while also becoming sacred Scriptures to believers and pious ones.

Human beings have advanced in thought, in spirituality, in cultural, and socially the last 2000 years. The world is ready for a text that reflects great universal truths and reflects the human advancement, e.g. on rights and equality. Some, especially Baha'is, believe that their Scriptures written by Baha'ullah do this. Indeed, the Baha'i Scriptures, written in the later half of the19[th] century, are the most modern of any Scripture of the global faiths. But while the Baha'i Faith strongly asserts the continuity of all the past religion manifestations, it significantly departs from its predecessor monotheistic religions which also originated in the Middle East when it comes to the doctrine of Heaven and Hell. All the other traditions: Zoroastrianism, Judaism, Christianity, and Islam all believe in Heaven and Hell as literal places, but the Baha'i Faith does not believe in these are real places, only states. The Baha'i founder was from an Islamic context, but he appears to have also been influenced by esoteric inclinations and Gnosticism which are points of departure from the Abrahamic faiths thus presenting a real challenge to the Baha'i faith to be truly that bridge for all these established traditions that preceded them.

It was not just some social aspects that need to be updated and brought into the 21ˢᵗ century but even some notions, practices, and development of theology. The Hebrew Scriptures are remarkable in achieving the concept of a universal God, but it was still a practicing temple-centered cult of animal sacrifices until the Second Temple was destroyed 70 CE Western civilization for a significant portion was founded on the legal moral codes going back to Moses, and civilization advanced, but the Scriptures were locked in their ancient past; they need to be updated, brought into the present;

The majority of Christians that the author has been acquainted with have a pessimistic view, believing we are living in the End Times, soberly and not eagerly awaiting the dreadful eschatological prophecies to come, as they understand. And this may be true, which means that more tribulation, even the Great Tribulation, is still to come. This can be a frightful thing but God does not want His peoples to live in fear. We should not forget about the beautiful optimistic prophecy of Gen. 12:3 which also has not been fulfilled either. Why not emphasis this one and get more positive? Both views arise from different prophecies in the same Bible. This Scripture emphasis a positive view to balance the predominate pessimism of today, and inspire fellow human beings.

Finally, there are some people of the biblical faiths that may say that producing a new text breaks the Scriptural command "not to add to it nor take away from it" (Deut. 12:32) with penalty of receiving the plagues in the book or one's name being taken out of the book of life (Rev. 22:18-19). The author takes very seriously the whole of the biblical Scriptures and these verses in particular too. But his view is that one who thinks this Scripture is breaking those biblical Scriptural is misunderstanding, misinterpreting, and misapplying those two verses. The proper interpretation of both Deut. 12:32 and Rev. 22:18-19, the author submits, is first a pre-canon interpretation. The Deuteronomy passage states it applies to any of God's commands. We can apply it to all the commands in the book of Deuteronomy, then also all the commands in all the Torah/Pentateuch, such as in Exodus and Leviticus. And the Rev. 22 passage says "the words of the prophecy of this book" which means the book of Revelation. But later on, after each of the Testaments got canonized, some may come to apply these stern warnings for the whole of Scripture. And the author would say it is safe to do this. It is better not to tamper with Scripture at all than for, say a monk in copying a biblical manuscript, to have inserted a couple words to flesh out the meaning, at least the meaning he thinks was intended, but the monk could be wrong. This is a brand new book written ages after the biblical Scriptures. It does not add or take away from any of those words as the author understands it. Many of the teachings in this book begins with a biblical basis, and then brings discussion of these topics up to the contemporary time, providing some continuity via teaching, but not actually adding or taking away from the words in the biblical Scriptures.

These eight points lays a rationale for the producing of this text that has come to the authors' mind. You may have a few thoughts yourself or different ways to express the essence of my points.

THE PURPOSES AND GOALS OF THIS BOOK

The purposes of this Scripture are fourfold:

1) to manifest a Scripture, founded on the great Scriptures of the past, from a monotheistic viewpoint, that presents the faith in God anew and relevant for the 21st century,

2) to maintain the relevancy of faith in this age of rationalism and secularism,

3) to strengthen the faith of believers or would-be believers in this generation and time to come, and

4) to be saturated with goodness and peace, sowing a foundation of religious peace for the 21st century.

The goals therefore are that these Scriptures serve as a bridge-builder of understanding among the faith traditions, bringing together motifs and topics, being honest about the differences but striving for unity in areas where unity can be achieved. In regard to relevancy, it has goals of touching these dimensions of human life: religiously/theologically, culturally, socially and scientifically-sound. The heart-intent of this work is to help bring people on earth draw closer together spiritually.

Not everyone will see it this way. A popular view among scholars and other educated persons is that all Scriptures are merely human inventions, along with the many epics, myths, sagas, tales, legends, and tragedies. Story-tellers, in their view, spun all the epics and tales including those of gods, fashioning them often in man's image. But this position fails to see the true God of Heaven and Earth. Yes, there have been many story-tellers through the ages. But the Spirit of God can also use this gift to craft stories that tell sacred truths of Heaven and Earth.

Historic sacred Scriptures, having a long living history, are dynamic in their received audiences, interpretations, and applications. The original authors for the most part did not state their agenda, or rather, their specific goals they personally may have wanted to accomplish by their writing. This author, being the single author of this text, is advantaged by this hindsight to state his agenda for this book. If he were asked, it is these five goals:

1) to instill and strengthen a global, universal faith in the Creator and Supreme God;

2) to increase sacred knowledge, wisdom, and truths in people around the world;

3) to educate and nurture a strong value in the sacred stewardship of this Earth and all its resources, underpinned by the belief that this whole Earth belongs to God, who has given us humans a responsibility to take good care of it;

4) to lay a solid and sure foundation for global peace (as much as a religious text could do); and

5) build a stronger bridge in the religious and ecumenical communities.

This book takes a bold step in calling itself "Scriptures." Only posterity will truly tell whether these Scriptures become sacred Scriptures received by many, received in their hearts, or simply a well-intended and religiously rich book shelved in libraries. The dream is that one day it will be accepted in the world's sacred Scriptures Hall of Faith.

With this in mind, the author looked to the Bible for inspiration as a model for the basic structure of this Scripture. Initially, a three-fold outline was established: Narrative, Prophecy/Poetry, and Wisdom/Teaching. It was amazing to see how the many thoughts that came to the author beginning in 2004 all the way to 2012, who diligently wrote them all down, beautifully fell within this structure. As the book was being compiled, the Poetry section was made its own section, and a fitting final Exhortations section was added at the end. All the sections are fresh material for this age but often spring out of the foundation of former sacred Scriptures especially the Bible.

The Narrative section begins with the story before the beginning of the Creation, which may not have ever been written in such a way and to such detail in a Scripture before, but brings out some truths held by many in a fresh way. Ancient Scriptures speak of the various heavenly beings like angels, Yazata, cherubim, seraphim, and "elders," but none of the prior texts describes their creation, that the author is aware. The next narrative on the Creation of the Material Universe is meant to parallel the Creation account in the Bible in many ways and yet bring it into the 21st century in line with the much greater scientific knowledge we have today. The observant reader who is also familiar with the Genesis narrative will quickly find that there are also seven days of Creation in this text, but what happens on each day progresses much more in sensible fashion of the formation of the universe, solar system, and Earth, based on our scientific understanding. The author is aware that Bible fundamentalists may be unhappy with this changing the story. The author suggests that fundamentalists view this text as good reading if nothing more than fiction, not as Scripture. The author reminds the readers that this work attempts to harmonize modern humanity's understanding of this universe scientifically on the premise that God did create this universe. Science, while it is flawed, still tells us a lot about this universe, and there should be no conflict between science and faith in God, in theory anyway. But in reality, contemporary atheistic scientists are debating with believing scientists, and the issues get politicized.

The Prophetic section is written with a distinct prophetic voice, and it is distinct from the Narrative voice and distinct from the Wisdom-Teaching sections, yet the whole book is unified in its view and worldview and connected themes. Prophets are great discerners and "judges" of spiritual condition, judging goodness from evilness, morality from immorality, based most often from a standard from God according to former Scripture.

On occasion, the prophets of old could put the fear of God in people using the threat of God's judgment for trying to get the right faith and behavior from people. The reader should always distinguish this type of discerning-judging thought from God's judgment of the eternal destiny of all individual human souls. God alone, who is no mortal being, judges peoples souls. The preaching of hell by some preachers in the last 2000 years is not in the spirit of preaching the Good News, and they sometimes error in crossing over that line whose power to judge the eternal destiny of souls belongs to God alone. This is one of the convictions expressed in this book, something that seems to be held to be true by most monotheists. The gross preaching of hell that seems only to turn most people away from religion. There are these two realms of judgment, the temporal (earthly) and eternal. The fuzzy line to distinguish is that God, however, has given His authority to His prophets to bring His word to many people and that word has included condemnation of sins and warnings of eternal consequences. People of faith, when their hearts and spirits are receptive, recognize the voice of God when they hear it. The author strives to present a clear voice of God for today, expressing a prophetic voice. Prophetic voices often calls for discernment and judgments. The readers are not to interpret this as personal judgments of the author but as a true prophetic voice, if the message can be separated from the messenger, while attempting to be sensitive to today's audience including gender sensitive issues.

The Poetry section is a creatively fresh section. God blessed the author with some degree of poetic writing skill, dabbling in it occasionally through the years. He had also written a couple hymns while serving in the former pastorate.

The Didactic/Teaching section is a series of teaching discourses by the teacher to disciples and all peoples of faith who are readers or hearers these words. The teacher tries to capture a universal voice who can be seen as a spiritual teacher, pastor, rabbi, priest, guru, depending on one's own tradition. The reader is invited in. His disciples have gathered and sat. Sit comfortably as you set aside the concerns and worries of life's demands, and learn and grow in your faith. The teacher views the disciples and all people who read or hear as his brothers or sisters in faith. He does not place himself on a divine pedestal. He does not claim to be an incarnation of a deity. The same Spirit in Him has breathed through many sages, prophets, and disciples through the ages. The style of language is didactic, distinct from the voice of the Prophetic section and the Narrative section. But there are some exact same topics between the Prophecy and Teaching sections that are correlative and complementary.

This book is an imperfect work that no doubt could undergo many revisions in the future.

As you enter these Scriptures, may you engage your spirit and mind. With your God-given intellectual mind, may you think and ponder the messages, may you make spiritual and intellectual connections of truths, religious ideas and how they relate, and may you gain a much better historical understanding of this topics within the faith communities and history in general.

You are invited to this feast of beautiful religious words. You have entered in through the opening verses, which may have already touched your heart, soul, or mind. As you enter in the Scriptures that continue below, the author's prayer for you is:

May you find many truths that ring out from these pages. May you draw strength of faith for this life even unto the hereafter. May you find comfort and be assured of a blessed eternal hope. May these words bring you to greater spiritual understanding. And may these words truly touch you with goodness, hope, and spiritual nobility.

PART I
NARRATIVE

IN THE BEGINNING

The Story of the Pre-Material Universe and the Creating of the Heavenly Beings

God...the Eternal One, the Progenitor of all things ("the Source"), before the beginning of the world, was perfect, holy, secure, and absolute. God was alone, as humans would understand it, yet complete and not needy in His aloneness. There was no incompleteness in the Single Being of the pre-universe. But in this God-only pre-universe, there were three things that made no sense: kingdom, communication and companionship. A great king needs a kingdom which requires other beings; and other beings are also required for communication and companionship. With whom could God communicate? God could speak, but who would hear? In God's perfect planning, He willed create two sets of heavenly, spiritual, perfect creatures with whom He could communicate, share His grandiose plans, and receive praise and worship from. The first set are the heavenly Counselors, and the second set are the myriads of angels.

In this early Heaven's time, before the temporal universe and earthly time, by His Word, God created the first of two sets of heavenly creatures: the heavenly beings who would continually dwell around the circle of His glorious throne. In human words, they may be called God's Advisors or Counselors, but there is no counsel they could give God that God was not already aware of because God has perfect and comprehensive knowledge and intelligence. Yet, as heavenly creatures, they each had individual consciousness and they all desired to live in God's presence continually. As God's heavenly circle of Advisors, they were intimately close to God. They could discuss God's plan in their holy circle, and even ask God questions. They could not read the mind of God and yet they were so close to Him they knew His heart and will. They participate in and bear witness of all God's glory. They are continually in awe before His Majesty. They intimately listen to God, and adore and worship God continually.

Once the spiritual counselors were created, they were each placed in their positions, around the circle of God's holy Throne. Each of the Advisors had equal distance to God's Throne, and in equal standing. There was no Advisor ranked higher or more influential than another. They were newly created and newly brought together in this heavenly Advisor's circle around God's Throne. Being in full awe of the wonder and majesty of God, they began their continual adoration and worship of God. Their first response was to prostrate themselves in complete adoration, devotion, and worship of holy Creator, Omnipotent, Supreme, Majestic, Glorious Eternal One. They had instant awareness of themselves, God, and each other. They each had individual consciousness and yet each were so intimately connected to each other and God. Their worship of God continued for a time that is only known by Heaven's time. There was a break from the intense action of worship, a moment of holy pause. And this opened up a social moment between themselves to greet one another for the first time. They exchanged holy salutations. Periodically, in between times of more active worship, they would have holy conversations among themselves, but the conversations centered on the awesomeness, majesty, and love of God. They looked upon each other and yet there was not even the slightest taint of sin such as jealousy that another was slightly closer to God than him/herself. In their worship of God, they often did not feel the need to speak since the love-communication being exchanged between God and them was at a higher and deeper level, a heavenly telepathy of sorts.

The highest form of communication and companionship was established through the creation and presence of the heavenly Advisors. Their role of worshipping God, the highest act any creature of God can return to God, was one of their important roles. They also had the role of intimately hearing the heavenly words of God, including God's plans, and discussing it. There was one more special role that God gave the Advisors in addition to worshipping God and serving on the eternal heavenly Council: to record, write and keep Heaven's books. To call these heavenly beings "Advisors" does not convey the full reality of their purpose, function, and being-hood.

Now that God had the circle of heavenly Advisors in place, any upcoming plans that God in His perfect wisdom would plan, He would announce beforehand in His holy heaven. It reverberated out His holy Throne to the circle of the heavenly Council. The glory, majesty, awe, holiness, and wisdom which emanates from Heaven cannot be comprehended by people in their unglorified state.

God announced His plan for creating a second set of heavenly beings: Angels: Seraphim, Cherubim (collectively commonly called "angels," but most of them are not "messengers" to people on earth in human history). God communicated His grandiose plan when He announced that He was going to create myriads of

Angels: Seraphim, Cherubim, a whole heavenly host that could hardly be numbered. The Advisors fell down and worshipped God. They said, "Blessing and glory and might be to our God, amen!" They felt no insecurity from this announcement of having other creatures in Heaven besides themselves, because in their holiness and perfect trust in and love of God, they knew that His plans are perfect and pure.

God spoke, and a myriad of Angels: Seraphim, Cherubim were created, each according to their kind: the flying creatures, the bright fiery ones, and the beautiful cherubs, all very beautiful creatures. And God placed them in rows like a tremendous choir around a sanctuary, circling all around His glorious throne, outside the circle of Counselors. Most of them had wings with which they could fly around heaven, but they stayed stationary in their places, beautifully arrayed in three-dimensional space around the Throne, like the most obedient of soldiers, until God sends anyone of them or a whole company of them out for special tasks.

But what all the Advisors and Angels: Seraphim, Cherubim had in common was that they were heavenly holy creatures of God, they were all beautiful, they did not age, for they were immortal, and they all had sleepless eyes, eyelids that never needed to close for sleep. They could and did peer in and see the glory, majesty, and even see the Being of God, for they were truly holy, but the Light emanating from the Being of God is so bright that only pure heavenly creatures can steadily peer in.

All the heavenly creatures, the Advisors and myriads of angels came out of the Being of God by God's creative power. It could be said that God "begot" them all, but this is a human metaphor trying to express the divine reality. God does not have a consort and did not have children in the human sense. But all His creatures are His children. This is a mystery how myriads of heavenly angelic beings can come out of God or rather, how they were created out of nothing by the power of God. They were generated by the Word and by the power of the holy Supreme Progenitor Being: God. (God produced such a beautiful array of holy spiritual beings that later humans called angels that would dazzle the human soul and imagination, those who caught glimpses of them.)

Now after all the angels were created, God called the first holy convocation in Heaven with the Advisors and all the angels. It was the first grand worship service and celebration in Heaven. The Advisors and the angels saw each other and met for the first time, and there was no sin, not even the slightest hint of jealousy between these groups that the Advisors are a little closer to God than the angels, or that the angels get to move around and fly whereas the Advisors were basically perpetually stationary. That would seem to get old after awhile, but only if you are mortal. They are immortal and holy and never grow tired of being awed in God's presence, adoring and worshipping Him. All the created beings were in full awe and wonderment of God, the focus of everyone's attention. There was complete love between God and the heavenly creatures. The grand convocation began with God calling forth seven angels each with a trumpet, positioned around the circle facing out, blasting out a loud sound in unison in such a strength and tone that reverberated throughout Heaven and into the great Expanse although no one was out in the emptiness of the black Expanse to hear or feel it. And a holy hush fell upon every heavenly creature: Then, after a pause, the great voice of God spoke, "I AM." And all the heavenly creatures—Advisors and angels—in one accord bowed down before God on His Throne, and raising themselves up, jubilantly burst out the great heavenly praise song, "Glory and majesty, praise and thanksgiving, eternal kindness and love be to You, most holy God Supreme, for ever and ever!" This became the heavenly chorus. The angels, whom God also gifted with song, sung this holy chorus in a round between the divisions of angels, while the advisers continually prostrated themselves before the throne. The divisions of angels are not ranks like humans have ranks between the more powerful and the lesser powerful, but division by creature type: seraphim, cherubim, and messengers. And this worship celebration went on for a time which human time cannot delineate. This was the first grand convocation and worship service and celebration in Heaven.

The Angels, Seraphim, Cherubim were distinct from the Advisors in position, function, and appearances. The Angels: Seraphim, Cherubim were all around, but outside the circle of Advisors, but there was no barrier the circle created from seeing or being in the presence around His Throne. The Advisors and Angels: Seraphim, Cherubim, were all fellow heavenly creatures of God. Their position and role was also distinct from the circle of Advisors. Where the Advisors perpetually remained in their position around the throne's circle, the angels could move around. Some would later be sent as messengers to humans on earth. They have wings to fly whereas the Advisors do not.

Their appearances were distinguishable from the heavenly Advisors. The Advisors form was like that of a human being, always remained the same, and their robes were of fine royalty, and they had no wings. In distinction, the Angels and most of the Seraphim and Cherubim had wings. With the wings they could fly around Heaven and the Expanse. There forms, while also like a human being in form, was somewhat fluid and could change appearances depending on the specific powers assigned them, which is a mystery held by God.

In Heaven, because God and all His heavenly creatures were holy and perfect, there was no fear, worry, or insecurity that there would ever be a take-over of God's heavenly Throne, unthinkable, because God, though one compared to myriads of angels, is so much more. No creature could ever take the place of God. Moreover, the creatures were holy and full of love for God, and

God fully loved them. All the heavenly creatures recognized that God and only God was the Sovereign and Progenitor of Heaven who could occupy the Eternal Mysterious Seat of the Source.

Now that God had His heavenly Circle of Advisors established and the myriads of angels, He had His perfect Kingdom of Heaven, replete with holy communication and companionship felt between God and His creatures and between the heavenly creatures. Perfect holy communion was established in God's Kingdom first with the circle of Advisors and then with the circle of Advisors and all the angels. Adoration, praise, and thanks was the natural holy response from all the heavenly creatures to God's person, nature, and works. And this continued during this time of the pre-material universe that only Heaven's time knows.

The Story of the Creating of the Material Universe

Glorious light radiates out from God all around, 360 degrees and three-dimensional. God is eternal, and so there was always light before the day God created light in the material universe. He modeled the radiant gaseous material universe with all its glorious galaxies after Himself. When the sacred Hebrew narrative mentions that on the first day of creation, that God created light, it was the light of the material universe He created, but brilliantly glorious light radiating out from the person of God, centered at His heavenly Throne, had always existed in eternity. There is no place in Heaven nor in the great Expanse that can escape the knowledge of God, and He can send His Spirit anywhere, but the fullness of His glory and majesty is at His Throne, the center of Heaven.

There was a passage of a heavenly epoch of time that only Heaven knows, recorded in the heavenly books. Then at one light-blink, God called another convocation of all the angels of Heaven. Many of the angels sensed it was going to be something

– MARK AHAVEL –

special, and there was a stir among them as they flew their way to their stations around the Throne of God. The Circle of Advisors were there waiting for all the Angels, Cherubim, and Seraphim to gather, in anticipation of God's announcement. Though the Advisors and angels were so very intimately connected to the heart and will of God, the mind of God they can not fully know, since He is all-knowing, whereas the heavenly creatures only have finite knowledge. Once all were gathered together, the myriads of angels all hovering in their various stationary spots outside the circle of Advisors, the voice of God spoke, "A world I create, a universe in a temporal, material realm. It is to be a glorious material creation, but inferior to the glory of Heaven. We will place it in the great Expanse. It will begin at the center of the great Expanse. We will create gases at the center. And out of this center, we will expand out the gases forming elements as they expand out into the Expanse. We will create gravitational forces to help govern the material universe, and to spin many gases and elements into celestial spheres. It will all begin by starting with creating one gigantic ball of gases and then pumping tremendous energy into the ball. When it reaches its critical mass breaking point, there will be such a tremendous explosion that we will be able to stretch the gas and forming elements to create a beautiful universe on the otherwise empty Expanse. The Ether will remain. We will form this universe of beautiful swirling galaxies from these gases, flowing energy, and elements forming matter. We will create trillions of stars making up the lights in the galaxies and thousands of planets, moons, asteroids, and comets to accompany the stars. My Word will create all of this, the angels will be my helpers, and the heavenly Advisors will be the witnesses and recorders of the great event. In one particular galaxy, I will create one special planet and place it at just the right distance from a medium size star, the sun, and make it into a beautiful blue planet. I will wrap this planet with life-generating gases, creating

– 42 –

an atmosphere, and I will blanket this earth with lots of life-generating water. I will also create a lot of land rich in hundreds of minerals also necessary for life. And from all these elements of gases, water, and from land, I will create exotic physiological creatures of all kinds of diversity: creatures of the sea, the land, and the air, thousands of species of all kinds. There will be many types of land animals of four-footed creatures. But among all the land creatures I will create one that will be most special: like by nature and yet distinct from all the animals on earth. This two-footed creature will be humans. By physical nature, humans will be like the other animals, having flesh, blood, and bone, and the requirements of eating to feed the body to survive and live. But into the humans, I will breath not only the breath of physical life, but give them eternal souls within their physical bodies. Unlike all the other earthly creatures, they will be made in the image of God. They will have the eternal spirit and soul. Into them we will place a moral conscience and write upon their hearts the eternal divine Law. And they will have intelligence greater than all the animals on earth, abilities to think, study, analyze, abstract, speak and write, plan and design. They will be objects of our special love because, though their bodies will be mortal, their souls are immortal and are destined to dwell with us in my heavenly Kingdom when their earthly journey is complete. They will complete the filling of Heaven, living in glory forever. According to their physical bodies while on earth, they will have to eat to sustain the life in their bodies, and they will mate, male and female, for reproducing their kind, as so designed in all the animal kingdom. We will place these special creatures, humans, people, on the earth will be the crown of the earthly creation. They will not only be the crown of the earthly creation in the spiritual sense but also in the temporal natural sense. They will be the Earth's caretakers, keepers, protectors, and preservers of all its natural resources. They will be stewards and managers of the

Earth. Upon the land I will create an abundance of vegetation of all kinds, all seed-bearing to reproduce each their own kind, and many fruit-bearing shrubs and trees for food for all people and diverse animals of all kinds to help sustain all the earthly creatures.

There was a holy hush in Heaven as the Advisors, Angels, Seraphim, and Cherubim marveled at and pondered this grandiose plan. It sounded so wondrous, these galaxies and stars and planets. They rejoiced that God's Kingdom will fill with humans too. The heavenly creatures were full of the love of God. It was only natural that they would be most desirous in sharing Heaven with others. They were pure and holy, without even a tinge of jealousy at the thought of sharing God's Heaven with other even lower creatures. In their pondering God's word of the creation of the Earth, they could not relate to the idea of sex because as immortal creatures; it was a foreign concept. God made them, but not through the act of sex, and nor do they engage in sex. They could only ponder that aspect. The physiological functions, such as the flow of blood and oxygen to breath was also foreign to them since their heavenly nature, of a higher state, does not require blood or oxygen as physiological animals of the earthly material require.

As the Advisors contemplated God's plan of the creation of this universe, questions started to come to their mind, mainly at the philosophical level because of the great intelligence God gave them. For example, they asked what will be the flux, progress, outcome, and end of the universe, or will it reach a static state and exist forever from the point after the day of creation? And why is it that humans have to be mortal? What is death? God in His infinite knowledge, wisdom, love, mercy, and patience, said, "This material universe, as you know, is inferior to Heaven. This material universe is limited and subject to the constraints of matter and the laws which governs material stuff. Every living creature in the material universe, whatever part of nature, by default is subject to the constraints of matter. All objects big and small will be subject to opposing forces clashing from the atomic levels to the galaxy levels. Forces exert themselves upon solid objects. It is not a world or universe of comfort, tranquility, or peace that is created. The material is inferior to the spiritual, metaphysical. I create this universe for the inspiration of its earthlings, people, for them to catch glimpses and snippets of eternity[7], for their stepping stone into eternity, and for creating more creatures who will freely glorify and worship Me. In my infinitely wisdom, they are created in the material universe for My glorious purpose. The universe will continue to expand out, and after eons of time, it will eventually die, like a mortal. But then I will create a new universe yet more glorious, and I will be glorified. There will there be decay in the material universe until I create the new heavens and the new earth.

"What is decay and why does the material universe have to undergo it?" asked one of the Advisors. God replied, "Decay is the slow process of degeneration and dying. In the material universe, it takes almost as much energy to be sustained as it does in creating the matter, materials, elements. I place in the material universe a gradual falling apart, decaying, to prepare my creatures for a better world that will come to them. Decay is purposed ultimately to prepare for the glorious recreation to come, and it is intended to prepare each individual soul for their glorious life in Heaven (Paradise) to come. The spiritual principle of the movement from decay to glory will be etched all through the material universe. In regard to humans, this means a slow decaying process that leads to physical death. This is purposed so that their souls more earnestly turn to Me for guidance and eagerly look forward to their glorious life to come in the bliss of Heaven."

God continued, "Moreover, the earthly human life in the body will be a life of both pleasures and pain. They will be given senses for life in the physical body for not only surviving but for perceiving, for learning for living a full life. But to humans alone, my special earthly creatures, I will give a particular joy, the ability to delight at the smell of flowers, to marvel at the sight of beautiful clouds, sunrises, sunsets, mountains, and valleys, to take delight in the taste of sweet and savory foods, and to be touched in the soul at the hearing of a baby giggling or lovers mating. Humans will use their intelligence combined with their senses for the utilitarian purposes of the life in the human societies they will create. In regard to pain, I do not take pleasure in the cause of any pain or suffering of any of my earthly children." An Advisor then asked, "Do humans have to experience pain or is their any way to have life without pain?" God, in His infinite knowledge, wisdom, love, mercy, and patience, said, "Of necessity, their physical bodies will require the nerves that have the ability to send the pain signals, as with all the other animals. There are positive reasons for this, mainly to alert them when something is wrong. They will be designed such that pain could be experienced in the body through the nervous system serving more than one purpose. First, the system will be designed such to protect the body from injury. And secondly, it is designed so for the purpose of a warning system when there may be toxins or other foreign agents, or unhealthy developments. These things are necessary for life in the physical body. There will be another kind of pain they will experience which will be different than sensory nerve pain. It is emotional pain. The emotional pain will arise directly from their person-soul-spirit. This kind of pain, we will pay very closely to, in our care of human creatures. For they will be fragile creatures in an unstable world who need the stability of Heaven to look up to help and support. Through their struggles, we will embrace them, hold them, sustain them, love them. Though they may feel lost, abandoned, rejected at times, our Word will assure them of a glorious Paradise to come. The first humans will not experience emotional pain until the fall into sin in the Garden. The humans will need our watchful eye, our care, through all their days, help them on their journey to the glory and bliss of Heaven."

The Epoch of the Creation of the Universe

So God had made these plans. His Word oversaw, directed, and empowered all the divine creative action. He sent His angels to start pumping in the gas at the center of the great empty Expanse and continued to form it into a huge ball of energy, gas, light, and fire which would be the catalyst for the creation of the universe. He stoked the fire of this ball, aided by a myriad of angels. The angels continued to pump in, pour in a tremendous among of gas and energy and the other angels watched as this ball of gaseous fire grow bigger and bigger. Many Heaven-days took place preparing for the day of the great Creation. Shortly before that time, God called another sacred gathering of all the heavenly beings. Once the angels were all gathered, God announced that the purpose of this meeting was both for a sacred convocation, and secondly as a business meeting to give out instructions. God first gave out instructions to all. He told the angels that they will all be actively participating in this grandiose creation event. Their chief role will help steer and guide gases into the galaxies and into stars. The sacred convocation portion was a holy interlude of silence and contemplation. The thoughts of the heavenly creatures were both on continual awe and adoration of God and at the same time, a contemplation of the grandiose event was about to take place. All the Advisors and angels felt this awesome sacred time. A Heaven time passed in this state of quiet reverence before God and contemplating the great event. Then God said, "The beginning of this material universe is at hand, and the beginning of its time." And God sent out powerful angel trumpeters in Heaven, toward the empty Expanse, and in unison they blasted a long sounding note which would have pierced the ear drums of any physical creature if there was one in Heaven. The blast stopped, and a most quiet and expectant pause fell on Heaven, as all eyes were on the center of the Expanse with the great ball of gas, energy, light, and fire, …and then KABOOOOOOOOOOOOOOOM!

And the myriad of angels heard God's thunderous voice say, "Go!" And they flew out at the speed of light into the Expanse. Flying with the cosmic wind, riding on the gigantic energy burst and with swirls of energy all around them, a multitude of angels compressed the gases into forming billions of stars and a myriad of angels guided and channeled the gases and stars into millions of galaxies. They were on the most exhilarating ride of their lives, like thousands of roller coasters full of riders all in action at the same time. All the while there were millions of flashes of light and bursts of energy as gas particles collided with each other and as stars formed. There were tremendous whirls of energy and electricity and cosmic wind all around, rushing out from the center, dazzling rays, such a glorious site to behold never beheld before by the heavenly creatures. The Advisors around the circle of the Throne in Heaven intently watched it all, and were eager to document it all in Heaven's books. This was the most exciting, exuberate, and fun day of all for the angels. While they understood the seriousness of the creation of the universe, this day was also like a cosmic amusement park of fast rides. But there was no fear of injury on the part of the angels because they were of the heavenly nature. They could not burn from the heat. Their eyes could look directly into the stars, the same as they do into God, and not squint or blink.

It was by God's Word with the aid of His angels that He birthed the material universe in existence. God provided all the essentials in the creation of the universe: the gases and the energy, the building blocks to the elements formed from these. The angels merely helped guide the flows of energy with their hands. They played an integral role in the Creation, but they too are heavenly creatures God has not intended for worship. God alone is worthy of all worship. God is the Source of all things. At the beginning, God provided the mysterious energy, the power, and the laws by which He made the many elements, the stars, the galaxies, and the seeds of material life. This was the first "day" or epoch of creation.

On the second "day" or epoch of creation, God told the angels "Go," and they went out all around the universe to help guide the material pieces and chunks out there to form planets, as these materials were cooling from the huge explosion. They assisted in the condensing of the gases into smaller celestial objects called planets and moons. They facilitated the cooling of these new celestial objects, allowing energy to dissipate. Once all the planets and moons were formed that the Word of God determined, the angels stopped, and saw that there was some extra materials left over, called asteroids. Some mighty angels flew to God in the speed of light and asked what they should do with this extra material. And God said, "Let them be. All things are in beautiful order: the galaxies swirling and planetary systems orbiting around their suns. But this universe is not meant to be perfect. The asteroids, in their orbital belts, are signs of the imperfection in the universe. They are extra materials left over. They will be kept for their own purpose; some may be used as signs in the distant future. God put all the universe, with its moons, planets, stars, and galaxies in order and in an orderly fashion aided by His angels, all governed by His wise laws and principles. And all celestial objects were subject to laws and limits that God determined for the material universe.

God built the universe upon a balance of both mystery and comprehendible scientific knowledge. The mysteries are three-fold: the Ether, which is the fabric of space of the great Expanse upon which He expanded the universe, the mystery of atomic cohesion (what holds the neutrons, protons, and electrons of atoms together), and the mystery of the unaccounted portion of matter in the universe called "dark matter" by later human scientists, missing matter which human calculations accounts for a significant portion of the mass of the universe but which cannot not be seen though telescopes by astronomers after millennia of advancement. All three of these mysteries baffles the intellect and seekers of cosmic truth and understanding among all humans. The common thread of these three mysteries is that they are all invisible, and herein lies the key that holds the mystery. God is the Sovereign over the whole universe, the invisible and visible; all are under His reign. But humans later to come, no matter how intelligent they think they become, their limitations are in the visible and material realm. Even though they may later develop sophisticated instruments to detect stuff in the universe not visible to the human eye, they will not be able to truly comprehend these divine mysteries of the universe. God's secret formula of the universe includes the comprehensive cohesive invisible energy, a great riddle which human science will not be able to figure out. The day when humans think science has solved one or more of these mysteries, it is not by science, but by intuition, God-given intelligence conveyed through their soul from connection to the divine Source, or through revelation.

In distinction to the material universe, God's Heaven is of the heavenly nature. It is in a space and place but in another dimension from the material universe. And the center of Heaven is God's glorious Throne from which such a brilliant light radiates all around in three dimensions. The universe was modeled on Heaven, where the big ball of gas, light and fire at the center, the catalyst for the universe, was modeled from God Himself and His throne. The trillions of stars formed, points of light, are modeled from the glory of the myriads of angels. But whereas the material universe is capable of corruption, Heaven is pure and holy, and always will be in eternity. It cannot be corrupted like the material universe. God's holy counselors continued to fall down in worship of God as the angels continued to bring back reports of the creation of the universe.

On the third "day" or epoch of creation, God sent out another company of angels to take that planet Earth just formed and transform it into a most special planet of the billions of planets. "Let it be a beautiful blue planet with a life-generating sphere of gas around, and plenty of life-generating water upon the surface, and dry land," God said. And the angels went out and calibrated the key gases around the earth that would assist the germination of later life. And they formed together an abundance of hydrogen and oxygen to make water, so much in abundance to cover three-fourths the surface of the Earth. God placed the Earth at just the right distance away from its sun, close enough for the heat in energize life, but not too close as to burn up life that would otherwise form.

On the fourth "day" or epoch of creation, God created the building blocks of life. God said, "Let there be life on the planet Earth." The Spirit of God put the Word of God into action, aided by the angels, and first, starting with the water, amino acids, and other chemicals. One of those chemicals was deoxyribonucleic acid (DNA), a fundamental building block for life on Earth. Then He formed organic cells from these inorganic chemicals and minerals. God was the mastermind of all this, planned from before the universe began, but enacted now to the marvel of His heavenly creatures creating first the building blocks. God, with the aid of his skillful angelic helpers, created cells which contained such a complexity that would baffle the smartest biological scientists in the 21st century CE, complete with micro-systems and engines all seemingly guided by an unseen hand and unseen force, and designed by a Master Engineer. And from cells, God proceeded to make plant life on Earth, plants of many and various kinds, each according to their specific species, all by God's design. God created grasses, flowers, herbs, shrubs, and trees of thousands of kinds. His angels assisted the Word in carrying out the work of the formation of the many plant species with their intricate and various designs. Each plant species was designed to reproduce themselves most often through seeds.

On the fifth "day" or epoch of creation, God created animal life, living physical creatures: animals of the sea, the sky, and the land. Many of the living creatures He gave flesh, blood, and bone for their nature and structure. And His Word, guided by the skillful hands of angels, made zygotes to determine the sex (gender) for each creature. They were built into the nature of the animals and all designed with a unique DNA code. The Angels assisted God in carrying out the work of the many intricate and various designs. And when the animals were made, He sent them out to inhabit the Earth: birds of the air, fish and sea creatures, and land animals of various kinds.

The holy creatures of Heaven watched as life formed on Earth, plants and oceans, sea creatures, and land animals.

On the six "day" or epoch of creation, God created the first humans. The Angels assisted God in carrying out the work of their design and intricate systems needed for life, particularly eager in this undertaking, knowing the humankind will not be much lower than the angels themselves in spiritual relationship with God, though they start out as mortal earthlings. And God formed the first humans, and as the former Scriptures declared, God's Holy Spirit breathed into their bodies the breath of life (Gen. 2:7) which includes the living, that is, the eternal soul. According to their physical nature, they are bone and *besar* (Heb. flesh), blood, and breath. According to their physical nature, they are closely related to the animal kingdom. But God placed in them the living soul and a spirit, the part of them that lives on in eternity. They were endowed with special gifts above the animals, especially intelligence. By their physical form, the first humans were Neanderthal-looking, homo erectus-homo sapiens. God created them in this state to give them room to develop into the modern homo sapiens. Through the process of time, their systems could improve, strengthen, and adapt to environment.

God expressed some humor in the Creation in creating the primate species, apes and monkeys, to look remarkably similar to humans. But humans were created as the crown of creation.

God declared humans the crown of creation on account of their spiritual nature, higher than any of the animals. God made their form similar to the heavenly creatures, and God gave them the responsibility to be the caretakers of this Earth. All people have to work; all have work to do: gather, plant and harvest, tend crops, gardens, and flocks, raise and nurture children. They will need resources and learn how to sustain the Earth's resources. They too, along with the plants and animals, were designed to reproduce themselves. They are also prone to pain and fatigue. They will need daily rest and have eyes that close in sleep whereas the angels are of sleepless eyes.

They will experience pain and pleasure. God spoke to His heavenly creatures, "They will need our help through the physical life. We will hear their prayers and come to their aid in the appointed time."

At the end of each of the sixth "day" of creation, when the action work was finished, God led Heaven to pause and looking at the beautiful creation of the universe, of Earth, and human beings. As recorded in the ancient Scriptures, God said, "it was very good" (Gen. 1:31)

At the end of each of the "days" of creation, the first through sixth, the chief angels came back to the Council of Advisors and reported the details of all the actions and accomplishments. And the Advisors carefully and diligently inscribed every thing in Heaven's Book of Creation in perfect accordance with the Word of God.

On the seventh "day" or epoch of creation, as the ancient Scriptures declare, God rested (Gen. 2:2-3), and so did all of

Heaven, all the angels. With the work completed at the end of the sixth "day," God led all to cease. The Advisors also ceased from inscribing the Book of Creation, which was now complete, except the recording of the seventh "day." And God called a sacred gathering of all of Heaven's creatures on this seventh day as a day of rest. He consecrated and sanctified it as a day of Sabbath rest, as the ancient Scriptures declare. The heavenly became a model for the earthly weekly day of rest. All the myriads of angels, Seraphim, and Cherubim were gathered around the throne of God. The Book of Creation was laid open and placed on the altar before God's Throne in the center of the circle of Advisors. And the whole heavenly assembly, in one accord, began to worship God, shouting "Great and glorious is God Almighty! Wondrous, marvelous, and splendid are your works! To You be all glory forever and ever. May your creation praise you forever and ever." They prostrated themselves before God, and the Advisors waved their royal sashes. It was a very festive occasion. The angelic trumpeters, all the angels God gifted with music along with all the choirs of angels produced a beautiful melodious music and songs of praise to God with filled Heaven. They all continued worshipping on this seventh "day" in Heaven's time as is only known in Heaven. It was a time of rejoicing and gladness for all the heavenly creatures. God took much delight in all the worship and in the finished work of the creation of the universe. But God's delight was tempered by His foreknowledge of the corruption that would one day fall upon every human and spread to the whole Earth. But His love is steadfast, and His mercy and patience are enduring.

Time passes…and earthly time passes. God and all His angels are cognizant of the early humans and their development on young Earth. God regularly sent angels to Earth to peer and care for people in particular. Because angels do not reproduce and did not know sex, when they happened upon a husband and wife mating, they wandered in their pure way, not having been created through sex. They knew it was the way of earthly nature. They were just curious about what it felt like.

God periodically called the great Heavenly Council and Convocation of Angels, Cherubim and Seraphim together to worship and to discuss any Heaven business and happenings and needs on Earth and how humanity was developing.

Centuries pass. Humans have advanced to the point that their intelligence has sharpened, expanded more acutely into abstract thought, and into the contemplation of life, philosophy, the Divine Mystery (God), and the nature of the cosmos (universe). One angel in particularly was intrigued by this, and wondered how far humans will be able to advance. On the next heavenly Convocation, the angel asked an Advisor to ask this question to God, "O Supreme glorious splendid One, will humans ever figure out the mysteries of the universe?" There was a holy pause, not because omniscient God needed time to come up with the answer, but to acknowledge the greatness and comprehensiveness of this question. All in Heaven intensely listened to how God would answer. It was one of those holy hush moments. Then God replied: "Humans will continue to advance in knowledge and in technology such that they will discover many of the main laws and principles which govern the universe including the material universe's speed limit and they will even learn how to travel outside the Earth's atmosphere. They will learn scientifically what makes Earth and stars tick, and basically figure out the origin of the material universe and its life cycle. But there will be five mysteries they will not be able to solve:

◆ The mystery of the nature of Myself, God, the Source and Progenitor of all things, for not any of My heavenly creatures comprehend the nature of My essence;

- The mystery of Ether: the emptiness or fabric upon which I have stretched the Universe,
- The mystery of the "Dark Matter,"
- The mystery of atomic cohesion, and
- The mystery of Life.

They will imperfectly figure out the scientific aspects to a few of these but will never be able to completely unlock the mysteries because the missing component and cohesion is in the spiritual dimension. It is the power and extension of God Himself which goes beyond what science can discern. But God did create a wondrous mysterious cohesiveness between God's invisible dimension and the visible material universe. This same dualistic mystery is found even within each human being: their eternal souls in their material bodies. This mystery parallels the dualistic cosmic universal mystery. God is glorified in all His creation and in this the truth that "God is in all and through all" is known, as ancient Scriptures did reveal.

Moreover, in the creation of the material universe, there was a distinction of Faith and Science but no conflict. Faith focuses on the heavenly, metaphysical, invisible realm, and Science which focuses on the material realm. But in God's foreknowledge, He knew that some human beings, even some scientists, would not acknowledge the Creator. They would see only the material universe, and cause a conflict between Faith and Science. This is human's doing, not God's.

The Corruption of the Material World

God knew that the material He created, was prone to corruption and decay, whereas the spiritual realm of His kingdom is incorruptible and holy. And humans' physical natures were prone to this corruption, and while their soul was made in the divine image, it is so tied to the corruptible flesh while in the body not yet changed to the incorruptibile in the resurrection.

God, moreover, wanted people who would freely love Him, which meant giving free wills to all human souls, which resulted in some humans turning away from God, not loving Him, or choosing to not even believe in Him.

God's Assistance for Humankind

God, in having perfect knowledge of all His Creation, intimately acquainted with the human He made, said, "My heart goes out to every human I will ever make. I know the pains they will experience in life. I will ache when they ache, My Spirit will cry when they cry. It is not for that reason I make them. I make them to glorify Me. They will not be forced to glorify Me. But of those who freely chose, will enter glorious Paradise and Heaven after their earthly journey and will be full of blessing and joy."

God designed every detail, every aspect from sub-atomic particles to the complexities of microbes, the complexities of DNA, proteins, human genetics, and having intimately designed the human species. God, because of His great intelligence created some DNA strands that different species share with each other, even between humans and apes.

God knew the difficulties that life in the material body would bring. God does not take pleasure in inflicting any pain, ailments, or suffering on any of His creatures, but God had to build bacteria and viruses into Earth's biosphere which is necessary to serve different functions, such as to strengthen immune systems. Without a strong immune system, the physical body will be too prone and weak to overcome viruses and will not survive. In this world, tension, struggle, and yin and yang are necessary. It is in this struggle that living physical creatures become stronger, and a certain amount of strength is necessary for the survival of each living creature in the material world. The irony is that viruses are needed to attack the immune system to make it stronger to resist the attack of other viruses. When humans, who know their Creator and their ultimate destiny in Heaven, discover this physical reality, they may not completely understand why God had to design it this way, but they yearn more for their glorious eternal destiny where there will be no ailments, pain, suffering, sorrow, nor tears, as ancient Scriptures revealed (c.f. Is. 25:8; Rev. 21:4), and there will be no viruses.

And so God, knowing the human condition, eager to hear the prayers and cries of all His humans, also led Heaven's creatures to remember humans in their needs. And God regularly sends angels out in response to their prayers, and spiritually pray for them. God gave to many angels the task of spiritually ministering to humans in dire need, the comfort through the invisible angelic presence when a person who cries out to God in need of comforting, from the small precious child to the very old person on their death bed. It matters not where on the planet Earth or what race, nationality, or culture they are from. God hears and comes to the aid of those who call on Him. The angels ride on the Spirit of God in their coming to minister to humans in need. While angels have heavenly bodies in the spiritual invisible dimension, God has given certain angels the ability to manifest into the physical realm, and appear much like a human, when God has sent them on special missions for special messages, revelation, to God's chosen.

A Natural Story of Early Humankind

And God established people into families. Each man of age chose a woman for a wife, and they came together as husband and wife, and bore children.

For the first few thousand years of humanity, the human population was small upon the Earth. Out of the instinctual feeling of survival, fertility was a very high value among peoples. They formed different tribes and spread out.

As God's special representatives on Earth, God clothed humans with a sense of dignity, nobility, and potential goodness, as objects of His special love, creatures for which He was especially proud after the heavenly creatures. But these early humans had room to grow and advance, from the tendency of the men to talk in grunts to later dignified and intellectual speech. God built this time-factor in to allow human beings to fully develop into the modern homo sapien that they became.

To each of the human genders, male and female, God gave special qualities. God knew how much nurturing and security humans would need in a relatively unsafe world of wind and lightning storms, earthquakes, tsunamis, and volcanic eruptions. He especially endowed women with nurturing skills. And God knew earthly life would have many physical demands, and that humans needed to be strong. He particularly gave the physical strength to the man and the quality of being the provider for his family focusing on hunting, but the women also provided, focusing on the gathering. To both males and females, God has given abilities that reflect the divine nature of the universe, to contemplate the Creator, and the sacredness of life and the Earth. God gave humans the ability to establish homes for their own families to be safe from the elements and beasts, and to begin to collect possessions, tools and supplies needed for life. And to both, God gave intelligence equally, not one gender more intelligent than the other (but many men later would think women are less intelligent because they tend to be more emotional). Later patriarchal societies, following the Neolithic Age, will arise, marked by a male domination over the female, but this is the way of man, not the way of God.

A Universal Story of Humankind

In God creating human beings uniquely, above the animals of the planet, He gave them all additional gifts. These five sacred abilities God has given to all humans: a *mind* by which he/she is conscious and thinks and reasons, a *heart* by which he/she feels, a *soul* that is the holy and eternal habitation for the conscious being, the *spirit* which takes in life from the breath of the world and exudes life, and the *body* of flesh, bone, and blood, the earthly vessel for his/her earthly journey. All these, God has wondrously made and fashioned into each whole human person. None is left without a soul or heart or spirit. God has blessed every fiber and space of His creation, and has placed within the soul of human the capacity to receive His love and blessings. God has wondrously made humanity, a whole creature of body and soul/spirit, and the crown of all the earthly creation.

God gave humans ten fingers, and these ten are a sign of the *ten gifts and faculties* the God has given to humans which also make them unique and the crown of the earthly creation: *intelligence, will, conscience, creativity, imagination, intuition, spirit, character, virtue, and love*. Without these, a human is not a human being that God has intended. Together, the five sacred gifts and these ten faculties gifts unpack the meaning of "made in the image of God. And together, they make humans His special creatures among the earthly creation. To all, God have given the capacities for these ten, but they are to be taught and nurtured by parents and teachers to the young and continued to be developed into and through adulthood. Some of these are like muscles. If they are not used, they atrophy.

Moreover, God endowed humans to ascent to several virtues on their path to spiritual maturity and nobility. The five main virtues are *chastity, charity, kindness, humility*, and *patience*. The five sacred gifts, the ten faculties gifts, and the five main virtues total twenty, which is the same number of fingers and toes most human beings have. So parents can teach these to their children, using their children's fingers and toes as signs.

With all these gifts and faculties, God has enabled people to walk as confident representatives of God on Earth wherever they went or dwelt. Some ascented to their spiritual nobility and called them "noble ones" which is what Aryan means (Hopfe and Woodward p. 235). But their fears, insecurities, distrust, and jealousy between themselves and others, between tribes, led to conflicts, skirmishes, and some blew up into full battles and war. People fought over territory, for power, domination, and out of revenge from previous killings. This was not the destiny that God planned for humans. But in time, humans accomplished much, built roads, bridges, tall buildings, produced beautiful art and magnificent architecture, made cars and airplanes, and made so many research discoveries from the smallest atom to large galaxies, imaginatively reaching for the stars. These are visible signs reflecting the great destiny of humankind as God planned, inspired by the great wondrous universe that God has made.

Without the knowledge of the truth that God gave all these gifts to us, humans would credit themselves with all their abilities and accomplishments. But this is delusional. All has been given by God, and to whom deserves all the praise, glory, honor, and yes, worship. God has not appointed to humans the nature of divinity. God through His Spirit has inspired humans to call on God.

The Spirit of God penetrates the inner nature of humans. he Spirit discerns the thoughts and intentions of the heart and mind. None can hide themselves nor their thoughts from the Spirit of God. The Spirit of God knows the good thoughts and the bad thoughts that humans have. The Spirit of God knows the insecurities that humans have. The Spirit of God knows the spiritual weakness of humans, pulled down by the flesh with cravings, desires, base urges, and lusts. Some people give in to carnality.

And God has endowed certain individual humans of various places through the ages with nobility and grace, leadership and confidence, knowledge and wisdom, to whom common people have often looked up to in much admiration. And some of these noble ones on which God's spirit rested have later been deified by other humans, usually posthumously. God honors the giving of honor to all upon whom His spirit of grace and wisdom has rested. God would not have peoples to forget the humanness of all spiritual teachers and founders of religions. The Spirit of God knows the human limits of comprehension, our weaknesses and our frailties. He knows our tendency to be enamored by the beautiful, the eyes of men falling for a beautiful woman desiring to make her into a goddess. God does not condemn us for our love for others, but He is displeased with ignoring the Maker and glorifying creatures in place of God. God understands the belief of some who see God in a human vessel, a human, such as a guru believed to be an incarnation of a god or God. God does not condemn belief. God wants His beloved creatures to look to Him, and give full honor and glory to the Maker of this awesome universe in which we live.

Enlightened ones look around at the cosmos and by faith, see the order of God. Unenlightened ones, those who lack faith, look around at the same cosmos and see chaos. All are looking at the same cosmos, but what one sees is empowered by faith and the other sees without faith.

God willed that humankind through the ages would flourish in civilization, in theology and philosophy, in the arts and literature, in science and engineering, and crafts and trades, desiring all to glorify Him. How wondrous that God through His Spirit has enlightened the minds and souls of His seekers from ancient times to modern days, theologians and philosophers given to contemplate and attempt to define, and articulate the mysteries of life and the cosmos. How terrestrial we human creatures are, yet imaginatively heavenly.

The way of all the enlightened, man or woman, seek God. They seek to be purified by God's cleansing spiritual waters. The enlightened seek the right knowledge of God and how to rightly live out days before the blessed journey to eternity. The enlightened seek truth that reaches beyond the senses. The enlightened seek wisdom for this life and the life to come. And the enlightened are generous in sharing the Way, the knowledge, the wisdom, the love and compassion with whom God brings into their lives. The enlightened seek to live peacefully and to abide in God's peace now and into eternity. Truly blessed are all God's enlightened children.

The words of this book are spiritual. They are not of the flesh.
These words are spiritually minded.

The prophets of the blessed past called their peoples to meet God
of their faith, each in their appointed consecrated places. In time,
these places became sacred, each in their own homelands of origin.

How does a person, O man, O woman, get right with God?
Will 1000 prayers bring down His platonic love?
Will 1000 meditations mediate it?
Will 1000 right intentions gain it?
Will 1000 fastings fix it?
Will 1000 prostrations prosper it?
Will 10,000 sacrifices secure it?
Will 100,000 rituals seal it?
How can we get right with God?

PART II
PROPHECY AND PRAYER

OPENING WORDS

From the land of a lion, these Scriptures go forth, Forged from the fortitude of faith, they fly out to the peoples.

From the inner chambers of the most sacred in the heavenly realm, the Source of light and inspiration has shone on the souls of prophets. By the Spirit of God, and in the spirit, not the flesh, some souls have been brought into these sacred chambers not only to catch glimpses of glory but more importantly, to receive most blessed thoughts to share with humanity that touch the hearts and souls of millions with goodness, to enlighten human souls, and lead to humanity's spiritual growth toward spiritual nobility. Many a sage and prophet came in this spiritual place. It was from this place that the Preacher of Ecclesiastes received this thought: "He [God] has made everything beautiful in its time. And He has put eternity in their hearts..." (Eccl. 3:11 NKJV).

It was while in the place of sacred prayer, that my soul was brought to the inner spiritual sacred chamber, where the Source has given me many beautiful, wonderful thoughts to share with humankind, to spread the Light, to publish the words on Earth.

In His infinite wisdom, God established the three-fold source of revelation for confirmation for human souls (c.f. Matt. 18:16). One is direct revelation from God's Spirit or through an appointed holy angel. Another is this inner sacred source where the spirit of the human receptive vessel enters in and by the Spirit, communication with the Source is actualized. A third is sacred Scriptures previously revealed. In the words of the Preacher of Ecclesiastes, a "threefold cord is not easily broken" (Eccl. 4:12b NKJV).

And there is a fourth source of revelation: natural revelation.

APPOINTED FOR A PROPHETIC ROLE

God called me to be one of His truth-bearers, to bring these words into the 21st century, to carry the prophetic word of God from the past Scriptures along with fresh words for this generation and the years to come, to make truth known, and strengthen the peoples of faith around the globe. The words will continue long after my name is forgotten on Earth. God's truth and His Kingdom is from everlasting to everlasting!" (c.f. Dan. 7:18) To His dominion there is no end. To Him be all the glory from now and forevermore! (c.f. Rev. 7:12)

During my first year in seminary, one day, while I was in my room alone studying, I felt a sudden need to take a break and pray. I knelt beside the bed. As I began to pray in a whisper tone, the Spirit led me to speak the vocables, "*ta ethne*," meaning, "the nations" (New Testament Greek, which I had learned earlier that year). And when the vocables came off my lips, the Spirit of God overwhelmed me and I began to weep for the nations. This was the first sign of a prophetic role God was giving me to the nations.

I never aspired to be a prophet or have a prophetic role or ministry to the world and neither is it a coveted position.[8]

Every prophet has felt the burden of their message. None have run to their Calling, knowing the turmoil they often face.

THE NAME OF GOD

The Name above all names, beyond all names, before all names, and encompassing all names-God- to be exalted above all names, alone fully worshipped and adored, worthy of all trust and faithfulness, the beginning and finisher of all things; His word is absolute and certain, more certain than frail mortal human existence.

O splendid souls, light has come to you. The bright light of God has enlightened your minds. When we speak of light, we speak of two kinds, the direct, actual, glorious, radiant light of God, and the spiritual light of truth and revelation to our minds and souls. Scriptures exude with the light. Its' abundance goes forth when their words are read or spoken. God has channeled his light of revelation and knowledge through humble human vessels, men and women, sages, prophets, and priests through the ages. There are some who want to seal up the light and control what is let out and what is kept from the peoples. God desires for the light to get out to the peoples. He will judge the ones who try to squelch, resist, or control God's glorious light.

LIGHT AND DARKNESS

Most wondrous, glorious, brilliant is the reality of your light that emanates from You and from your throne, for all creatures in a state of holiness are able to see, but their eyes cannot penetrate. You are clothed with such splendor O Lord God. All the glories of valleys and canyons, suns and moons, pale in comparison to your awesome glory.

In the world you have created, you have made light and darkness, many points and light and darkness in space and in the shadows created by celestial bodies. These are the sanctified light and darkness in the universe, that which You have ordained, and to which the Psalmist praises You: "Even night shall be light about me; Indeed, the darkness shall not hide from You, but the night shines as the day; the darkness and the light are both alike [to You] (Ps. 139:11b-12 NKJV).

O great God, You have given your servant understanding in many things, in the heavenly realm and the earthly realm, in the realm of the metaphorical and the realm of the literal. I searched this truth out, and found that there are really two truths, which has caused confusion among the peoples on Earth because we are using the same terms. The light and darkness mentioned above is that which is sanctioned by You, and both are holy. It is this holy darkness which I have seen in a vision of the tranquility of a vastness of space, when I tapped into the source for the many words you have given men. When I saw the darkness, I was a bit confused myself, since we humans often use dark and black to represent bad and evil. That leads to the second sense in which people use the terms light and darkness: in a metaphorical sense. The use of the term "light" as metaphor for divine knowledge, wisdom, and revelation is a good metaphor to use, and several faith traditions have been speaking of the light of God both literally and metaphorical for as long as sacred Scriptures were first penned, and most likely by oral tradition even further back in time. And so likewise, "darkness" has been associated with bad and evil deeds. This is quite understandable since bad people tend to come out at night to do their "dark deeds" so as not to be caught by the light of day. And so "darkness" is used metaphorically for bad and evil in general. God has declared that no amount of physical darkness will hide evil deeds, for He knows and sees all. The darkness is a light to Him. The darkness does not stop the expanse of His awareness.

O God, lead your peoples of faith to become radiant with your light and peace in this world, beaming with truth, righteousness, and justice, cloaked in humility. May they, radiating with your light, be steady waves upon the shores of a darkened world that takes pleasure in self-willed, displeasing, and godless ways.

Arise!

Arise! Let God's radiance lift you, the Divine Life-Giver lift you to new life! His Scripture of ancient days says He "renews His mercy day by day" (c.f. Lam. 3:22-23).

These Scriptures are Spiritual

The words of this book are spiritual. They are not of the flesh. These words are spiritually minded.

God is Good and Loves All

God is good! His goodness is everlasting. His love is incomprehensible. He loves all humanity: black and brown, red and yellow, pale and white.

A Vision Of God's Glory On His Throne

A vision came to me on the night bed, while I was yet awake. The Spirit showed me a beautiful vision of God on His glorious throne, eternal before the Creation. The vision was like unto Isaiah's vision of God's Throne with the train of His robe filling the heavenly temple, with beautiful seraphim and cherubim around. My vision turned to focus on the center, the great and brilliant Light emanating from God Himself. And I knew that I was in the Spirit, for in the fallibility of my raw humanity, I could not look into the great and holy Light of God; I would have to look away. But here, my eyes peered at it, spellbound, but without the blink of an eye. But the light of God was so brilliant I could see no form, if God even has a form as we may humanly want to think. The heavenly Advisors' or angels' eyes cannot even penetrate through God's glorious light emanating from the center of His Being. Its majesty and glory is beyond all description. Somehow God had removed my sin in this spiritual realm, allowing me to see His glory. Somehow I knew this glorious peering was going to last but for a moment. Somehow I knew that I had not died, that my life was still bound to the earth. I knew God's Spirit must have had a purpose, which must be to share with others, to inspire them to the glory that awaits. It is this vision alone with the related insights that I received that led me to set out to pen the narrative of the pre-Creation and Creation in these Scriptures.

THE KINGDOM OF GOD

O God, your Kingdom is from everlasting to everlasting (Dan. 7:18). O God, it is not enough that your peoples ascent to this truth, as though mere knowledge. We would yet still be restless all our days on Earth if we do not know with a certainty of faith that we will live in your blessed Kingdom forever in the hereafter! And this we know we do not deserve. How can we cast off our sin and come up to You? How can we atone for our past sins? Is there any amount of good works, prayers, or rituals or treasures in the Treasury of Merit that can guarantee our passage into Heaven? Only by your mercy and grace, through forgiveness of our sins will You grant us into your eternal Kingdom.

O marvelous are your Scriptures through your apostle who spoke in the present tense, that You have already granted this Kingdom to us! (Eph. 1:3). We do not see your Kingdom on Earth, but we believe. When we see fellow believers, we are seeing the Kingdom of God on Earth, albeit in imperfect earthen vessels. To some extent, religious houses, organizations, and institutions on Earth represent God's Kingdom. But whether they do a good job reflecting it depends on their degree of upholding God's word, having integrity, and welcoming my Spirit.

O houses of God on Earth, clean your houses. Let my Spirit in to breath a fresh breeze of spiritual life, integrity, and power to be my faithful witnesses on Earth.

THE SACRED LAND

The land above all lands, the stan above all stans, the khan above all khans, the eretz (Heb.) above all eretz, the Zion above all Zions, is the sacred land into which every soul taps when it seeks out the sacred and the Divine. We enter this spiritual place through our soul.

THE HOUSE OF GOD

O marvelous are You, O God, that You desire to dwell with your people on Earth. You have inspired faithful and pious ones across the lands from ancient times on, to build for You places where peoples meet You, learn of You, worship you, and offer sacrifices. Splendid have been your houses and temples in many lands, but they pale in comparison to your heavenly glory, majesty, and holiness beyond our comprehension. You have given the prophets of old glimpses of your glory, and even kings out of your covenantal peoples attune to your Spirit. To king Solomon, You moved to pray at the dedication of your temple in Jerusalem (the first of the Jewish temples), "But will God indeed dwell on earth? Behold, heaven and the heaven of heavens cannot contain You, how much less this temple which I have built! Yet regard the prayer of your servant and his supplication, O LORD my God, and listen to the cry and the prayer which Your servant is praying before You today...then hear from heaven, and forgive the sin of Your servants, Your people Israel...then hear in heaven Your dwelling place, and forgive and act..." (I Kings 8:27, 36a, 39a NKJV). Mightily and most wonderfully did you speak, O God by your Spirit through the Prophet Isaiah, "for My house will be called a house of prayer for all nations" (Is. 56:7d NKJV). Even before Isaiah's day, the fame of your holy house in Jerusalem spread across that lands and down the caravan routes all the way to Sheba in southern Arabia.[9] In king Solomon's day only a few years after the first Jewish temple was built, its fame and also the fame of Solomon's wisdom spread far such that it stirred the Queen of Sheba's heart to come and hear Solomon's wisdom and see the great temple (I Kings 10:1-24). And holy Jesus centuries later You did send, and arriving at the temple, the zeal of your house consumed Him as He was angered by the corruption of the money changers in the temple area (Jn. 2:17 based on Ps. 69:9). After turning over the tables of the money changes, the Jews asked Jesus for a sign, and He spoke this wonder, "Destroy this temple, and in these days I will raise it up," (Jn. 2:19 NKJV) to which John adds an even greater wonder, "But he was speaking of the temple of His body (Jn. 2:21 NKJV). And wondrous is your word in the holy Quran speaking of the holy house, the Ka'aba at Mecca, "Remember We made the House a place of assembly for men and a place of safety; and take ye the Station of Abraham as a place of prayer; and We covenanted with Abraham and Isma'il, that they should sanctify My House for those who compass it round, or use it as a retreat, or bow, or prostrate themselves (therein in prayer).[10]

...O God, peoples on Earth, yes, religious peoples, have been envious of one another over the renown of each of their holy places, perceiving that the other is better than their own, or even conveying superior attitudes. You know, O God, how we all have sinned. Lead the nations and religious communities in confession of their sins to one another, and come to love each others places as much as their own, without having to convert to the other religion, but to love the other religion's and people's holy sites out of love for the people themselves, flowing abundantly out of the Golden Rule.

THE PLACE OF MEETING GOD

(The following word is an edited excerpt from the author's blog: http://globalofaith.blogspot.com. It also connects with the "House of God" article in the Wisdom/Didactic section)

The prophets of the blessed past called their peoples to meet God of their faith, each in their appointed consecrated places. In time, these places became sacred, each in their own homelands of origin.

The great Hebrew prophet Isaiah wrote, "Now it shall come to pass in the latter days that the mountain of YHWH God's house shall be established on the top of the mountains, and shall be exalted above the hills, and all nations shall flow to it. Many people shall come and say, 'Come, and let us go up to the mountain of the YHWH God... (Isaiah 2:2-3a NKJV)

O peoples of the Earth, let us go up to the spiritual mountain of God, joined in the common cord of faith in God, and in our common humanity. May there be peace and unity. May praise and jubilation break out in city streets, villages, and farmlands, from the mountaintops across the seas: from the east to the west, the north to the south.

In this new millennium and early 21st century, it is dawning on more and more people of these faith traditions, lay and ordained alike, that God cannot only be the God of only one place on Earth, but the God of the whole Earth... the global God. O peoples of the Earth, meet God in the sacred houses that you can go or travel to, in a place that reflects or accepts your faith or is similar enough to feel comfortable. There meet the Transcendent One.

TRUE WORSHIP

Rabbi Y'shua (Jesus Christ), according to John, said, "God is Spirit, and those who worship Him must worship in spirit and in truth (Jn. 4:24).

Hear, O peoples, God receives true worship wherever you are, when you turn to Him through the spirit in truth, by prayer, devotion, mediation, chanting, singing, prophesying, sermonizing, speaking in tongues, dancing, or studying.

True worship is not by magic which seeks to control the Source which alone is controlled by God. True worship is not mimicking others.

True worship can be by mantras, when the worshipper's heart is directing worship in truth to God. But mantras stop becoming true worship as soon as they take their focus off God and place it on something else. And repetitions of any mantras earn no divine grace or favor, they only create an effect upon the human soul.

True worship may be melodious music unto God. It is not by magic or mimics, nor by repetitious mantras, but by melodious music and meditation in truth to God.

The Same Spirit Through The Ages

At a time in which I was receiving messages and insights almost daily, I was enlightened to these words:

The same Spirit of God who hovered over the waters of the young Earth after its creation has enlightened the souls of many of God's servants: sages, prophets, priests, and kings, and common people too, all who look up to God, seek Him, thirst for Him. The Spirit reveals God personally and intimately to those who earnestly seek, in every generation.

God Visits Every Soul

Likewise, at a time in which I was receiving messages and insights almost daily, I was enlightened upon this awareness:

The Spirit of God comes personally to every soul at least one time in their lifetime, of every human soul ever born on Earth from the most ancient of days to the present and into the future, until the end of the earthly ages and the new heavens and new Earth. The timing is chosen by God. For some, it is when the soul is a child. For some it is when they are a teenager. For some, it is when they are a young adult. For some, it is when they are around mid-life. For some, it is when they are in their senior years. And for some, it is when they are approaching death. God's ways are mysterious, and His providence of His wisdom is beyond our comprehension. Some souls are receptive to God, and feel His presence when the divine visit is made. Some souls are partly receptive but partly unreceptive. They sense the holy presence too, but their mind is cluttered with other possibilities and perhaps dismiss the feeling of God's presence due to an outburst of radon gas escaping through the floor of their house, or some other fumes making them light-headed. And some others are virtually unreceptive and scarcely sense God's presence at all. God has given every soul the capacity to believe and to feel God's presence, but some souls turn away from God not long after they come into this world, when they begin to crawl.

Saints before us have experienced the visits of God's Spirit. Some theologians and songwriters have called it "God passing over." Many more saints have experienced the personal visit of God's Spirit, but many of their stories were never recorded and preserved.

The purpose of this most special divine visit, words cannot perfectly reveal. It is like a once-in-a-lifetime spiritual examination. God reads you like a book from cover to cover and instantly knows every detail about your life, good and bad. It does not matter if it is in the cold of the winter when the Spirit visits you and you have four covers on you in bed. It is as if you are completely naked before Him. No darkness, nothing can hide the Spirit of God's eyes from giving you the most thorough spiritual examination you will have in your whole life.

MY SPIRIT THROUGH THE AGES

My Spirit has been hovering over the Earth from the beginning after the Creation when It hovered over the waters (Gen. 1:2) through time. My Spirit has witnessed the formation of saints and the formation of diabolical sinners.

My Spirit has been the companion and still small voice in guiding those upon whom the Divine light fell, upon Akenaten (Amenhotop IV), Moses, Zarathrustra, and many later prophets. My Spirit was there in guiding the minds of the Chou (Zhou) dynasty who attributed their rulership to Me, whom they called Shang-Ti. My Spirit was there to help guide many rulers, all who sought Me.

My Spirit aided in the light upon the great kings of the ancient Near and Middle East: Naram-Sin, Sargon, Hammurabi, David and Solomon, Cyrus, Darius, and others, giving them magnificent kingly rule reflecting imperfectly My Divine rule, giving them much wisdom and inscribing the first legal codes, praise songs, wisdom literature, and charter of human rights.

My Spirit was there as a witness of great battles, grieving the loss of great numbers of lives. My Spirit through the aid of angels carried these millions of souls throughout time to their resting place.

My Spirit was there in the form of a dove bearing witness to Jesus the Christ (Lk. 3:22).

My Spirit was there when Constantine received the vision of the cross with the message, "conquer in this sign." And My Spirit was there on the heart of empress Helena to establish churches in the Holy Land.

My Spirit was there enlightening the Arab peoples on one God at the time of Muhammad.

My Spirit was there giving wisdom and courage to both sides of the battle, to both Richard Lionheart and Saladin.

My Spirit was there to give faith, courage, and grace to king Louis IX in going across enemy lines and approaching the tent of the Muslim general.

My Spirit was there channeling the light of knowledge, truth, wisdom, reason, and science to great scholars of the Middle Ages: Maimonides, Aquinas, Averroes and many others.

My Spirit was there to aid in the courage of the reformers of the great Christian Reformation while caring for My peoples on both sides.

My Spirit was enlightening the modern principles of freedom, justice, and equality to many leaders of different Western nations in the modern era.

My Spirit has been there throughout the ages hearing the longings of the human heart and cries of distress for all who have called out to Me.

My Spirit will continue to enlighten and guide ones whom I choose, and no powers on Earth can stop. My Spirit is a Spirit of peace, and guides saints in reflecting the peaceful Kingdom of God on Earth and all places in Space that humans may travel.

God's Revealed Messages Are Pure, But...

Of a truth, however, is revealed here, that God can by the power of His Spirit and presence communicate directly to a human soul, a chosen vessel, on spiritual or temporal matters. This knowledge is pure, yet all people are fallible, eclipsed with corruption. None of us can perfectly hear, receive, and understand any of God's messages. But the Spirit aids in our receiving and understanding it, especially for those who are receptive vessels of God. In holy moments, we may feel God purely, but our earthen vessels keep us from perfectly understanding the messages.

You could have been born an African, an Asian, a Middle Easterner, Turk, Russian or Mongolian, an Aleutian or Pacific Islander, a European, an Hispanic or Latino, a Native American, or an Anglo-American, or a mix of two or more of these (except which one of these you may be), but did you have a choice when you came into this world? Do you know a single person who made this choice? Herein lies, oddly, evidence of a spiritual truth. We know how much our lives and our identity our wrapped up in the family in which we were raised. But if we were only material creatures (not spirit or soul), these questioning within the human soul of "I could have been born in other place to another tribe and different race) is a clue to our spirit being within us, that we can figuratively momentarily get outside of our bodies and peer in, in relation to a broader humanity. Native American religion understands this spiritual dimension well (although remaining quite nature-based), and for Hindus, they understand it within their belief system and worldview of reincarnationism).

But you were born into the body with its specific race and family and tribal ancestry that your soul found itself. Here you are! In whatever race, ethnicity, or tribe you were born, this was the beginning of your journey toward God and discovering his purpose and overall design for your life. God wants to fill Paradise with not just millions, but billions of people of all races, tribes, nations, and language, all giving praise to Him. On the Day after the great Transformation, it will be the biggest party ever, because all the myriads of angels will join in the heavenly celebration along with the millions or billions of glorified human souls!

You could have been born into a Buddhist family, a Christian family, a Jewish family, a Muslim family, a Hindu family, a Farsi or Zoroastrian family, a Shinto family, or a Baha'i family, or a family without a religious identity (except which one of these you may have been born into). So which one is true? Let God be true and all humans recognize that humans are religious who in part created various religions themselves, flowing out of the spiritual drive God placed in the human soul. And then upon prophets, sages, teachers, priests, and founders, great and pure insights came, but all human beings, fallible and corrupt, receive these messages and instructions imperfectly. They could only understand the messages dimly. And so every religion by default gets corrupted in relation to the standard of the perfect divine thought, as soon as the original message coming out of the mouth of the original recipient falls into the ears of other human beings. Some gladly received the messages, and it took time for it to sink in. Buddha established his *sangha* (Buddhist community) with his five friends. It took days to persuade them, and weeks to convert them. The priests, Pharisees and later Rabbis dedicated their lives to teaching the Hebrew and Jewish people. Jesus chose His Twelve Apostles and commissioned them to take the Gospel to all the world and teach all nations. It takes time for the messages of God to sink into the minds and hearts of human souls of earthly lives because of their limited cultural lens, because of their less than 100% spiritual aptitude of receiving the divine messages, and because mostly being occupied with daily needs of earning bread and caring for selves and family.

Righteousness And Divine Justice

O you who have sought the righteous life, and all you peoples of faith, O how righteousness of God desires to live in the Earth! But some people of every generation are godless, and try to stamp out the light of God's righteous. Every generation needs willing and courageous souls to uphold the righteousness of God, to lift it high, to broadcast its light from country to country, across deserts and plains, from coast to coast, and across seas to islands. Let God's righteousness shine like the beauty of the stars in Earth. Magnify, O God, a love for your word, your light, your truth, your righteousness in the hearts of your peoples. Send it into us like a burning flame that we must pass on to others.

Your righteousness has been written and prophesied in Scriptures. Open our spiritual eyes and hearts to understand and grasp, and then be your instruments to send it out to the world, to be your lips, your pens, keyboards, your printers, and your mobile devices.

"With righteous judgment, You judge, O God," the Scriptures says. And every soul will meet your divine justice. Have mercy on all repentant souls.

HEAR GOD AND CONNECT WITH HIM

Hear, O soul, attune your being to the voice of God and you will hear Him speak. He speaks: "I love you with a perfect love, and desire good for you, not harm nor evil (c.f. Jer. 29:11)."

O soul, a mystery we cannot understand in our earthen minds, that though God is Spirit, He knows the pains and struggles we experience in the body in this life, and He is full of empathy. The mystery is the connection of our spirits to His Spirit. Herein is the interface of communication between our souls and God through His Spirit. No matter where we are or go on Earth, sea below, or outer space, He knows (c.f. Ps. 139), and because of His care, He feels what we feel, by His design because He loves us. He knew that in creating the material world which is imperfect by nature, there will be struggle because of all the forces around and limitations and opposing wills. Know that your life on earth is but a short time compared to the glory of eternity in Heaven. Keep the faith. Stay the course. Accept the fact of the internal struggle in life, and some tribulations from the outside, motivated in hope for the glory that awaits. Tomorrow shall be your dancing day, where there will be no more struggle, suffering, pain, or grief.

But the sure promise of glory in Paradise, many souls feel is not what they deserve. In their honesty, they know their sin. Even when they believe that God loves them, they know they do not deserve such a great gift of Heaven. The truth of God's grace, that Paradise is a gift, has enlightened upon millions of souls on earth.

SIGNS

God has given signs all around of Himself, in nature and in humanity, big and small, objects and symbols. The sun and moon are two large objects as signs of light, being temporal celestial objects of light partially disclosing the glorious permanent Light of God in Heaven. The sign of day and night as the sun makes its circuit across the sky, that God has created the day and night for humankind and all Earth's creatures, reflecting His wisdom and teaching us distinctions of work and rest.

God has given covenantal signs such as the wondrous rainbow of the sky after rain, a sign of God's care and mercy of the Earth and a sign of His grace pouring down on humankind (c.f. Gen. 9:11-17). He also gave to Abraham the covenant of male circumcision which in time became a distinct mark of the Jewish people, set apart from other peoples of the Earth. The Spirit of God, knowing the jealousies in human hearts, sent other messenger-lights to emphasize the spiritual interpretation, that the outward mark on the flesh was a sign on the inward circumcision of the heart, as the apostle Paul had taught (c.f. Rom. 2:29; Gal. 5:6-15).

God, endowed peoples with the gift of writing, have given them to rich ability of many signs and symbols at all literary levels: a letter, a word, a phrase and sentence, a message, an oracle, a chapter, and a whole book. Each of these signs represents a reality. Even the word "God" right here on this page is not God, but a sign of the reality of God.

There are many kinds of signs, each with their assigned and distinct meanings all carried by the sign. There are natural signs from the heavens, from Space, and the atmosphere, to natural signs on the Earth, on land. The sign of a black cat crossing one's path in ages past many interpreted as a bad omen, but blessed are those who can rise above those superstitions. And there are the many signs that humans have fashioned, literary signs and works of art.

Some signs, like objects, are realities in and of themselves, and they have particular functions and purposes. There are signs that merely convey a utilitarian purpose and meaning, and then there are signs with divine significance. Wise are those who can distinguish. Some divine signs can only be rightly interpreted in accordance with given revelation.

Blessed are all souls who can rightly and wisely interpret all signs. All things are subject to God. There is no power that exists in the universe that God is not aware. And all things are designed to bring glory to Him. Therefore O peoples of the Earth, cast off superstitions but keep the true faith in the God whose Spirit rightly guides in the interpretation of all signs, for those who diligently seek.

Be cautious, O impressionable children of Earth, of those who teach of signs in esoteric ways suggesting that God's words are hidden and only the few can obtain their understanding. God desires all believers, peoples of faith to have the understanding of signs, from the simple to the advanced disciples.

The Vision Of The Flower Fertilizing The Whole World

In a time of daytime rest upon the bed, in that state coming back to consciousness from a peaceful unconsciousness, I had this vision of a large white and yellow flower, a trumpet-like lily. As my gaze fixed upon this beautiful flower, I sensed it full of life and energy. Then all of a sudden, it inhaled, then it let out a large puff of spores. And the puff became a cloud, and the cloud expanded in all directions, and the wind took it in all directions and it fertilized all the lands around the world. The Spirit asked me, "What is the meaning of this?" I replied, "Is this not a symbol of God's good news spiritual Kingdom spreading all around the world and planting in peoples hearts and minds?" "Right on," said the Spirit. "And you will see some of this in your own lifetime."

THE VISION OF THE GRAFTED TREE

I visited a church member who was a farmer. After visiting in his house a little while, he led me out back to show me his various citrus trees. He pointed out the branches in which he had grafted one kind of tree into another kind of tree, such as a lime branch on a lemon tree. I was amazed, having never seen this before. And while I stood there contemplating this, I entered a deep contemplation, and I looked again, and saw another branch of a different tree grafted in. And I blinked, and looked again, and saw yet another branch grafted in. And the tree looked fuller. And I looked again, and the tree now had dozens of different kinds of branches grafted in, and they all looked healthy, vibrant, and filled with fruits of all kinds. And the main tree and its trunk was no longer a dwarfed citrus tree, but became a mighty oak. And its branches grew out in all directions, east and west, north and south, as if reaching out to the world. And then I heard the Spirit's voice: "This is the faith that I desire upon the earth. Peoples of the Earth have divided by language, tribe, nationality, culture, and also religion. But in these latter times I am planting seeds towards uniting peoples around the world in a common bond of heart and understanding, though their differences remain."

BLESSED ARE PEOPLES OF FAITH

Blessed are the peoples of the faith of Abraham, for the light of revelation they have received, the truth of the Creator God, the covenants, righteousness, mercy, and justice.

Blessed are the children of the faith of Jacob, mighty in faith of God they have been, witnesses to the great acts of God, deliverance from Egypt, miracles in the wilderness, the Shekinah glory of God inhabiting the Jerusalem Temple; blessed are they for their faithfulness, for their returning to Me through the great crises of faith, and for preserving My word for generations to come, and for upholding the holy standard of My commandments and holding the light of good ethics for the world.

Blessed are the people of faith, the submitters of Allah God for accepting the light of the truth of one God and proclaiming My sovereignty of the universe to the world.

Blessed are the Farsi people of the faith of Zoroaster, the faith of the one God Ahura Mazda, for keeping the light of the truth of one God where you have gone, and for maintaining the light of the good ethic and for preserving the sacred fire.

Blessed are the faith of the peoples of central and northern Asia for receiving the light of the truth when it was brought to your lands, and trying to maintain the light in a cold and sometimes dark but beautiful land.

Blessed are the peoples of Chin for their accepting the light of the one God Shang-Ti, and for their deep respect for their ancestors and parents, and for their humility.

Blessed be the peoples of the islands of the rising sun for their deep respect to their ancestors and their parents, and their deep respect for nature and their devotion to live in harmony with nature.

Blessed be all the Pacific islanders who contemplated and grasped faith when the light came to them.

Blessed be the peoples of faith of the dark continent who received the light when it came to them, and for their intense, vivacious devotion to God.

Blessed be the peoples of the Americas for their deep respect to their ancestors and their deep respect for nature and their devotion to live in harmony with nature.

PROPHECY TO PEOPLES OF VARIOUS FAITHS

O peoples of Zoroaster, Farsis, do not rely on your tradition to save you. Go back to your Scriptures. First, purify your Scriptures by having your priests remove the polytheistic corruption that was added to Avesta long after the prophet Zarathrustra wrote the Scriptures and died. Then rekindle your true worship and relationship with Me through the pure Scriptures. You do good in focusing on your religious motto, "good thoughts, good words, and good deeds." But this will not save you. But your faith in Me and My imputed righteousness alone will save you.

O peoples of Judaism, such clear and brilliant lights of My truth, My word, My heart, have I sent through the prophets of old. And you have been so faithful in preserving these Scriptures. But you do not uphold the Scriptures equally, but lift the voice of Torah only at My voice, but all the other Hebrew Scriptures as commentary. You therefore have failed to hear my living voice for every generation. This caused you to not really hear the word of my new covenant (Jer. 31:31-34). Thus, when I sent the Messiah, your minds and hearts were closed off. I, the Lord God, never intended to create two separate religions, namely Judaism and Christianity. My Scriptures are brilliant light of one God, one voice, and one heart. But in the Common Era, you did fashion your rabbinic religion separate from the Messianic religion, and emphasized your tradition more so than the full Scriptures. You did not want to get along with the people of the new Christian religion.

O peoples of the Christian religion, you who think you are the truest of them all are to take a deeper look into the mirror of humanity to find the truth that you are not better than any other peoples in the world that I have created. In your Scriptures, I have given such clear light as to My nature as a loving God, and this you know, but in your sin, most of your evangelizing is motivated by pride and superiority and not true love. I have given my former prophesy through My blessed servant John, warning of being lukewarm, and losing your first love (Rev. 3:15-16). Return to the true love, as also many of My peoples around the world have. Do not be jealous of My love for others who are different from you. Finally, I have called you to be one of the leaders of peace in the world in the End Times, along with servants of other faiths, and instead of making bridges of peace, you sometimes conjure up painful military memory and imagery when using crusader language. This is to your shame, for none of the killing in the time of the Crusades glorified Me. My Kingdom comes peacefully. All military and fighting terms are not helpful to My cause for peace in the world. Do not again sow pain and discord, leading humanity into centuries of more of conflict when the world needs to be healed from the tragic religious killings of past.

O peoples of Islam, purest you are among all in submitting to Me. But I have called all my peoples to a relationship with Me and toward spiritual maturity. You have been hung up and stuck on the submitting. There is much more to live in God than just submitting. I desire compassion and love. You give lip service to Me as the Compassionate All-Merciful, but I want to see in evidenced in you. Your culture is known much more so for harshness, brutality, and lovelessness. Receive My stern reproof. I give My stern reproof because I do love you intensely, as I love all My peoples: the children of Abraham and Shem, the children of Japheth, and the children of Ham, and all the children of the East, West, North, and South.

O peoples of Baha'i, some of the most beautiful spiritual people on Earth, you nobly desire to embrace all peoples, all faiths, all religions, seeing them all as manifestations from the one God. You have ascented to this noble truth which few on earth have climbed. But do you properly understand Scriptures including the blessed Baha'ullah in making the world one? I, who have created such an abundant diversity of peoples, languages, and cultures, do I now want to obliterate all differences? Is it My will to create one earthly political kingdom that rules over the whole earth? Do you not understand that when there are different nations, this by its very fact creates spiritual growth opportunities for the people each on their own side, to learn how to come to peace with each other. This is one of My purposes for dispersing the peoples around the earth in ancient times, and create national and cultural diversity. Earnestly seek My will on these matters, for could it be that the spirit driving your thrust in creating a one-world nation, government, organization, or system is not My Spirit but a spirit of this world. I have formerly spoken through one of My prophets of the Antichrist who will come and take his seat in the temple. He who is discerning and wise, let him guide the brothers and sisters in faith with humility. Lastly, I alone am to be worshipped. I already know, but you yourself know in your hearts when you cross over that line of giving more homage to the human person of Baha'ullah that what any human is spiritually entitled you. And yet, blessed are all those of compassionately and lovingly remember all their founders, sages, prophets, leaders, pastors, and apostles who cared for their people and nurtured them in the faith. Are they not all lens through which God's glory shines out to the peoples?

O all you non-theists: Buddhists, Jains, Confucians, and Taoists, do you eat from the bowl or drink from the cup and yet do not recognize the bowl-maker and cup-maker? Why is it that you fail to recognize Me, Creator of the Heavens and Earth? I formed you in your mother's womb (c.f. Jer. 1:5). I have created, designed, and fashioned all life. All my other peoples of the world not only recognize Me and My hand behind all in Creation, but they gladly honor, praise, and worship Me. But you do not. Much better for your souls to recognize Me during your life on Earth than to wait to be shocked and Tremble on the Day of Judgment when your soul will be brought before Me for to determine your eternal destiny. And what will be your destiny? To fear, believe, trust, and love me today will lead you not to be afraid on Judgment Day. But woe unto souls who have received knowledge of Me in this life but chose not to believe in Me. Great fear will come on their souls at the Judgment.

My Spirit leads peoples of faith to true religion, spiritually understood; and My Spirit is the spiritual force that connects all peoples of faith with the Divine and to some extent mysteriously connects people to each other everywhere.

BROKEN FOR A BROKEN PEOPLE

The Spirit led me to a Jewish synagogue to worship with Jewish brothers and sisters. This was not unusual but neither was it my custom. For over twenty years, I have occasionally worshipped with Jewish believers in both the traditional Jewish and Messianic traditions, particularly on festivals. But this particular Shabbat evening in 2011, the Spirit moved on my heart, making it very memorable. During the service, in the secret meditation of my heart before God, I was utterly broken over the horror that these people experienced through the Holocaust. I was about to weep, but held myself back so as not to draw attention to myself in the assembly while we were in the middle of the Kabbalat Shabbat liturgy which contains several joyful praise psalms and a few sober prayers of remembrance. What I experienced I knew was from the Lord. I talked to God in the spirit, "I have been to many Jewish services before, but never before did you lead me for my heart to be broken." I was in seminary at the time the movie "Schindler's List" came out and saw it. It really impacted my mind, but my heart was not yet broken. I knew that God's Spirit was continuing to form and groom me to be a bridge of understanding and peace among peoples of faiths. God was preparing me now in a more full way.

A WORD FOR FOLLOWERRS

As I reflected on the reality that most people are followers, my heart melted as I was reminded by the fact that people are capable of almost blindly following fallible human leaders, charismatic yet void of grace and God's way. It was as if I heard the Spirit's voice, a thundering echo across the sky out to humanity: "Remember the lesson of the horror of Hitler and Nazism." God has brought His swift and powerful judgment upon his soul according to the great responsibility he had, and leading millions astray, committing mass murder and all who participated in this atrocity. The people who were followers were also judged for virtually blindly following the mass murderers. God has planted in every human soul a basic conscience and morality, that they know its wrong to hate and kill other people. God has given this sense even to simple-minded people. When such evil, ungodly, wicked leaders arise, God does not obligate the common peoples to follow them. They are to be civil and obedient in all ways as possible, but in cases such as these, God excuses civil disobedience and even righteous opposition bands. But never does God sanction violence. Bands that call themselves "righteous" but then raid and pillage villages, oppress peoples or kill them, are corrupt. In these cases, God gives authority to the main powers that be, even though they do not recognize God, to maintain order, because order is a prime purpose of the state which facilitates safety, health, and peace among all its citizens.

Because of the great destruction of souls the Nazi dictator perpetrated, his soul will experience his own soul's destructions millions of times in the deep outer darkness and will never see the Light.

My heart went out again as I thought about the peoples of the world who are like sheep, but they do not have caring shepherds to care for their souls with grace until the day of eternal grace is gained. But they have spiritual leaders who are as much if not more concerned with temporal politics, enticed by worldly ambition, and lacking love, care, and grace of their flocks. Though they believe and teach they have the "true religion," their religion seems more like a guise for their earthly political ambition.

My heart went out to the millions in countries where little is known about God and yet these people seem good-hearted and humble people. They surely have a religion, actually more than one to chose from, and in fact, they can hold to more than one at the same time. They meditate. They may visit shrines. They may contemplate in nature. They may refrain from any actions. They may rhythmically chant in sacred communities, They may study sacred texts. They may practice various rituals, incantations, or magic chants. They may believe they are enlightened, and hope to achieve salvation. But for most, salvation is a vague, unclear, uncertain concept. "O God," I prayed, "Bring your light to these millions. Let them drop superstitions and fall in love with the living, loving, global God."

FAITH: THE WORLD'S STUMBLING STONE

O faith, the world's stumbling stone! Moderns dismiss it as tales and fictitious myths, however moral, but humanistic creations. But the truth of God endures, and the stories in His Scriptures for peoples on Earth are faithful and true. Faith in God is the key that unlocks which door of our eternity destiny we will step into. The faith of God unto His righteousness grants us eternal bliss. O faith, through the ages even to this age, you are the world's stumbling stone.

THE DREAM OF THE FOLLY OF FALSE MYTHOLOGY

I dreamed this dream. In the dream, an angel took me, brought me into this building. Coming into the entrance, I saw a hallway going to the right and one going to the left. The one on the right was full of light, and above it read "Truth." The one on the left was dark and above it read "Folly."

The angel took me down the hallway of folly to the left, and I did not know why. There were several doors along the hallway that were closed. The angel opened one of them, and led me in. I looked at the angel with uncertainty. He nodded for me to go in. The room was very dark. My eyes began to get adjusted to the darkness, and I could see it looked like a movie theater. The angel motioned for me to sit down, and the angel sat next to me. Then on the screen up front a motion picture began to show, an epic of gods and goddesses, their interactions and play, the follies and emotions, the love and their battles, their incest and their warfare. As the movie played, I became aware of the audience of many people in the movie theater watching the same movie. At the end of the movie, the audience energetically applauded. It was revealed to me that it was all just entertainment for them. They did not believe in any of these gods and goddesses. They were just myths of human imagination. But they could relate to them because the lives of the gods and goddesses depicted were much like themselves.

I looked at the angel, and I could tell that he knew I was marveling. I was marveling that this was a holy angel of God, and could someone come down to this world where there is folly, and yet remain pure, uncorrupted. The angel then led me out of the hall of Folly, and down the hall of Truth. Then the dream had ended.

A WORD FOR ANIMISTS

This word came to me, as I reflected on animism, the belief in spirits all around us on Earth. These thoughts came: O you who fear the spirits all around, your belief is unfounded, rooted in superstition. But fear the One, the All-Powerful One, who can send your soul to Hell or bring you up to a glorious eternity. He has given us the light of His revelations which gives true knowledge, leading us from darkness and ignorance of superstitions to the truth and true light of His all-encompassing power, His majesty, glory, and Sovereignty of the universe. His light moves us from unfounded fear to trust and love of Him. Cast aside your unfounded fears, and receive a new life in the light and truth of God!

O you who think you have to appease these other spirits of your imagination, come, listen to me, and I reveal a higher way. One only is to be appeased: God Supreme. Almighty God has created all things in heaven above, on the Earth, and the seas below. He has given us humans to have dominion over all things on Earth. Consider those spirits, if you cannot dismiss them from your minds, as your equals. You need not fear the forces you sense when you realize they are all under control of God almighty who is not out to get you, but cares about you, yes, loves you! Be subservient, yes, to the One, that is, God. Re-orientate your spirit to this view of living in harmony with both God and nature, the Source of nature."

FREEDOM OF WILL

God says, "I have given freedom of will to all my human children. My desire and law is that they all chose good, and enter into a free, loving, and blessed relationship with Me their Life-Giver. But some do choose evil, and in their evildoing, often cause pain or suffering on My children. And My heart is broken whenever evil comes to any of my children causes pain or suffering."

THE LIGHT OF PLEASING GOD

O souls whom I desire to delight in, know you not the things that please me: to believe in Me, to listen to My word, to let My word guide your life, to fear, trust, and love Me above all things, to let My righteousness penetrate into your soul, and then to do righteousness and justice on Earth, to be kind and show kindness and compassion, to love your family members, and to love others in the community and society as you would have them love you (Golden Rule). Am I also not pleased with these: to be trustworthy and honest and fair with others and in your dealings, to be controlled and tempered, and to be sharing and generous as you have the means. And do I not delight in souls who study and meditate on Scriptures to get to know Me better, and to live in a relationship with Me. But knowledge can be used for good or evil.

I am more pleased with a 5-year old child who innocently prays to me, thanks Me for all I have given them, than with a philosopher whose sharp intellect can expound on metaphysics and the nature of the human soul, but who does not glorify me with his/her words or in his/her heart.

My Spirit has revealed to many souls through the ages, anchored by a conscience orientated to the holy Divine, that God is the All-Knower and Judge of all our thoughts, words, and deeds/actions. I brought light to Moses, Zoroaster, Isaiah, Jesus, and Muhammad. I also brought light to Gautama Buddha, Laotzu and Confucius, who each received it through the filter of their culture and understanding. They too taught the truth of the conscience and good morality by believers and in society.

I have been reaching out to peoples of the Earth through the ages, to lead them on the path of truth, goodness, civility, and spiritual nobility. My truth has come to noble souls and ordinary souls. Upon them was enlightened the truth that human beings are tied to their character, and character is tied to our thoughts, words, and actions.

God-fearing, seeking, and contrite souls have been enlightened to the truth that in all things: our thoughts, intentions, motivations, attitudes, the words we say, and all our actions and deeds come under My awareness and judgment. Nothing can be hid from My knowledge.

It has taken centuries, even millennia, to get human beings to begin to grasp that My main motive and character is love, pure unconditional love for peoples. But this world, I know, is not easy. So many things can go wrong or bad, that you feel that I'm out to get you. Do not believe that. The world does not provide the light of truth to you. My word provides the truth. Listen to Me, follow My instructions, and I will delight in you. Believe, fear, trust, and obey, and My righteousness will shine through you, and you can come confidently before Me in the Day of the Great Judgment. My Spirit places truth in your internal conscience within your soul, and this will guide you through life, and life pleasing to Me.

GETTING RIGHT WITH GOD

How does a person, O man, O woman, get right with God?
Will 1000 prayers bring down His platonic love?
Will 1000 meditations mediate it?
Will 1000 right intentions gain it?
Will 1000 fastings fix it?
Will 1000 prostrations prosper it?
Will 10,000 sacrifices secure it?
Will 100,000 rituals seal it?
How can we get right with God?
How can we lift ourselves to Heaven to claim it?

Is this not the righteousness of God to believe in Him (Gen. 15:6) and His word (c.f. Jn. 6:29), and then in response to His word, live by faith (Hab. 2:4), do God's righteousness and justice (c.f. Mic. 6:8) brought to Earth through His Word made live in human hearts, minds, and souls.

God loves human hearts that look to Him, call out to Him, and love Him. But no amount of religious rituals can get us right with God. It is God's Spirit who empowers faith in our hearts to believe, and from believe, His righteousness is imputed (Gen. 15:6). "All your man-made religions on Earth," says God, "gives you plenty of ritual. Many of the rituals are helpful in preparing souls to turn to Me or get in the right spiritual mind. But do not cling to any false doctrine or hope that any number of rituals, performed rightly, and with the best intentions of heart, mind, and soul," will grant you special merit or favor from Me; from human-made institutions, organizations, religious teachers and gurus. I look for the pure heart who desires to commune with Me, and none of the rituals no matter how many you perform will gain you the grace that will be sufficient to enter Paradise. Believe and trust in Me and My Word. And I desire obedience as well as faith."

THE WORKS OF HUMANKIND

Take care, O man, O woman, as to the works in your life, that they are not in league with darkness. All human works will go through the great holy fire. And only the works that make it through the holy fire will be accepted by God. They will have been purified. All other works will be burned up. Be careful, O soul, that you do not come before God in the great Judgment with no works to show forth to please God. In one lifetime, one can produce abundant works acceptable to God. Taking a percentage of your income to give to God through a religious organization or character, caring for your family, acts of kindness. But be assured all human works of darkness on Earth that does not give glory to God will be incinerated.

CORRUPTION OF HUMANKIND

My Spirit has revealed my previous words, that I tear down, but I build up (c.f. Hos. 6:1-2). I judge, but I restore. I have revealed My heart of mercy. But as a truthful God, I call a spade a spade. Humanity is corrupt, but not hopeless. Were it not for My power, Spirit, and word of restoration, transformation, glorification, there would be no hope for human souls or humanity for a blessed eternity.

I sought the Lord God as to why so many people want to deny corruption in human beings, though its heard or shown practically everyday in the secular news.11 The Spirit revealed to me that it is not just a spiritual condition of spiritual obstinateness or rebellion before God. They are completely saturated in its tainting and its all around the environment, that they just don't realize it is all around. It is like asking a pig in a mud hole what clean is. It is like two people on a hill and far away is the view of a beautiful lake. But they can only see it through the telescope they have, and the telescope has a permanently dirty lens. No matter how hard they try to see the beautiful lake, it will be marred by the dirty lens.

God is pure. We can imagine and contemplate His purity, but we cannot fully see it or comprehend it because our natures are tainted, saturated with a corrupted element.

I, says God, do not desire the eternal consequences on human souls for corruption. Each soul did not cause the state of corruption in the world. But each soul is a part of the collective corruption. It is like mercury in your flesh. It is hard to get out. But I desire to restore all souls to a state of purity, all souls who turn to Me, and I have the power to purify. Unpleasant it will be for your souls to go through the purification process of my holy fire, but many times worse will be the hell-fire. After the purification process, you will rejoice along with all the saints after the purifying process.

THE DISPLEASURE AND JUDGMENTS OF GOD

I have spoken abundantly in the Scriptures of the past the things that displease Me, yes, even the things that I hate: Through Solomon I declared these seven things I abhor:

"an arrogant look, a lying tongue, hands that shed innocent blood, a heart that devises wicked plans, feet that are swift to run to evil, a false witness, and one who sows discord among the believers" (Prov. 6:17-19 MT).

Even these things cause me sore displeasure, and I will sternly judge:

> Killing of innocent people,
> Meditating to murder,
> Plotting to destroy other lives,
> Bearing false witness,
> Slandering an individual,
> Slandering a race or tribe of people saying they do not have souls;
> Spiritual slander of putting oneself in God's place and saying who will make it to Heaven and who will not; Lifting oneself in the place of God is a grave sin; Corrupting my Word;
> Lying and deceiving;
> Taking from widows,
> Abusing children and orphans;
> Stealing, Merchant gouging, cheating for one's own gain,
> Schemes of the wealthy to get more from the poorer, Corporate corruptions of all kinds,
> Immorality, fornication, sodomy, rape, pedophilia,
> Adultery, marital infidelity, and
> Gross pollution and careless treatment of the Earth, earth, and all its resources.

I will judge all these souls according to their sins before Me. There are no corporate sins or crimes that are immune. They have no protection nor can they hide from My judgment. All things are known by God. None can escape My judgment. Divine wrath will come upon souls who have sinned greatly and remain unrepentant. The holy terror of God will come upon their soul that they will not be able to escape from at that time, whether to flee, hide, or intoxicate. For some, the fires of hell will be inescapable.

GOD'S JUDGMENT ON CHEATING DEALERS, MERCHANTS, CORPORATIONS

I saw the demon of greed go out into all the world. It went out to people of all kinds and in every land, from wealthy bankers and corporate executives down to poor street vendors and peddlers. It enticed many people to gouge, cheat, swindle, steal, lie, and deceive. It led them not to be satisfied with decent salaries. It stirred evil within their hearts. It corrupted their minds to not be satisfied with healthy competition. "We must destroy the little guy," was what came out of their mouths in their private boardrooms. "We must tarnish the image of our competition." "We must be king." We want it all. We want to control all the assets."

God's judgment is swift about all these souls. No business name, building, or offices are off limits to God. They cannot hid from the all-knowing Spirit of God. Their business name or structures cannot protect them. He observes and knows all dealings. All dealings, all conversations, all files, all safes, all vaults are wide open to the Spirit of God. He looks on the inside of people, even their inner thoughts and hearts. All is made bare before God. When all along they thought God was a myth, or dead, or your business deals off limits of faith, the Day of the God on these souls will be a trembling terror. They will writhe in His presence. They will fall on their knees, not out of humility to confess His name but agonizing over the reality of God, His judgment, and their shame. Great corporate executives will suddenly become as small helpless impoverished children. They will have wished they had not succumbed to greed. But their remorse will be too late.

O man, O woman, do not think that the demon is to blame. The wills of all these people were in league with the demon of greed. There was no one who led them on the path of greed out of duress. It was their our heart and will that welcomed it in.

O do not be deceived. Have human beings really advanced through the ages? O yes, technologically, and if technology is your God, then you would affirm "Yes." But peoples in the faith of God do not confuse earthly creations, not even all the gold in the world, with God. Human beings have only gotten more sophisticated at their cheating, conniving, and back-door dealing. Corrupted and illegal dealings taking place in private corporate offices is common place, but no corporate door can shut out the Spirit of God. Some of the illegal corporate dealings are kept a secret, only known by a handful at the top, but the systemic corrupted corporate culture is that all employees are to keep quiet about anything they see are hear wrong. Employees and officers are expected to pledge their loyalty to the corrupted corporations. The beds they sleep in are ruffled with deceiving, cheating, conniving, customer gouging, and cover-ups. All their sins are known by the Spirit of God who searches all things out. The searing heat of God's retribution will come swiftly to them all, especially for making more people poorer and making the rich, richer still.

THE SIN OF USURY

The world has gone its own way, says God, not according to My will or word, but led and driven by the greed of worldly financiers and leaders. My judgment is against all who have forsaken my word on usury. My judgment is not against anyone making an honest living, but on those who burden high debts upon the poor in order to make the wealthy even more wealthy. My judgment is on all who rig the financial systems to feed more of the wealth to those who are already wealthy.

PAIN AND SUFFERING

O cry out, precious soul to God. Especially in times in pain and suffering, we ask why God allows it. Why did God even create it to begin with? Has God created it to deliberately inflict it upon us? Especially in a moment of intense pain, it sure may feel like it is a deliberate plan of God.

But precious soul of God, do not turn your back on God. Instead, lift your soul in faith to hear God's word, "My precious beloved. I know that you do not fully understand now. In your present human state, the pain is real and can be intense, it may even seem torturous. My desire is not for any of my children to abide in pain, agony, or suffering. My child, trust and be comforted that none of My children are lost. Not one life is snuffed out by evil or accident without my Presence to carry that precious soul to the blessed eternal habitation. You too will see your loved ones who have gone before you. Trust My divine purposes for allowing pain and suffering in this life.

"My heart delights whenever a soul looks up to Me and earnestly seeks Me, and trusts in Me even though you don't understand the reason for the suffering. My heart delights when the suffering you experience builds character and virtues such as humility and patience. My heart delights when the suffering you experience builds faith and trust in Me and love toward Me. My heart delights when a child of mine who has the tendency to be wayward or rebellious turns their heart back to Me. At times, I use suffering to discipline my children. At times, suffering is to lead a child of mine back to Me.

"Do not think that all suffering you experience is for your sins or that the suffering should lead you to feel guilty. My Soul delights when guilt in a child of mine is freed and let go. You know in your heart whether you have been disobedient toward Me or not. And you know that I desire for all my children to live in spiritual freedom, not to carry a shadow of guilt around with them.

"The patience and endurance that suffering produces strengthens your spirit, builds hope and trust, preparing you for your blessed eternal habitation. The pain and scars you have today will be removed, and you will fly to My Glory, and the former sorrows forgotten."

FOR THE DISCOURAGED OF FAITH

O you, precious soul, who has been discouraged by your own religion, believing it to be the truth, the true way to God, only to find corruption as you moved up the ranks to those in power. God is God, is He not? Put your trust in Him. He loves you and desires for you to one day live with Him in the glory of Heaven. But God is not finished with your life on Earth. He has brought you to this time and moment. There are others as yet who do not know Me, though they hold to your same religion. For them, it is only a religion, a custom of man; it is the accepted thing in society. But have desired to know Me. I desire others to know Me too. Take My word to them. Share the message of a living God who desires to care and love all people.

SPIRITUAL MATURITY

I was considering the state of people everywhere who hold to some religion but who cannot hardly talk about religion with people different than their views, without getting negatively emotional, defensive and perhaps argumentative. I was driving at this moment, and I saw a flash of light across my vision. At first I thought it was a flashing light from an emergency vehicle, or lightning. But I did not see any of those. It was, as I concluded, a prophetic flash, which I had never had before that I recall. Then the thought from the Spirit of God came, "This is the state of the level of human spiritual maturity. There is much room for improvement. After thousands of years of development, humans still remain relatively spiritually immature, but not all humans. Some have attained high levels, usually prophets, sages, gurus, and some mystics. But the majority of people spend most of the time and energy focused on earthly concerns. God knows the needs and difficulties of human life. But more can be challenged to a higher spiritual level, when their ministers or spiritual leaders and teachers on Earth so help to equip them through messages: sermons, books, CDs, DVDs, TV broadcasts, radio, seminars and conferences.[12] Too many settle for mediocrity in their lives. The next thought that came to me, that I believed was Spirit-led, was "Write." Write the many words I have been given you in these last few years.

THE AGES OF HUMANITY

The Spirit guided me to see prophetically the ages of humanity. I saw long ago in which many people lived relatively in darkness, just having a little light from natural revelation, but lived mostly as superstitious animists. Then I saw great ages that came that elevated in culture, civilization, and thought, birthing some great philosophers. But this age and civilization was viewed as still darkened in their paganism by yet another age of faith that came after them. In every age, God has been trying to speak.

As I had contemplated the spiritual ages of humanity, I saw a great light that appeared to be a divide from all ages past and all ages from that time forward. The insight that came to me, Spirit-guided, flowing out of the biblical Scriptures, is that the final sacrifice, the holy Lamb, Jesus Christ (Jn. 1:29), if you are willing to receive, completed the age of sacrifice and ushered in the age of non sacrifice, except the spiritual sacrifice or offerings of thanksgiving, praise, worship, tithes, charity, almsgiving, and service. No longer has God looked to nor expect peoples on Earth to perform bloody sacrifices, such as animals, and certainly not humans, to atone for, propitiate their sins and appease the judgment and displeasure of God to gain His favor. The author of Hebrews revealed that this Jesus offered Himself up "once" for "the sacrifice of sins forever (Heb. 10:10, 12) and "perfected forever those who are being sanctified (Heb. 10:14 NKJV). Not everyone will receive this word into their hearts, especially for those not raised on the Judeo-Christian Scriptures.

There have been spiritual awakenings, revivals, renewals, and rebirths in the last few centuries in particular, but has human nature really transformed yet? Many teachers and spiritualists are claiming that they feel "in the spirit" that the Earth is being or has undergone a transformation." May a transformation of souls from those who once lived for themselves, ignorant to God, to believing, honoring, and praising God come to the whole world.

I also contemplated the pride that people have for themselves, their people groups, their culture, and their nation, A degree of pride is acceptable for all peoples and nations; but there is a degree to which it rises arrogantly as stench before God. The word of wisdom, adage, which applies to this spiritual condition is, "Pride comes before the fall." Remember the pride and lesson of the Titanic. Refrain from saying or believing that your age, culture, or nation is the greatest the Earth has ever seen. In our pride, God may decide to send such a catastrophe upon that nation to teach it the lesson of arrogant pride.

Let us all live humbly before God, fearing, trusting, and loving Him, knowing that if we lift ourselves in gross pride He could cause events upon the Earth to bring our culture or civilization back into the Dark Ages.

THE NEW AGE

A glorious new age is coming, and it is already here by faith! The glory seen through faith on a peoples enlightened by His Spirit, a peoples who do not sit in darkness as in bygone ancient times (c.f. Is. 9:2a), but enriched with the spiritual gifts of God: faith, hope, comfort, and a vision of the glorious Transformation to come. Some see that Transformation as already happened spiritually. We need just to open up our spiritual eyes as in the Celestine vision (Redfield). Others in blessed faith see that new age having been ushered in by a man God appointed in modern times. Others in faith see the beginning of the new age through the Cross of the glorious Christ and Savior, but who now await for His return. The greatest New Age is yet to come, O peoples of faith around the world, when God makes all things new in the heavens and Earth, and all in faith are glorified, transformed, and lifted up to their places of eternal bliss.

God's word in Scriptures past mainly was to instill faith, inspire hope, and give comfort. In the same Scriptures, He also gave warnings of hell and hell fire. Receive, dear soul, which of these words your soul needs to hear. If you are in gross sin or spiritual rebellion, then take in the warning. But if you have humbled yourself before God, longing for Him, desiring to live with Him, then take in the Good News into your heart. Let God's Spirit guide you in the wisdom of applying the appropriate word to your spiritual condition, whether word of warning or word of good news.

Arise! Let God's light shine on you. You can reflect the blessed New Age in your life!

THE STATE AND FATE OF THE EARTH

Praise and thanks be to God for the invaluable life and sustenance provided by His Earth, our mother-ship of life, our enduring earthly home. Be diligent and wise in taking care of all of it from pole to pole and around the whole circle of earth. In essence, God has charged us humans with the care of the earth.

In the beginning, did God not command us to take care of the earth in the words "to tend" (Gen. 2:15). And do not corrupt the meaning of God's command to the first humans to "have dominion" (Gen. 1:26, 28) over it the living things on the Earth as an excuse to extract any elements or minerals carelessly from it. Many opportunists have interpreted the "dominion" command to mean "exploit."

Lament, O soul, over the misuse, carelessness, pollution, and rape of the Earth, carelessly extracting ore, elements and minerals for profitable gain.

O you who carelessly extract from the Earth. Learn the spiritual lesson from the Native Americans. Say a sincere humble prayer to God before extracting, asking first for permission from God's Earth, then thanking God for the resources that He has provided. To not recognize God in this process, judgment has come to your souls, a judgment you will later regret.

Lament, O soul, the path of conflict and destruction that humanity chose through technological revolutions: from stone weapons of adze and arrow points, it became copper and bronze points, swords, and shields. Bronze gave way to iron points and swords. Then came gun power which led to speeding bullets and cannon balls. From bullets and cannon balls delivering instant death to dozens, came bombs delivering instant death to hundreds and thousands; and out of this arose that atomic and nuclear bombs capable of instantly killing hundreds of thousands or millions.

Reckon, O soul, the great need of humanity with its huge population of billions in this age. Did not God know that one day this day would arrive? It almost seems that God hastened it on in His first command to human beings from the Hebrew Scriptures "to be fruitful and multiply (Gen. 1:28). God knew the end from the beginning. He knew that history would race forward to the time humans are capable of such massive self-destruction. It is not that God was eager for the destruction to happen, but He foreknew that this was the path that humans would choose. So

He let them play it out, but God from ancient times promised such a beautiful day of restoration of all things to come. Humans in their depravity pollute, corrupt, and sometimes destroy. But God in His goodness restores and gives the gift of living eternally in His glory for all who believe and trust in Him.

NOT BY MIGHT, NOT BY ARMS

O peoples who claim a faith, do you still not hold to the things of this world like a clutching baby's hand? How quick you are to raise the arm in conflict. Shame upon those who cause violence, incite riots, or kill in the name of God throughout the ages. The "name of God" is but an excuse for their own hearts inclined to evil. Have you washed yourself of your sins and the sins of your forefathers?

And you, precious souls, pure in heart but naïve, easily led astray by charismatic leaders. Learn and remember the lesson of Jonestown and Waco. The first was a deluded leader who lead his followers to commit mass murder. The other had delusions of an armegeddon and stock-piled guns and ammunitions, and it ended in a blaze that was warmly invited, a kind of self-fulfilling prophecy to the point of self-destruction. This deluded leader led his followers to that tragic end.

It is not by might nor by arms that the kingdom of God comes on earth. The prophet Zechariah, speaking through the word of God, said, "Not by might, nor by power, but by My Spirit says God" (Zech. 4:6 MT). Cast off your carnal minds. The kingdom of God is spiritual. The apostle Paul said, "The kingdom of God is not food and drink, but righteousness and peace and joy in the Holy Spirit" (Rom. 14:17).

In your human weakness, if you feel the need to, keep one weapon in your home for your personal and family's protection. But when it comes to spiritual matters, walk and live by faith.

He is your protection. And He NEVER sanctions violence to advance His Kingdom on Earth nor should any person of faith use violence in God's name and thus corrupt their religion. The noble religions are spiritual and wholly dedicated to the goodness of humanity in their pure state. But religions are possessed by impure people. God's Kingdom, however, is not the ways of humanity saturated in corruption; nor is it the way of conflict and competition.

In former times in human history, such a diabolical ugly head raises, bent on mass murder, in the midst of a society with a strong community of faith, and the community of faith, meeting in secret, determine that this diabolical human leader needs to be assassinated. They will ask God to forgive them, and God will forgive them for planning the assassination and attempting it, whether successful or not. Wisdom leads such a community of faith to be so secret that it is just a small handful of skilled men who are zealous for God's cause, and to keep the knowledge of such a plan away from most of the people in the community of faith so they have not even a tinge of blood-guilt on their souls.

THE WARFARE OF HUMANITY

I looked out on the sea of humanity through the ages, and I saw what seemed to be countless warfare battles, bloodied bodies by the thousands here and there, lying around for acres, and some piled up like refuse, time and time again, age after age, virtually all tribes, races, and nations. When I saw the sight, I became so distraught, so weak to the point of collapse, falling on the ground as if myself mortally wounded. I cried out to God, "Why?! Why?! Why did this have to be? I listened to the voice of God. There was no great thunderous voice from Heaven. It was like the still quiet voice, the whisper of the Spirit which revealed to me: "These things are because of the nature of human beings. Until their nature changes from the inside, even in their internal spirit and soul to transform them, these ways will continue. But a glorious transformation will come." As I began to think about the glorious transformation to come, my spirit was revived, and I was able to get up.

RELIGIOUS CONFLICT ON EARTH

I cried out to God over the fact and tragedy of the much religiously motivated violence on the Earth through the ages. "Why, O God?!, I lifted up my voice in the spirit. And the thought that the Spirit implanted in my mind is, "Humankind is corrupt. They identify with a religion or they adopt one, but their nature is not yet transformed. Only through purgation of the soul from its corruption, which some attempt while yet in the body of flesh, will transformation come."

And I complained to God, saying "But religious peoples or people motivated by the religion inflicting violence makes their own religion look bad in the eyes of others. These things should not be!" And it was as though I heard the wise and quiet voice of the Spirit say, "When they engage in the bad behavior, they know it, and I will judge them for it. Some are them of the world who do not even know Me, though they became a religion. They do further injustice. All violence is inexcusable. Peoples of faith today need to be warned and learn the lessons of the past to not repeat the inexcusable acts of violence. I have appointed you to get this word out in the world. The majority of people will only partially understand, and their natures will not be transformed by it, but some will heed and vow to live to the higher calling of peace and spiritual nobility.

In time, the work of these words and other peaceful Scriptures will continue to be planted in many souls to bear a blessed and abundant harvest of peace in the future.

PROPHECY FOR AMERICA

The following word came to me on October 14, 2011, the first conscious thought I had when I woke seconds before the alarm clock went off.

O the land of the great Eagle, land of the red, white, and blue. Great you have risen upon the Earth; you have risen among all nations; had risen above them all in great strength of ingenuity, industry, and led with a vision as a moral beacon to the world. Is it not also by My Hand that I have given you your ingenuity, strength, and vision?

O great Eagle, do not lift up your self in pride, and follow the way of Babylon into so great a fall. You are not without sin, like every other nation. On your hands have been found corruption as among other nations, from the top governmental chambers to the military in the foreign fields to municipalities, in institutions, schools, and homes. As yet you are given opportunity to repent of your sins. You are not finished.

I have raised mighty interceders across the land of the great Eagle who come before Me earnestly in prayer for their nation, to turn it in repentance back to its moral founding and grounding, and to once again be the beacon of light to the world. You have slipped from the height of your glory. But the decline of your glory is not irreversible. Your fate has not been sealed. I do not delight in your downfall. I desire prosperity for the many. I desire for your moral beacon to be restored. God desires all nations to be blessed, and He eagerly awaits for repentance and humble hearts turning to Him, and He hears all the prayers lifted up to Him.

Therefore, do not lose heart. Your glory days are not gone forever, if your peoples throughout the land especially its leaders, do humble themselves, pray, sincerely repent and change the ways that need to be changed, then I will give strength to the Great Eagle (c.f. II Chron. 7:14).

And even if too many leaders and the people under the wings of the great Eagle do not acknowledge their Creator nor repent, and I send my judgment upon you, can I not raise up another Eagle to continue as a beacon of light to the world? This Eagle from the Great one may be slimmer than the obese one, the Great one that grew in the land of fat and abundance. I can send disasters, draughts, floods, hurricanes, and earthquakes. I can also send rains and great harvests, abundance, and prosperity.

O you who have been nurtured by the Great Eagle, you have heard fellow inhabitants who live under the wings of the Great Eagle begin to speak of its decline like a sealed fate, prophesying its end. Do not drink from this word of hopelessness and despair. But look to Me, Trust in God. And lead many to pray for repentance. And I, the Lord God, can still bring prosperity back to the land of the Eagle.

THE DELUSION OF ALIENS

A great delusion has come upon the Earth in this age. Apostolic Scriptures did prophesy this day would come. They speak, in fact, of "delusions," more than one, and they have been displayed before our very eyes in this age. This great one I speak of is delusion of an invasion of aliens, extra terrestrials from outer space. If it were the case of just a few novels and movies for entertainment purposes, then probably little harm. But human writers, movie makers, and produces have been saturating audiences year after year to epic delusional proportions. Many will still consider these just for entertainment purposes, but they are not unaffected. The power of a movie picture impacts every viewer, and their makers and producers know this. Their agenda is unveiled.

Indeed, God created all things in the universe, and could have created other intelligent beings on some other planet light years away. And they too could develop high tech space travel such as to lead them to explore and find other intelligent creatures in this universe besides themselves. This speaks to a universal truth that indeed, we intelligent creatures do not want to feel alone, which itself reflects that we do feel alone to some real degree. God alone can fill that yearning. Just the sheer curiosity of the possibility has been enough to wildly stir the imaginations of people around the world in this space age that we live, after we humans invented means of projecting ourselves out of Earth's orbit into space.

O beautiful creatures, if there are any living creatures somewhere far out in Space, then God has made them too and given them intelligence. To discover them in actuality would be the greatest discovery of all times. But the way aliens are depicted by Hollywood is a great delusion. The great delusion is the great unanimous tradition depicting aliens as monsters, body snatches, evil, inter-global terrorists who want to take control of the Earth, in all darkness and diabolical delusion. The various evil ways these demented and perverted minds depicts their deeds of invading and infesting human bodies, filled with all uncleanness; and then disseminating these diabolical portrayals around the world through all media, especially movies, the most powerful way to brainwash the masses, is a diabolical plan. The writers, directors, and produces are in league with darkness. The Spirit of God's anger has been greatly kindled against all behind this delusion. As elsewhere in this world, money is their god. The true God will judge all their works and return to them the portion of darkness on their soul that they poured out on millions.

I lifted my voice up in complaint before God, saying, "O God, the deception of alien invasions like a massive propaganda through books and movies has spread like fire all across the globe, getting a hold of the minds of the people of the world even influencing peoples of faith. Send down your holy fire, O God, and burn up all their works and erase the memory of these fabrications from the minds of all!" I listened in the Spirit as to what God would reveal. It was as if I already knew the answer, for previous Scriptures have spoken, they have prophesied of these deceptions which have now come upon the Earth. Why God allows them, I did not know; why God allows these deceptions to go out, unholy propaganda to be published and proliferated. Why does God not now make anew the heavens and the Earth, and bring all His children into Paradise? While we do not fully understand the why of God's timing and the why of allowing deception and evil on this Earth, we can be certain that He has us here for a purpose, and one of those main purposes is to make a positive difference, to be His lights in this world in which there remains a stronghold of darkness.

TRIBULATION

Life has enough stresses and troubles. Do not add to this worry about some future tribulation. True is the adage, "ignorance is bliss." But searching minds want to know, even good disciples of God's word and ways. What more has been revealed that has not already been revealed about tribulations to come? Indeed, some great tribulations have already taken place. The great tribulation of the Jewish people in the Holy Land by the Romans is the first century C.E and the destruction of the Temple and Jerusalem in 70 CE was one of those events which the prophets and the Son of Man saw and regarding which they prophesied. But not all tribulations have come and gone. There are yet others to come, even a great tribulation of famine and pestilence. In these times, God always has servants to care for the hurting, the lost, the lonely, the destitute, and the disillusioned. Know you not that you are in God's hands both in good and bad times. If you are a God-fearer, do not need to fear tribulation upon the Earth. You have been sealed already by God's loving seal, as John revealed through the angelic revelator (Rev. 7:14, c.f. Eph. 1:13). But if you are not a God-fearer, then be afraid, for fear will come to your soul on the terrible day of the great tribulation.

Jesus Christ said according to John's Gospel, "In this world you will have tribulation, but be of good cheer, I have overcome the world" (John 16:33 NKJV). The Greek word for "tribulation," *thlipsis,* means, as used in the New Testament, more fully: stress, distress, hard circumstances, trouble, and suffering, (CGEDNT p. 83).

Jesus, here, spoke more broadly about the stresses and distresses of life. But He also prophesied of "tribulations beyond the normal stresses of life. He spoke of persecutions and His followers (c.f. Matthew 10:15-22; 13:21). And Jesus prophesied of: a "great tribulation." Matthew wrote Jesus said, "For then there will be a great tribulation such as has not been since the beginning of the world until this time, no, nor ever shall be" (Matt. 24:21 NKJV). The things mentioned before this verse are these portents: deceivers and wars, which are "the beginning of sorrows" (vs. 8), persecution even unto death, false prophets, the gospel of the kingdom preached around the world, and the abomination of desolations! So bad is this great tribulation, that Jesus said, "Unless those days were shortened, no flesh would be saved" (vs. 22). This great tribulation is yet to come in the eschatological days in which we live. But God does not desire for His people to live in fear. His word of exhortation is "Be strong and courageous. The victory is mine, and I have declared you victorious because you are My beloved children."

THE COMING GLOOM AND GLORY

Be wise and plan, O people of faith, for you do not know the exact time of the coming global panic and financial pandemonium. O yes, we will see the signs, but all shun at the idea of the reality when that day arrives! All except the evil opportunists, just as night brings out thieves and predators, so also such great disaster and unknown tribulation will bring out devourers. But peoples of faith, as dreadful as this day sounds, know that you are sealed by God's seal, as our former blessed brother prophesied (Rev. 7:3). Some of you will already have shed the mortal life on that day. Others will still be on the Earth. Especially for you, plan and be prepared. Do not be caught off guard like a thief in the night (c.f. Matt. 24:43; 2 Pet. 3:10). It will not be merely a collapse of the global system but collapse of the worldwide Internet, which the people of earth have not only grown accustomed to but depend on for vital financial transactions. At a time after the world has gotten dependent on the whole digital and Internet system will their be a major shut-in, as if in one day, as if the dark spirit of this world has planned it all along. Panic will break out in the streets. Pandemonium in city after city, millions, billions in sudden distress. The panic will increase in the days immediately following as millions of people scramble for needed supplies. Grocery stores will be flooded, bombarded, raided, and people will run through the markets and malls. Millions of people who once has instant access to their money and direct deposits of paychecks from their employers will not transact. In this time of great distress, women will beat their chests in the streets, crying out to the sky. Vigilantes will arise and run or drive through the cities, raiding supplies. Mansions will be seen in the distress ablaze in fire. Great indeed will be the distress of the world at this time such as the world has never seen, like multiple Armegeddons around the world. The distress of Jerusalem besieged in 70 CE and 1099 CE were only foreshadows of this day to come.

But do not lose heart, beloved in faith, because God does have all His children sealed who are on the earth (Rev. 7:3). It will still be very trying times, but it will not be hell for you, though it seems like hell is happening all around, God's Spirit will give you peace, comfort, and send protectors. God will also send agents of provisions, even from strangers, to keep His people fed, clothed, and in safe shelter. It may seem that the evil of the night is right at the very door, but the evil passes by, because of God's angelic hand of protection.

Just as there is all economic strata in society, from the very rich to the very poor, so it is also among the people of faith. Generosity is called upon the wealthy to help the poor. In these days in particular, help one another. Care for one another. There will be moments of joy, happiness, and sacredness when a mother gives birth to a child, or when in singing sacred hymns and praise songs in the night that waft up in the sacred space of the sanctuaries where you are gathered.

So be wise and prepare for the day. It does not mean not to use the online system. But safely keep in hiding a cache of coins, cash, and other tradable valuables for the day when all electronic transactions collapse, that you will have means to obtain food and other supplies for a time.

Do not lose hope in a future. God keep you in peace and faith during the trying hours. There are yet better and brighter days ahead. For some, it will be sooner as they enter into Paradise. For those who remain, things will improve. After a period of time, pandemonium will subside, after some horrible riots and killings. Stability will eventually return by a powerful leader. God exhorts us to pray for those in authority. Earnestly pray during these days, for there is no Paradise yet on Earth, but at least stability will be restored by a powerful hand.

THE CONSUMMATION OF THE AGES

Through the ages, I have spoken of the consummation of the ages to come. The Earth's history will be wrapped up and a glorious re-creation of the heavens and the Earth. Because this day tarries, many people do grow weary in their faith. Look to Me, whether you live or die, you are my precious soul. I have given my prophecies of the coming consummation to prepare humanity, but each soul, believer, should not live in angst about its coming. Live your lives on Earth, try to enjoy it while living morally, and always in faith toward Me, and I will bless you. So whether this consummation comes tomorrow, or next month, or next year, or 900 years from now, do not worry. Sufficient is this day for your concerns (c.f. Matt. 6:34).

THE BLESSED DAY

Blessed is the Day of transformation.
Blessed is the Day when there will be no more pain.
Blessed is the Day when there will be no more grief or sorrow.
Blessed is the Day of the healing of the nations.
Blessed is the Day of the gathering of all the purified souls.
Blessed is the Day of the gathering of all the souls in glorious Heaven.

THE GREAT JUDGMENT

I have declared, says God, in revelations of your past of the Great Judgment of all souls. Let My Spirit penetrate the truth of this great day. I know all things. I see the end in the beginning. It is as if My judgment has gone forth. For you in human flesh in the temporal world, it is still to come. Fear Me! He who does not fear Me in their life of earthly testing would wish they had had such an attitude after they arrived at the place of condemnation. No human soul will be allowed to opt out or take a rain check. On that day that I call your soul to appear before my great Throne room and court in Heaven, you will come. Prepare during your lifetime by living in faith, in prayer, in thanksgiving. Do not be caught in shock or terror of your soul before My awesome presence on that Day.

HELL

The prophecies given through the Prophets in past ages have spoken in clear and vivid imagery: a place of punishment for the wicked, fire and pain, ghouls and torments. The prophecy of Jesus further clarifies it as a place of everlasting fire where souls sentenced there will wail and gnash their teeth (Matt. 13:42). The Spirit has spoken. The prophecies have gone out to the world, to those who heed the warning, and not dismiss them as myth of human imagination, fear, and guilt.

PARADISE, HEAVEN, EVERLASTING LIFE

The Spirit has spoken. The visions of Paradise and Heaven of Scriptures past have been rich, beautiful, and just enough, not too much, to continue to inspire earthlings and invite wonder. With a rich variety with beautiful imagery the Spirit has given. In one imagery, it is a happy family joyfully eating under a fig tree on a beautiful day. In another, a perfect pastureland with a flowing brook of clean water. To another, it is a beautiful seascape on a lush coast with perfect climate. In other visions, it is a celestial habitation above the clouds in Heaven, invisible to us now. The oldest, most enduring and popular visions is that of The Garden, the Garden of Eden. This Garden is perfect, idyllic, serene, in an enclosure which bars all sin or evil from gaining access, Picture it as the most beautiful park, with colors so vivid, perhaps in a lush valley with a stream flowing through the middle, with trees and a variety of plants, and the people therein, most content, sinless, holy. And animals are found there too, from large giraffes to lions and tigers, to goats, sheep, dogs and cats. But none in ferocious or flesh-eating behavior. There, the lion lays down with the lamb (c.f. Is. 11:6). Add to this image an abundance of fruits to eat, partaking of its delights: figs, dates, pomegranates, grapes, and olives, and grains of all kinds. The imagery from the Scriptures of

Arabia depict Paradise in Arabian terms: arriving at a grand oasis to be so refreshed, shaded from the intense desert sun, water to quench the thirst and eating of the delights from the date palm trees. And add to this picture, young dancing women, delights to men's eyes, applied now to the vision of the heavenly Paradise: feasts and dancing virgins, no end of this delight. God's Spirit has given the inspiration of Paradise and Heaven in terms that their cultures related to.

Some visions reflect a surreal and heavenly place, totally other-worldly, in or beyond the clouds. Other visions have seen Paradise as a real place between Heaven and Earth, a place that is beautiful and free of corruption and sin. And yet others have spoken of a Paradise on this Earth that we know, but that which will be purified, all sin removed, on a great day of transformation to come.

The crossing over from the life in the body of flesh and blood to the permanent state is the entering of everlasting Life. God's Spirit has desired to give people faith, hope, and comfort in this life to prepare them for the glorious life to come. Some Scriptures speak more clearly with these words of faith, hope, and comfort. Other Scriptures reflect a people pre-occupied with their worries of leadership in temporal affairs, but the Spirit still reaches souls by the miracle of God.

I heard a soul on Earth cry out to God, "Why do we have to suffer in this life?" Then I heard the Spirit answer, "The life in the body of flesh and blood soon passes away. The short-lived suffering there makes Paradise all more sweeter."

Some souls while in their earthly life wrestle through these issues, and seek God's face. Others postpone these issues and do not properly prepare to cross over. They also risk being shamed by God and cast away from His presence. There will be a purification that all souls will go through before allowed to enter into the glory of Paradise, Heaven. God's purifying holy fire will burn up all unholy thoughts, will, and deeds. There will be various degrees at agony in souls in this process lasting a short time, depending on their preparation or lack of it. This comes around the time of the Judgment of souls. No soul can purify themselves. This is God's action, after His judgment of His imputed righteous through the blessed Advocate, the atonement of sins, for all who believe in God. At that moment is when the angels guide them through the holy purification tunnel. Through this process, they are transformed into the glorious state, and the glory they see at the end of the tunnel is so beautiful that nothing in the world compares, indescribable, all-glorious, full of splendor and brilliance is the holy Light of God, and so beautiful is the sight of myriads of holy angels!

CONCLUSION

O peoples of faith, do not live solely on the fumes of your past glory age, but live a living faith built on the past foundation, lived in the present reality, looking for the expectant hope of future glory. Live everyday anew by God's living word and faith, through the journey from the earthly to the eternal glory which far exceeds the earthly.

SEALING THE PROPHECY

I knew that these prophecies were not to be sealed up as in "shut up," closed, until some distant future, as Daniel 12:4 says of that end of the Old Testament age prophecy, but these are sealed, that is, certified as trustworthy and true, and made visible on paper by the penman, guided by God's Spirit, to then be sent out to this generation in the 21st century. But I lifted up a concern to God in regard to peoples' interpretations of these Scriptures after I am gone. "Will not some misunderstand these words?" When I lifted my concern to God, the Spirit brought these thoughts to me.

"There will always be some who misunderstand and some who are lesser enlightened. Do not concern yourself with those who lack understanding, or even with those who may try to corrupt these words. My Spirit can raise up rocks to prophesy to people in the world. I will deal with any who may misuse these words. These words will be a living Scripture for people. They will be opened and freed for as many who will receive."

In God's Garden is a place of light,
In God's garden are revelations of delight.
In God's Garden of inspiration,
Is your truth, tranquility, and revelation.

PART III
POETRY AND PSALMS

GOD CAN SPEAK

God can speak through theophanies,
God can speak through philosophies.
God can speak through prophetic voices,
God can speak through human choices.
God can speak through cosmic rays,
God can speak through the Ancient of Days.
God can speak through heavens light,
God can speak through earth's delights.
God can speak though whirlwinds,
God can speak through caves and dens.
God can speak from East to West, from North to South,
God can speak even through a donkey's mouth!

SPEAK, O GOD, AND I WILL HEAR

Speak, O God, and I will hear. Open my spiritual ears, and
     I will listen.
Your word is precious, more than gold and silver. (c.f. Ps.
     119:127)

Bring down your word, and I will listen. Give me an
obedient heart.
Open my lips to praise You,
And give me boldness to confess your name before others.
Open my mind to your wondrous thoughts,
and I will come to know your marvelous ways.
Bring me to know You most specially,
Radiant in all glory and majesty.
You have given me life;
Your holy Spirit is welcome in my earthen tabernacle.
Material things are lifeless,
They are dead compared to your living presence!
Cause me to trust in You and your word above all (c.f. Ps.
119:42)

IN THE GARDEN OF GOD

In God's Garden is a place of light,
In God's garden are revelations of delight.
In God's Garden of inspiration,
Is your truth, tranquility, and revelation.
In the garden Heaven and Earth meet,
A snippet of Paradise lays out on a sheet.
In the garden is fullness of delights,
Sun and pools, and flowing fountains,
Flowers and foliage dazzling in the light.
In the garden wafts fragrant aromas,
Of gardenias, honeysuckle, and rose.
O Garden of Eden, O Garden of Zion,
O great Pool Garden of Isfahan, O paradisiacal Gardens
of Rizvan,
Here, You inspired prophets and poets,
Here, You have invited thousands of visitor pilgrims,
And Your Spirit touched their minds, hearts, & spirits
In them you have inspired Paradise into peoples hearts;
In them is pure love and delights.
I sat in the garden meditating on this inspiration,

O Lord, how I love this habitation,
O how I desire to dwell in your Garden unto glorification.

GREAT IS THE RICHNESS AND DIVERSITY OF FAITH TRADITIONS

Rich and diverse are your houses, O faith traditions,
Rich and diverse are your places, O sacred spaces,
Rich and diverse are your faces, O peoples of faith,
Natural and made-made are your sacred structures.
Some of you are ornate, and some of you are simple.
Some of you are colorful, and some of you are plain.
Some of you are cavernous, and some of you are small,
From cathedrals to the spaces of a home living room.
Diverse are the sounds from your places
Loud and quiet, hard and soft are the sounds that fill your
     spaces,
Diverse too are their range from natural sounds of God's
     outdoors,
To beautiful-sounding man-made musical instruments
     through which the spirit soars.
Diverse is the resonance of these sounds within diverse
     houses
Reverberations and echoes around large stone cathedrals,
To muffled sounds from smaller carpeted structures.
Diverse are those man-made sounds,
From soft organ music to triumphant organ blasts,
to solos to multi-voice choirs and inspiring vocal praise
     bands
to meditative sitars to rhythmic acoustic guitars,
to the beats of the bass and loud electric guitars,
to drums and cymbals,
Some prefer the quiet and meditative place,
Where their soul feels closer to God, drawn up in the
Sacred silence or quiet background music, where they
Feel at peace and listen to God
There is a time for jubilation and rejoicing,

There is a time for quiet sober reflection.
Some are accustomed to loud music,
Reaching mostly to young souls mantric.
Great is the richness and diversity of sacred places in the
  Earth.
May God be praised in many places, in abundance of
  spaces.
May billions be blessed in sacred places.

PRAISE TO GOD FOR THE FAITHS

Praise be to God for the Jains for their great care of the
  Earth, down to the smallest gnat.
Praise to God for the Hindus for their outstanding
  devotion to deity.
Praise to God for the Buddhists for their great
  concentration on good.
Praise to God for Judaism-Jews for their love of God's
  Torah (instruction, word).
Praise to God for Zoroastrians (Parsees) for their ethics
  and preserving the sacred fire.
Praise to God for Messianic Jews for their love of Y'shua
  Ha'Mashiach.
Praise to God for Christians for their love of Jesus Christ
  and zealousness for the truth.
Praise to God for Muslims for their passion for the truth
  of one God.
Praise to God for the Baha'is for their spiritual nobility to
  see all religions manifestations from the one and same
  God almighty.
Praise to God for all nature and spirit-based religions
  who both see with their spiritual eyes and feel with
  their beings that all things are connected and part of
  the one ultimate force that holds the whole universe
  together.

PSALMS
Praise to the Creator

Praise to the Creator
Praise to the Maker of all things
God is mysterious and awesome;
His universe beyond comprehension.
We may be small in comparison,
But significant, esteemed in His eyes.
From His creation of the first homo sapiens,
The tribes of the Earth have sprung,
Many and various peoples sung.
Diversity of animals and people,
Of flora and fauna too,
He made all with such variety.
He painted the world in an array of colors,
Browns and greens, blues and purples,
Reds and yellows,
And placed in the sky rainbows.
Upon the skin of humans He fashioned the tones:
Dark and browns to yellows and pales.
God gifted humans with languages,
The creative center for communication,
And endowed them with intelligence above all creatures,
God set all the elements for life on earth,
The sun as the power driver, light and warmth,
Water, the incubator of life,
An atmosphere and magnetic field to protect life on Earth
    from harsh solar rays, and for breath of life for humans
    & all mammals
God gave an abundance of food upon the earth for life,
Many kinds of fruits, variety of plants
Renewable, reproducing, regenerating to sustain life,
Grains and meats to complete diets.
God sent humans to spread out upon the face of the Earth,
Seeking space, food, and new habitations as their numbers
    grew,

Propelled also by a sense of adventure,
Braving even crossing seas into the unknown.
God is a God of peace,
And He, heartfelt looked upon humans lacking peace,
Fighting over land and property through the ages,
Grieving God's Spirit.
God has been communicating to humans through the
    ages,
Many have heard His messages, some have listened and
    received, others did not listen,
And for all who have heard, they but partly understand.
God desires peace between family members,
Peace between neighbors,
Peace between communities
Peace between states and nations.
Praise to the Creator, the Maker and Giver of all things.

The Rock

We praise You, O God, for the rocks of the Earth that reminds us of your permanence; your steadfast love remains forever.

Praised are You how you have created so many elements and minerals, and shaped them together in pressures of the Earth to form such solid forms; compact with marvelous wonder and weight, lines and textures. O wondrous in your Creation in making a foundation for all the habitations of the biosphere. The firmness of the rock points to the firmness of the faithfulness and steadfastness of your nature and character. While the rocks can crack, tumble, and wear, You alone O God are completely solid, firm, and faithful.

Ironic is it as solid as rock is, it transfers all the quakes and shakes of the Earth, assisting sudden Tsunamis which cause instant fear in animals and people. The earth we thought was solid can become unstable in a split second manifested in an earthquake. God has built this into the Earth to continue to lead people everywhere to look to God for His help and salvation. Blessed be the God. God calls thousands home in one disaster. Grieve is poured out to the thousands of families, and yet also blessed is God, for He has not lost a single soul. He has taken them to the land of Glory. Praised be God.

The Woods

Blessed be God who made the woods. Among all the environments on Earth that God has made for humans and animals for habitation and enjoyment, unique is the experience of the woods, unlike the environments of plains, deserts, tundra, and seas. Humans had sensed something special about the woods back before they even had the word "sacred" in their vocabulary. There are special life forces that seem more concentrated, which we feel in the woods, but do not see for the most part. This experience has been intriguing to the inquisitive souls through the ages. On top of that, we hear sounds in the woods that we do not hear quite anywhere else: the sound of the wind blowing through the tree tops, the crackling and popping of the trees as they sway in the wind, the pattering of rain upon the leaves. Moreover, the woods are a haven and habitation for many animals who hide in the woods by day and come out to feed at night. We feel their presence in the day, through we do not see them. Praised be God for the connection that You have given us to all your creatures. May we take care of them all, from the lowly animals that live in the ground or slither around to the animals that live in the canopy above, and the birds of the air.

The River

Praised be God for the amazing gift of water, and the flowing streams that He has made, the basic gift of life on this planet on which we all depend. We praise you for the rivers, and flows of water down the mountains, through the lands, and to replenish the seas after first giving drinks to all people and animals who need to along the way. And praised be you not only for this gift for drink, but for bathing, washing clothes, and for frolicking. And praised be God for the sacredness of water that symbolizes the washing away our sins, providing us forgiveness. Blessed are millions every year who make their pilgrimage to sacred waters, exercising their spiritual faith and freedom, in their own way or tradition, to draw closer to you, O Giver of all waters, rivers of the Earth.

The Ocean

O Praised be You, O God, for the great expanse of the oceans that you have created, to remind us people that though you have made us the crown of Creation, we are greatly humbled at the expanse of the oceans. The sheer size of them and their awesome power especially during mighty storms races fear into the human soul and we cry out to you for help. You, O God, hear our voices even through the roaring of the wind and seas, since no where can we go to escape your presence (c.f. Ps. 139).

In contrast to the fear and trembling that the seas can cause in us, the great oceans have also inspired sages and prophets for centuries to speak of the ocean of your mercy, grace, and love.[13] Praised be God for the oceans of the Earth which He fashioned to humble humanity.

The Desert

Praise be to You, O God, for the desert that you have created on Earth. Blessed are all those who not only find the physical beauty, but spiritual refreshment in this land of contrast of dry and wet. Blessed are the hundreds of monks and hermits through ages past that made their way through wildernesses and deserts on not as much a physical journey as a spiritual journey in faith.

Faith takes us from the seen to the unseen, ultimately to peer into the presence, purpose, and place of God through their eyes of faith. Blessed are all souls, not only monks and hermits, who experience this sometime in their life, past, present, and future. Praise be to God.

The Cave

Praise be to God for the cave. Blessed are these natural shelters, dens of the earth, that both humans and animals sought shelter, rest, and solace from the outside elements. Blessed are You who have also made it a place of spiritual haven, connection to You mystically. You led mystics by your Spirit to realize they may move closer to You through dedicated intentional prayer during a time of fasting, coupled with contemplation on your Word. So several in the ages past have had special cave experiences. In the case of Muhammad, the Prophet of Islam, in the cave of Hira, he believed he received recitations of the very word of God through the angel Gabriel. There are other accounts. The Oracles of Delphi, received in a cave in Greece that had a vent from the earth below which released gases, enabling visions. There are others too. Blessed be God for the gift of the cave for shelter, protection from the elements, for solitude, and for contemplation on the things of God.

Praise the Lord, You Voices of Industry14

A Modern Industrial Psalm of Praise based on Psalm 150
Praise the Lord God!
Smelting fire, glow in glorious praise!
Molds and presses, clap your hands,
praise God with all your might.
Nuts and bolts join together,
unite in praise to the Maker.
Drills, spin for joy to the Author of vortex.

Hammers, swing in gladness,
pound without meekness,
to the Maker of matter and force.
Electrical currents, race in praise,
feel the good pleasure of the Eternal Power.
All moving parts, dance in glee.
Forklifts, lift up your hands in praise.
Pallets, bear your burdens in joy for the Lord.
Trucks, toot your horns in praise.
smooth running engines, move in harmony.
O cranes, lift up your heads in praise to the Giver
of the morning sun, and bow down before Him.
Ships, sound your signals in praise to the Sea-Maker.
Large sounding noises, praise the Lord!
Booming sounds, declare the voice of the Lord.
Whistles and horns, blast in praise.
Let everything that moves or sounds,
praise the Lord God!

PART IV
WISDOM AND DIDACTIC
(TEACHING)

OPENING ADDRESS TO DISCIPLES, READERS, LISTENERS

O peoples far and near, young and old, female and male, of all classes, from urban, suburban, and rural cultures, and everyone in between, reflect on these words, ponder them, savor them and save them in your heart. Take them into your mind. Let them roll around your mind, mutter and meditate upon them. Study and learn them. Let them sink into the sacred place of your soul, created in the image of God. When I say, "my disciples," I am a brother of humanity to you. If you are a youth, then perhaps I also am a spiritual father to you. I am an earthen vessel like yourself, dedicated to God, who has given me much knowledge and wisdom to impart to you, O peoples of faith. I am no self-acclaimed guru claiming to be the incarnation of a deity. I may be called a "teacher," as in function, for so is the gift God has given me, and considered a spiritual and religious teacher, but always remembering that God, His Word and Spirit, is alone the Master Teacher, the Teacher of all knowledge, wisdom, righteousness, justice, and peace. The Spirit of God leads and guides us to the truth. Human teachers, gurus, and masters are fallible; they could disappoint us, but God is the perfect one who never disappoints. Many prophets, gurus, masters, and spiritual teachers have pointed their disciples to the Source of All, the Being of all Goodness, Creator of the Universe. Thanks be to God for all the willing human vessels through the ages who have ascented to and then reflected the Divine light to others.

WISDOM IN VERSICLES

There is the way that moves closer to God and His Light,
And there is the way that moves away from God and His
    Light.
There is a way unto holiness, and there is a way unto
    unholiness.
There is the way of the right path, and there is a way of
    the wrong path.
Easier it is to follow the wrong path, harder but blessed to
    follow the righteous path.
Broad is the path and many paths there are that lead to
    unrighteousness,
But distinct is the path that leads to righteousness, and it
    is usually a narrow one.
There are many paths in life, many of them are temporal,
    spiritually neutral.
And there are many spiritual paths on Earth out of the
    diversity of human cultures.
Some of these spiritual paths are co-relative and mutually
    supportive,
Some have concepts that are very different to each other.
    Wise is the one who can understand these distinctions,
    keeps a faithful heart toward God, and strive for peace.
Choose the path that not only makes sense to you but
    which you feel the Spirit lead you on, the one in

your very being you know is best, most blessed, most assured of heavenly bliss or the ultimate noble goal, in accordance with your conscience, not simply the one that will please your parents, grandparents, or ministers, or teachers.

The way of forgiveness is the way of the blessed,

Unforgiveness grieves the Spirit of God, and grudges only hurts the soul who holds it.

Blessed are those who diligently work; they glean the fruit of their labors.

Blessed are those who bring peace into their homes; happier will their families be.

Blessed are they who are charitable and generous; God rewards them in the ways God chooses, whether spiritual or tangible blessings or both, and sometimes multifold.

Blessed are they who have integrity, character, and who are respected in society,

They who are so by character and not simply to get honor by people in the community.

Strive to live in peace with all, and follow your conscience.

Eternally blessed are all those who keep faith in God, relying on His mercy and grace, not their own merit, for salvation, transformation, and entering Paradise and Heaven.

DIDACTIC [TEACHING] SECTION
From the Mountain

On this mountain, you all have gathered, beloved children of God, from so many nations, tribes, races, and languages. We all have God in common. Together we hold the common belief in the eternal Sovereign Supreme God of the universe who is mysterious and powerful, to be feared, yet He loves us unimaginably.

You have come in the Spirit of truth to receive a greater understanding of the truths of Scriptures past and present.

Preparing for the Teaching

O you, and peoples of the Earth, seekers of knowledge, seekers of truth, and disciples of many traditions, partake of these many teachings below, whether you have had little education or much. The many teachings below cover an array of topics and doctrines that are held by billions of souls. Many of these are foundational teachings, yet they go beyond the basics into a religious, historical, and cultural depth that should stretch many minds. These teachings are mostly for our minds, but O peoples, how could we and why would we ever want to disengage our souls and hearts in this process or with any activity in life? Indeed, at least one wise Jewish sage of the past said that God's instructions and the study of His word leads us to worship, and that the greatest form of worship is to study His Instruction book. May they touch your heart and soul while stimulating your mind. These teachings are rooted in the great scriptural foundations of the past and carried forward to into the 21st century for the religious and spiritual benefit of many peoples of faith. Seek to attain full knowledge, and by the aid of the Spirit, may wisdom come on its wings, applying them in the heavenly, spiritual, and earthly realms. Seek, inquire, delve, dig, digest, explore, meditate, and rest in the richness of knowledge, not for knowledge sake and your own enlightenment alone, but to be that vessel of light to reach to others; and to share and fellowship in the knowledge of many truths with your fellow brothers and sisters of humanity.

There are levels of knowledge from the basics and foundational to the deep, complex, symbolic, metaphysical, esoteric, and mysterious knowledge. Let us not succumb to the corruption of some esoteric ones and Gnostics who want to keep hidden the knowledge and truths for themselves, to elevate their own power and to keep others from having it. Rather, let us share it all with others to empower them. God has desired from the beginning for the light of knowledge and wisdom to go out to all the peoples, as discerned in the Abrahamic blessing (Gen. 12:3). The Spirit of God grieves when the few keep knowledge and truth to themselves purposefully.

In your study and quest for spiritual truth and knowledge and ultimately salvation, study the sacred Scriptures of the past ages as well as these Scriptures. Search out the wisdom of the ages in many books, if you so incline and can find the time. Many prophets and teachers have come before, and their disciples have left books for posterity. The teachings of Zarathustra, the Buddha dharma, Moses, the Hebrew prophets, Jesus Christ, Muhammad, Guru Nanak, Baha'ullah, and others have all been penned. The controversies among peoples on the Earth are not caused by God; they really reflect the power struggles of corrupted human wills. Do not give any place to those who are divisive. The Spirit of God has been trying to communicate to souls around the world from the most ancient times to the present. Hear the Spirit communicate through blessed teachings. Gaining much knowledge, may you not be puffed up with knowledge but found clothed with the spirit of humility. Be blessed gaining a more complete truth. Strengthen the brothers and sisters in the faith with the teachings.

God: Absolute, Supreme, Eternal, Creator...

God is the Absolute, Supreme, Eternal One!

O blessed disciples and peoples of faith, there are many teachings which are dear to our hearts, but the teaching of God Himself-this is most dear and most holy, beyond all reverence, that is, all our earnest reverence falls short of what He deserves. Nonetheless, we come to ponder these basic truths of God because it is in our nature so to do, a desire God has placed in us to learn and love Him more, endlessly ponder His great majesty.

God is Absolute. God alone is God of the universe, Creator of all things, Determiner of all things. This makes God the Absolute

One. He is the one who established all the principles governing this universe including time, space, and gravity. As the Absolute One, He is the standard by which all things are judged.

God is the Supreme One. Many peoples in ancient times believed in many gods while at the same time having a vague sense of the highest, supreme God. For the ancient Semites and Canaanites it was El Shaddai (Heb. "God Almighty" c.f. Gen. 17:1). In the human imaginations of many people, there were many deities in their conceived hierarchy. But the Supreme was always on top, and the true God, which more and more souls through history began to see and understand. There have always been others that want to believe in and pay tribute to other deities, usually nature-based ones since they are more tangible for their minds to deify. But upon many others the truth in God Supreme, the Eternal One, has dawned. This God is the Source and Progenitor of all things. This light of God Supreme has not been static through the ages, held equally everywhere throughout time. Several scholars, such as Mircea Eliade, have pointed out the common belief among ancient peoples in the remoteness of creator God, who distanced himself in the sky. But this "celestially structured supreme being preserves his preponderant place only among pastoral peoples…that tends to monotheism (Ahura Mazda) or that are fully monotheistic (Yahweh, Allah)" (Eliade p. 122).

God is the Eternal One. This concept of the eternalness of God is unfathomable to the finite human mind, existing always before in eternity past and will for eternity future. In our heavenly glory will understand this a little better, but will by no means comprehend it even there, since we are created beings.

God is Creator of all things in the heavens and the earth, indeed, the entire universe.

Former Scriptures, perhaps most clearly in the Hebrew tradition, articulate the Creator God, as is found in the opening two chapters of the Bible. God created an orderly purposeful Creation. But I submit to you that God did not create order out of chaos as has been commonly held by many commentators, teachers, and philosophers in mythic understanding. The Creation account in the book of Genesis speaks of "darkness and void." But rather than interpreting this as "chaos, I submit to you it was a blissful emptiness. The interpretation of it as chaos is actually reflecting darkened minds of the fallible human interpreters with possessing only partial divine light. The human darkened understanding that developed this tradition of "chaos" and this notion from ancient times spread around the world in the ideas of man's imagination, not enlightened by the Spirit of God.

And it is immediately after the mention of darkness before the Creation in Gen. 1:2, that we also encounter the Spirit of God. In this first encounter of the Spirit in the Bible, the Spirit is "hovering over the face of the waters" (Gen. 1:2). At least two important characteristics are evidenced in this verse. First, beginning with the definition of "spirit" (Heb. word is *ru'ah* which is the word also for wind or breath) as well as from this context is the picture that God's Spirit is amorphous, that is, without form. The second thing the text reveals is that the darkness does not seem to inhibit the movement of the Spirit at all. It has special vision in the complete darkness equipped with divine Universe Positioning Sensing (UPS) and keen spatial skills in this primordial universe when as yet there were no fixed points in the sky or on the Earth for referencing, since the Earth nor the physical universe had been created yet, at least as Gen. ch. 1 indicates.

Now taking a more doctrinal approach instead of an exegetical approach, we have this truth: "God is Spirit." When we speak this truth that "God is Spirit," what do we mean by it? This is one of the several attributes of God's nature, along with His eternalness, His supremacy, His omniscience, His omnipotence, etc. Is it to be equated with the "Spirit of God"? These two can be distinguished and yet inseparably from the same Being. The first time we encounter God's Spirit in the Hebrew Scriptures is at the very beginning in Gen. 1:2. God's Spirit is amorphous. And yet God Himself dwells on His Throne in Heaven. These two seem to be quite different and distinct, and yet many ascent to this truth although our minds fail to penetrate this mystery.

His power pervades through the whole universe, and His knowledge expands throughout all space-nothing can escape His knowledge.

Is God male, female or neither? The Spirit of God leads us to know the truth that God is beyond gender as we know it on Earth. This question tries to impose an eartho-gender-centrism upon the Divine Being of the universe. To very briefly summarize great Scriptures of the past, perceived masculine traits such as power is prevalent. And yet in Scriptures, we find caring, nurturing, feminine aspects too. In brief, the Hebrew Scriptures lays out the seminal passage of God creating male and female in creating humankind in His image and likeness, "male and female He created them (Gen. 1:27). The creative genius and acts of God, His progenitor role of the universe we may consider masculine. But His care and nurturing of souls is generally a feminine characteristic. His Spirit itself is gender neutral, as evidenced in the Koine A Greek of the New Testament. In the Hindu tradition, the equivalent for "God" is Brahman, which is in the neuter case and means "ever growing" (Hopfe and Woodward, 385).

In these teachings and in this text, I cannot help but to refer to God when using pronouns in the third person masculine pronouns such as "His." This is used as a convention and custom, and in part by default and because of the fact that in English, the neutral gender "It" is so impersonal. From the perspective of the view of a personal monotheistic God, it seems disrespectful, but it may be acceptable in the Hindu tradition.

Our ascriptions and praises to God could be endless, O peoples of faith, but let us briefly highlight yet more truths of God's nature and character upon which many through the ages have been enlightened.

God is holy, righteous, and just. God is kind, merciful, and loving. God is the gracious ruler of the universe.

God is knowable, and yet mysterious and not fully knowable by human limitations of knowledge, comprehension, and understanding. God is personal and yet impersonal. God is mysteriously in you, in all His children and yet throughout space in the universe too. Do not be deceived to think all His power dwells in you. Our mortal bodies could not even contain one atom of all His power. Our bodies would explode apart if it tried to contain God's power. And yet spiritually, we can have such an intimate personal connection with the God of the universe whose glory and majesty is beyond us in Heaven, out of which the universe flows. He is unseeable through mortal eyes and yet seen throughout all His works of creation in the heavens and on the Earth.

God abides in the Light. God has created both light and darkness. God's presence is everywhere in light and darkness and nothing escapes God's knowledge. God is all-knowing.

For those who have come to faith in the one God have taken that first major step of submitting to Him, not by their own human will alone but by the Calling and power of God's Spirit.

O peoples of faith, the pre-creation Narrative in this Scripture depicts a concentration of God's presence in Heaven on His glorious Throne. This itself creates tension with the concept and belief in God's omnipresence. If God is truly everywhere, can there be a Throne of God at all, implying a specific location, or is it merely a metaphor? First, we need to be careful not to let a human-made concept and doctrine called "omnipresence" override the Scriptures which most believe to be the word of

God. The Hebrew Scriptures speak: "God's throne is in heaven" (Ps. 11:4), and "Your throne, O God, is forever and ever" (Ps. 45:6a NKJV). So how can God having a throne, which implies a specific location, or heavenly region, not everywhere, not conflict with the belief in God's omnipresence? These two are in tension to some degree, but what helps to resolve this variance is to turn to the same Scriptures, again, a source text for the omnipresence of God, also found in the Hebrew Scriptures. In Psalm 139 we find, "You [God] know my thought from afar off" (vs. 2b), and "Where can I go from your Spirit? Or where can I flee from your presence? If I ascend into heaven, You are there. If I make my bed in Sheol, behold, You are there" (vv. 7-8 NKJV). An important aspect of properly interpreting Scriptures, people of God, is to let them all speak with basically an equal voice. It is when others pick out certain verses they like and disregard ones they don't, they ignore the whole of God, they slant the text their way, they fashion their own interpretation and sectarian interpretations have created hundreds of denominations. *Human beings create religions but God's truths are universal.* Therefore, let the Scriptures, even the whole counsel of God, speak with equal voice. Keep them held in a blessed tension, a tension for us while in our imperfect minds on earth, but will be more clearly understood when we are glorified in body, mind, and spirit.

The discussion of the Throne of God regarding its location, which is still a mystery to us earthlings, is a worthy aspect, but we should not overlook, of course, the more important and theological meaning. Namely, God is the Sovereign over all the universe, period. There is no other who can compete for this spot. And none of the angels in Heaven, which He created, aspire to usurp His Throne, because they are full of awe, adoration, and love of God. They have no desire to do so. They are perfect and holy.

Some scholars of religion and humanists or social scientists have taught that human beings have fashioned God from their own need and imaginations. A good example of this is the God as Father image. Humans have fathers and understand the need for fathers. A paternalistic culture applied this need to the concept of God, they teach.

There is also the fundamental issue of whether God is a personal Being or an impersonal Being. The Eastern religion of Hinduism has not historically had the concept of God as a personal being, but Brahman is prevalent force of the universe. Instead of asking the simplistic question whether West or East is correct, we should consider the reality and validity of personhood and individual consciousness. If our premise is a Creator God, which itself directly implies personhood, and we are individual persons with individual consciousness, then it does make sense that God too is a Person, the Supreme Person of the universe, which humans in our current estate cannot fully comprehend.

Let God be praised, and endless are His ways, and all His truths inexpressible.

The Oneness of God

God is…one. Praise be to God for being God!

Dear friends of God, companions of faith, we come to yet another foundational teaching. This truth of the oneness of God is held by billions. Welcomed also into this teaching are others who hold to other concepts. We have things we can mutually learn from each other in a time of dialogue and sharing.

O dear disciples and peoples of faith, upon many of you has the truth in the oneness of God enlightened your hearts, minds, and souls. I need not teach as though I would be unconvinced of your belief. You know this truth in the oneness of God has dawned on millions, even billions of souls from ancient times to the present. Let us first, though, highlight the light of the oneness of God in the Scriptures of the Abrahamic traditions.

In the Jewish Torah (and Hebrew Scriptures), we have the clear ringing declaration: "Hear, O Israel, the LORD our God, the LORD is one! (Deut. 6:4). Coming to the Christian faith, the New Testament Scriptures clearly bear witness that God is one, flowing out of the Hebrew tradition. The apostle Paul writes "one God" (Eph. 4:6). In John's Gospel, Jesus' prayer to His Father, "… whom you have given Me, that they may be one as We are…that they may be one just as We are one" (Jn. 17:11c; 22b). And in the Muslim faith, the Quran, Islam's sacred Scriptures, "Say, He is Allah [God], The One…" (Holy Quran 112:1).

…Now dear disciples, let us go into greater depth of understanding of God's oneness through the sacred Scriptures.

The light of one God dawned on ancient Egypt in the 14th century BCE upon Amenhotep the IV, also called Akenaten, who hailed Aten, the Sun God, as the sole God (Fletcher pp. 52, 87). Moses, who was raised in Pharaoh's house, came on the scene around a century after Akenaten, most researchers and scholars believe. It is quite possible that Moses had heard of this one God Aten during his first 40 years of life in Egypt. But even if this is the case, this should not negate God's direct revelation to him at the burning bush (c.f. Ex. Ch. 3). Historically, it is quite possible that the seed of monotheism was planted in the younger man Moses. From the Hebrew Scriptures, we also know that there were other Semitic nomadic monotheists in this region, such as Moses father-in-law Jethro. So God's direct revelation of Himself to Moses ("I AM WHO I Am" Ex. 3:14) was not the first dawning light of monotheism on Earth. God stated to Moses, "I am the God of your fathers, the God of Abraham, the God of Isaac, and the God of Jacob" (Ex. 3:15). Moses may not have been the first man to receive the revelation of God Almighty and His oneness, but the witness of Scripture progressively gets clear through the Torah/Pentateuch when we come to the clear witness of God's oneness in Deut. 6:4. Here, we find the unequivocal clear truth:

"The Lord (YHWH) our God, the Lord is ONE" (Deut. 6:4). The book of Deuteronomy, the "Second Law," may have been penned in the 7th to 6th cent. BCE The 7th century BCE Hebrew prophet Isaiah likewise gives such clear prophetic witness of the universal God being the one God (c.f. Isaiah 45:5-7). In reality, the world of these times was still very polytheistic, and being a monotheist was very unpopular, but the light of monotheism was growing brighter.

Moving hundreds of years forward, we come to the age of Christianity. The Christian faith is solidly rooted in the monotheism of Judaism via the Hebrew Scriptures, the Bible of the earliest Christians. Christianity developed into more complex theologies its first 400 years, and adopting terms such as the "Trinity" to explain the "Father, Son, and Holy Spirit" of God. The foundational Christian belief that Jesus Christ was and is the Son of God, and possesses divinity, along with the doctrine of the Trinity, has made it a unique religion in the world but also a bit of a stumbling block for the strict monotheists of Judaism and Islam.

We come to Islam which historically was birthed in the 7th century CE in Arabia. One of Islam's foundational beliefs is the oneness of God to which they strictly hold to, perhaps more so than any other religion. There is but one or two verses in the entire Quran that clearly states "God is one." But oddly and almost in contraction with these one or two references, the rest of the Quran, actually often speaks in the plural "We," which the pious interpret to be the voice of God. Why does this "We" so often occur in the Quran? This point has baffled many imams and Muslims. The Spirit of God leads us to all truth, and we can go into any Scriptures to see what truth may be contained there. Here, I give a very sensible explanation to the Quranic occurrences of what is presumed to be God speaking in the plural. We start on the point on which we all agree and believe to be historically true. All are agreed that the Quranic verses are from the blessed Muhammad's recitations in Arabia from 610 to 632 CE Many of these oracles were given by Muhammad speaking to the Muslim community (Arabic *umma*). The "we" may very well be meaning "on behalf of" the community of believers he addressed. This is not to deny God's revelation through him. Many pious ones, once their Scriptures are compiled and taken to heart, elevate every word as if it fell down from heaven. Orthodox Muslims do believe that every word in the Arabic Quran is the very word of God, even the eternal word of God. This explanation is not what pious Muslims hold to, and it is not given to offend any pious Muslim, but to reason together in regard to the truth of its historical cultural context. This interpretation resolves the one problem of a one God speaking as "We," but it creates another major problem for the pious ones of these Scriptures lessening some of its words from being the "word of God" to being more human than their souls want to admit.

In growing to spiritual maturity, sometimes we need to take steps out of our preconceived notions of truth from religion traditions, or rather, man's interpretation of them. In this process, we may discover that some traditions within our own faith may be man-made traditions, not truly from God. As seekers of the truth, we sift through piles of human traditions to get to the reality of God.

Moving from the "great Abrahamic faiths" of Judaism, Christianity, and Islam, it is not till the 19th century CE that the Baha'i faith is born. The most basic motto creed of the Baha'i Faith is "One God, one world, one people." From both perspectives of a Baha'i believer and a religion scholar, we see a continuity of the belief of one God through the ages, through the Abrahamic faiths and continuing in the 19th century CE-21st century.

Let us highlight one more religion on this topic of the oneness of God, oddly, from a religion which is known to be perhaps the most polytheistic, namely, Hinduism. Hinduism, like most of the world faiths, is really a label that encompasses several traditions. The closest equivalent to the concept of "God" as understood in the monotheistic traditions is the concept of Brahman in Hinduism. Brahman is the Ultimate Source and impersonal. In addition to this ancient Hindu teaching, the Upanishads are generally understood to be written from a monistic or oneness of reality perspective. With the Upanishads influence on popular Hinduism, in turn, has influenced countless Hindus through the centuries to understand all the Hindu deities as manifestations of the ultimate Being, Brahman (Hopfe and Woodward p. 87). This is therefore a connecting point that monotheists will have with Hindus. Even though the popular religion of Hinduism has thousands of local and regional deities that they worship. Many Hindus today believe that all these deities are manifestations of the One. Therefore, to some degree, there is an aspect of the oneness that monotheists and polytheistic Hindus have in common.

But for those of us who are monotheistic, God is one and sole. The thought of worshiping other deities viewed as human concoctions and idols is repulsive. We focus our worship on the one Supreme God of Heaven and Earth. There are no other gods or deities of the sky or on Earth demanding our worship, obedience, or to appease them.

May the supreme one God and His reality enlighten all His children on Earth with truth in Him.

The Reality of God

O learned disciples, along with the oneness of God, the reality of God has also enlightened your mind, heart, and soul since we believers do think of God as more than an abstract thought, but a reality. God as the Absolute Being of the universe, is therefore the Determiner of all reality in the universe and ultimate Reality on Earth. Because of the freedom of the will He has given human beings, some can chose to ignore the ultimate reality and choose not to believe, but even if all the people on Earth refuse to accept the truth of the one God, it still is true because only God is the Absolute and the Determiner for all things. This may be called a circular argument, but that does not make it untrue. Many modern humans repulse at this notion, because they do not want to cede to anyone on the top except themselves. Modern man has so lifted himself up to make him the deity, bowing to none, ignoring the true God, for those who have not accepted the truth in the reality and absolute supremacy of God. A popular question posed to college students in this modern era is this which follows. If a tree falls in the forest and there is no one to hear it, does it make a noise? The answer that many moderns want to give is "no." What this answer reveals is that it makes the human the center of reality. Moreover, it fails to even acknowledge God in the picture at all. Of course it makes a noise. Though no human heard it, there are the other creatures in the forest, and most importantly, there is God. But for you, O blessed learned ones, you have been enlightened, you have ascented to this truth or are in the process of enlightened ascent. Now ponder these thoughts too.

The knowledge of the reality of God, like many teachings and doctrines, first come to the soul as knowledge, intellectual knowledge. Then their spirit and heart begins to engage with it in time, hopefully, as they ponder the knowledge as truth, not just data. In the pursuit of truth, some come to the highest level.

The highest level of knowledge, in regard to the reality of God, even His presence, is experience. But this experience, while it is existential, it does not align itself with existential philosophy which puts humankind at the center of the universe. The experience of God encounters, when God visits individual souls on Earth in every generation, whom and where and how many He chooses according to His gracious will, is so powerful, way beyond mere intellectual ascent. The experiences are beyond words. The experience of the reality of God flows out of a relationship with the All Powerful one, initiated by Himself, for it is beyond our ability or fabrication.

When the Spirit of God breaks into a persons life, it will stop them in their tracks. With the reality of God the Spirit comes to a soul, it is like a major jolt, a sudden reorientation to one's whole view of life that they have been programmed to view through: their cultural lens, even their religious lens, since God is so much bigger than any religion, and the lack of faith the person had before that moment. All suddenly gets upset and catapults this frail human soul into the reality of God like launching from a NASA launch pad at full throttle. One's whole view of the world suddenly changes. All the filters placed on that person through what they were taught about God, religion, and religious tradition were suddenly removed, obliterated in response to sudden Presence. It was not that what they were taught about God was all wrong. It was just that it was primarily intellectual. And suddenly, instead of looking through a dim mirror, it is crystal clear, and the sudden bright and holy light is startling to corrupted soul. In the after experience, the soul wonders, was it really God or could the experience have been caused by some rush of chemicals in the brain suddenly over exiting some neurons, or gas? When it's the reality of God, the person knows it in their soul. While the experience will dissipate, and then becomes a memory, and yet the undeniable absolutely one-of-a kind holy touch leaves an impression upon that person's soul for a lifetime.

To whom does God come and bring such an experience and touch? The former Scriptures say, "The Spirit comes and goes as it wills" (c.f. Jn. 3:8) God knew very well that there would always be a handful of people who would want to try to control it for their own advantage, sense of power, sorcery, to whom God's word gives specific judgment to.

We can and should desire to draw closer to God in a relationship with Him, and to know His reality. But God can never be manipulated. There are many people who may try to manipulate God. We cannot control where and to whom the Spirit passes over to touch another soul, but we should be open to when God's Spirit comes to us, whether to teach us, guide us, comfort us, etc. When souls have experiences with the Spirit of God, they will then understand in a deeper way as a result of the experience. God reveals Himself to His peoples subtly. He does not shock us by bringing His full reality into our room. Sometimes God sends messengers to lead us to faith, to test us, etc. all according to His holy mysterious ways.

The Oneness and Unity of Reality

From most ancient of days to the present, O learned ones, peoples' beliefs and worldviews were profoundly marked by this fundamental understanding of the oneness of Reality. From thousands of years ago, how far back in time we know not, but human beings in most cultures perceived that somehow there was some unified invisible power that held all things in common, from Native Americans to ancient Asians, Africans, etc. And this deep perception from within the soul of humans, to all the reality around, did develop into clearer, more concrete beliefs. Philosophers would later call this belief: monism. Virtually all cultures have manifested at least some aspect of monism which sees one fundamental reality behind all things on Earth, the seas, and the heavens above. Polytheists, pantheists, monotheists, and even non-theists evidenced aspects of monism. For the non-theist religion and philosophy of Taoism, the Tao is that one fundamental reality, defined by that belief system as being completely impersonal. Pantheism is defined as "the doctrine that reality comprises a single being of which all things are modes…

or projections" (Runes p. 223). The Gaia (Earth) religion holds to a pantheistic view of the Earth, but herein is its great limitation: focusing only on the Earth itself and essentially ignoring the rest of the universe. We know from science that the Earth is one small sub-atomic particle compared to the vastness of the body of space with its billions of stars, planets, etc. Paul Clasper in his book on Eastern Paths and the Christian Way, in the Chapter on Hinduism, states, "The Hindu believes there is a common underlying unity to all of the religious quests for self-realization. He then highlights this ancient prayer from the Upanishads which reflects a unity of reality and which he suggests we all can pray, having "the deepest things in common" Clasper, p. 18):

From unreality lead us to reality,
From darkness lead us to the light,
From bondage lead us to freedom (Clasper, p. 18).

Clasper further explains the fact of "Hindu belief in the essential oneness of all diverse paths" (Clasper p. 28). There is "one Tree with many branches." Applied to the various religions, for example, the "Christian coming to know God through Christ is just one path of many to God" (Clasper p. 28).

For the monotheist peoples of the faith in God, Creator of all things, is the Source of all things in the whole universe. By faith, we strongly sense that it was God who placed this "law" in all human souls. Some people are enlightened to the reality that God is that fundamental Reality, and for others, they are not enlightened to this truth, though they still perceive the fundamental reality, such as Taoists, they are still shrouded in semi-darkness. They are still precious children of God, but they do not recognize God as the Source, a personal Creator, Sovereign of the universe, who knows all His creatures.

Each person usually believes according to the faith or philosophy tradition, with its worldview, they were taught. And each should be free to believe and practice according to his or her own faith. Blessed be the peoples of faith who have been enlightened to the truth of the unity of Reality and its Source. The oneness implies an absolutism.

Absolutism and Relativism

Dear learned ones, we come to these abstract terms, absolutism and relativism. We have previously portrayed a commonly held belief in the one God, who is the Absolute and Supreme. Since God is the Absolute of the universe and the Determiner of all reality, God Himself defines the absolute and is the source of absolutism.

In seeming opposite contrast, relativism has risen as a belief, viewpoint, and philosophy in the modern age, especially in the last few decades.

But are these two mutually exclusive? Without the teaching of the realms previously been given, discussion on absolutism and relativism without defining the scope (whether just earthly or heavenly/universal and earthly), the discussion would quickly get confusing. The Spirit of God has given me clarity on this issue as well. When we go beyond the realm of human habitation in the earthly, to the heavenly, we should rightly focus on the Absolutes. But in human society, where we are striving for freedom for all people, whatever their belief systems, there is a functional relativism. This sense of relativism is closely connected with level one tolerance in the teaching on Tolerance below. Each individual who has a distinct belief can believe that their belief is absolutely true, but accept the fact that in human society, there are all sorts of different beliefs, some of which agree with each other and cannot all be true.

Is it possible for both/and to live with either/or at the same time? And answer is yes. In other words, the same person of sound mind can hold to absolutism and relativism at the same time. Let us say this individual, person A is a monotheist who believes in one God who alone is Absolute and all truths of the universe was established by this God. Now person A lives in and recognizes that in society, all the peoples of the various different believe systems, most of whom assert their truth is the Truth, accept the fact of the different beliefs, creating a social relativism. Because person A and many others want to live peacefully in society, all agree to accept the fact of the many different peoples all living concurrently in society. And to maintain the peace, many will say to another whose faith is different, "That may be true for you but it is not true for me." Many people do accept absolute truths, and they hold those truths in their hearts before God. But they recognize human society is not the realm of God, but of all sorts of things, good and bad, points of light and corruption. The absolutists acknowledge this reality of imperfection, realizing it is not a Paradise on Earth. They do not have to cede to the relativism in the absolute sense, only in the relative sense.

There has been the absolutism versus relativism discussion and debates in recent years. Throughout the past ages, this was never debated because virtually all, at least in the West, were operating with the same epistemology, which was heavily Judeo-Christian based. But the Enlightenment of the 18th century changed that with a shift to a humanistic base as the center of all knowledge, led by the intellectuals and philosophers. This shifted the basis of knowledge away from God and the sacred Scriptures, the written revelation of God, to humankind. God and sacred stories became viewed as myths, and placed within the realm of human creations. Therefore, all sacred Scriptures were viewed as human books. None fell from Heaven. While it is reasonably true that none of them literally fell from Heaven, this understanding failed to see God's Spirit working through all the human agents, prophets, priests, and penmen.

In the last couple decades, a relativistic understanding has taken a hold on the predominate culture in the West in particular.[15] O you who do not like absolutes, search your own heart and mind as to why you don't like absolutes? Is it not because you do not want to have a higher power over you? This exposes your arrogance, even rebellion before God. No such arrogance in a soul will God admit into Paradise. Repent of your arrogance before the Almighty God who can snuff your life out any moment. Yes, you should fear Him you who are fearless of Him.

Dear special soul, are you one who shies away from absolutes? You need not shy away nor be afraid. God is the Absolute One and the basis for all absolutes, but He knows you and cares for you. Do not be swept away by the currents of the philosophies of man that lack divine light and truth.

Many people today, even the young adolescents or college students have gathered that part of the reason for the predominate acceptance of relativism is out of convenience to try to put all the belief and philosophical systems on the same table, in the societal realm-to accept this "politically correct" mores. Some can compartmentalize their life: in society, they may put on their politeness accepting the fact of all the beliefs out there are equal and in theory, there is no one absolute truth, but privately, they do believe in a particular faith, for example, the global God, and believe this to be absolute. This, my friends, is a lot better than not believing at all. We should not expect the other extreme of a believer shouting their own faith at other people including strangers in public. This latter behavior goes against the Golden Rule since we would most likely not like to be treated the same. So we do behave politely in public and recognize the broader societal structure which strives to treat all people the same and give all respect and the human dignity they deserve, and accept people of different faiths than you. But we don't have to accept that all truth is relative. The common statement that has been heard by various people in society: "What may be true for you is not true for me." This does existentialize truth and actually put the foundation on human beings. This has become the new truth for many people in the world today. While it may be wrong, since it does not acknowledge any absolute truth, each individual person should be respected. When you get opportunities to build trust with one such individual, you can gently lead and persuade them to discover the truth and goodness in the absolute.

Heavenly Kingdom

God's heavenly Kingdom, which is metaphysical in relation to our human perspective, is the most glorious realm. The center of this Kingdom is God Himself, the most Glorious, Majestic, Splendid, Supreme One. His mystery, glory, and eternity can never be penetrated by the mind of people nor angels nor His heavenly counselors.

Ancient pious priests and prophets, once earthly kingship became well established, began to view God as the King of the universe. In this sense, the theology of God's Kingdom developed as a result of reflecting on earthly kingdoms. This is not to say that pious humans invented truths of God and the heavenly Kingdom. But they are human terms that we can relate to, so long as we have kingdoms on earth. Kingdoms have, in modern times, morphed into nations, and thereby nationalism is the geopolitical map of most of the world today. The truth and mystery of God and the heavenly habitation for all souls whom He will receive is beyond what our human words can express, as the apostle Paul received the prophetic insight, "words that cannot be expressed" (2 Cor. 12:4)

Earthly Kingdoms

O disciples and peoples of faith, I need not teach about earthly kingdoms, since this is plain knowledge in this world, the earthly realm, which we learn about in school, from the news, in our jobs, etc. But there are some truths which you can glean or affirm.

The first truth, supported in Scriptures of the past such as the Bible, flows out of the belief in God as the Sovereign of the universe which includes the whole earthly realm. Similarly, since God created all things, the Earth is His too, and He has authority over all, which some people accept and submit to, and others who do not. From this flows the belief that all kingdoms on Earth get their authority from God. Historically, though, we can find some powerful rulers in various times that were grossly atheistic, such as Stalin. Spiritually, God is the source of all earthly power. But some rulers can misuse that power or use it in ungodly ways. By no means misunderstand that God sanctioned any evil or murderous acts of any rulers or dictators nor was God even indirectly responsible for them. It is God who has delegated authority to mankind on Earth. And there have been some righteous rulers throughout time, and there have been some evil rulers.

The Bible expresses this worldview and teaching of God's authority from Heaven to Earth. I will leave it to you to search those Scriptures for those truths.

God is concerned with human affairs and He knows human weaknesses. The spiritual dimension bridges the heavenly and the earthly temporal realms, and should touch the kingdoms on Earth, because they are made up of people, and God has made people having a spiritual dimension as well as our bodies of flesh. Rulers are subject to human weakness just as all people. Who among you believes you are perfect? Do you not take to heart Jesus' wisdom about not pointing the finger at someone else without removing your own sin? (Matt. 7:3). But true, rulers are held to at least as high a standard as the common people. In truth, people put them on a higher pedestal. When, therefore, they make mistakes, misbehave, or do wrong-doing, their actions get more harshly criticized than what the common people would criticize if their own family members or neighbors did the very same mistake or deed. This is the reality of human life.

Spiritually speaking and spiritually minded, we need to continue to pray for all our leaders, that God gives them integrity, wisdom, and a God-fearing heart, and that they lead with righteousness. May the light of God go out from even the centers of governments, even a holiness, such that the peoples of the nations will be in awe, and follow in righteousness.

Source of Revelation

O peoples of faith, search from within your beings to beyond, to the Source of all things: God. God is not merely an abstraction, but the reality of God, the ultimate Reality of all things. Is He not the source of inspiration above all? If created the Earth, life, and people, it makes sense that He, the all-intelligent one, would want to enlighten us with knowledge, wisdom, and revelation of many things including His goodness and character, His righteousness and justice, and desire for peace on Earth.

Previous Scriptures clearly declared that God has spoken through past prophets (Heb. 1:1). The apostle Paul wrote, "All Scripture is God-breathed..." (II Tim. 3:16). And Peter wrote, "...for prophecy never came by the will of man, but holy men of God spoke as they were moved by the Holy Spirit" (II Pet. 1:21).

What truly inspires human souls? Is it tantalizing tales of pagan fables and myths? Is it dragons and the year of the dog? Is it the hypnotic beat of traditional drums? Is it mantra chants leading to mindless meditations on emptiness? Is it coarse clothes and ascetic practices? Is it whirling dervishes? Is it the beautiful sound of a choir singing in a cathedral? Or is it ink on parchment?

The Spirit leads us back to the Source of All things: God. In getting in touch with God through the Spirit, when we return to Scriptures, we will recognize His voice more clearly. In the Scriptures, we find His light, knowledge, wisdom, and love, which gives us spiritual life. But His Spirit makes it alive for us in our souls.

Revelation: Its Kinds

O enlightened peoples of God, these teachings and this Scripture, as you find, is premised on a belief in one God who created all things and who is still Sovereign of the universe, and on the premise of basically two kinds of revelation to human beings: general natural revelation and special direct revelation. The general natural revelation has always been around for human beings from most ancient times all the way to the 21st century to self-discover. But the special is unnatural, divinely guided, usually direct and specific messages to peoples by God's Spirit, sometimes mediated through an angel and sometimes directly to the soul of the prophet by the Spirit's power. These Scriptures often use the word "light" as a metaphor for the special insights that have enlightened upon the souls of those looking to God, willing and prepared vessels as servants of His word. And most of these direct revelations, because of their recognition of being divinely special, care was taken to write them down to preserve them for posterity, especially for God's people.

Now let us ask an honest and intelligent question. Is this notion of "revelation" really a post-Scriptural concept that later traditions conceived of or contrived to give legitimacy to their Scriptures, or do we find the concept in sacred Scriptures themselves? An answer is unequivocally that we find the concept clearly in sacred Scriptures through and through. Hundreds of texts could be cited, but here I will cite just one, commending all

Scriptures to your own study to determine truth. This Scripture verse is from the book of Deuteronomy from the biblical Hebrew-Jewish Torah, which most scholars date from the 7th to 6th cent. BCE "The hidden things belong to YHWH God, but the things revealed belong to us and our children forever that we may do all the words of this instruction [torah]" (Deut. 29:29 MT).

This is one of the fundamental truths of faith that has to be nurtured in our children and youth. And it is a key point of engagement to peoples who do not believe. We should approach skeptical or unbelieving adults, whether work associates, acquaintances, or friends, with respect, care, speak in winsome ways. The light of God does not come by force or our flesh, it is wrought by the Spirit of God. We are enlightened by revelation. The sense of the sacred is a universal connecting point even with those who do not believe. Go forth in peace and with positive frame of mind.

The Sacred Place: An Intuitive Source of Revelation

Within the depth of the human soul is a vastness beyond our own body of limited space of phenomenal experience. Many through the ages have felt, sensed, and discovered this in their contemplation. Consider, O searcher of truth, that many a prophet, sage, and mystic tapped into this sacred space flowing out of the Source, and the Spirit being the connection of their souls to the Source's sacred space. From here, many a word and divine thought, light of revelation, came to the minds of prophets and sages. This sacred spiritual Place planted the seed of holy thought through which they found words to express in the language of their native tongue, to enlighten their souls, to warn and bless. To some, God gave a greater sense of intuition, and intuition is a faculty of the soul, not the fleshly mind. It can serve like an aperture of a camera lens opening up wider. There, in the sacred

Place, they sense things that are well beyond earthly concerns. The feeling in this sacred Place is magnificent. The serenity is much more peaceful and satisfying than any earthly pleasure. By God's power, He enacted many times with direct revelation to His prophets by means of His choosing, His Spirit directly to a chosen prophet or by direct words through an angel expressly sent for such purpose. But consider too that many a prophet and sage tapped into this spiritual well within the depth of their souls entering that sacred sweet spot connected to the Divine. This may have been the experience of Elijah on Mt. Horeb when he heard the "still small voice" (I Kings 19:12).

In many others, has not God also placed a sense of the Oneness, Source of the universe, in their souls? By faith from a global perspective, we perceive God has placed this sense in all human souls. In this sense is the seed to the knowledge of God Himself. When human beings break their routines of life, or get away for a little while from regular life, perhaps in nature or on a retreat, they instantly may feel more connected to the Source. All those mundane and tangibles of routine life and responsibilities which filled the mind, is put on hold, and then they suddenly discover or rediscover or feel the Source. We may ascent to a universal truth that all human beings can feel the sense of the sacred. It connects with and helps to unlock the truth of Scriptures becoming sacred.

Sacred Scriptures

Blessed are all who have read or heard the voice of God through sacred Scriptures established in ages past and in these Scriptures, and who believe. Your souls have gravitated to the revelation of God's mercy, compassion, goodness, and love. By faith, you understand that God's Spirit was behind the inspiration of these thoughts, the speaking and writing of them, and then compiling them in the books that became the established Scriptures, and in their passing from one generation to the next and their enduring preservation.

From the beginning of human existence all the way to our day, God has given humans the capacity to sense the sacredness in life, from birth to death. So also, God enlightened our souls with the sense of sacredness through sacred texts penned through the ages by pious persons wholly dedicated to God, writing the things of God, the spiritual kingdom on Earth, Divine narrative, salvation history, and wisdom for daily living.

Yes, are not these the reasons why these Scriptures have endured through the ages, in human terms besides the sheer fiat of God's Spirit: because they have penetrated to a depth of the soul that no other voice in the world has, they speak with a universal voice that rings true to so many of faith, and third, because they speak to and they get into our heart. Each soul that reads Scripture gets something particular out of it, sometimes speaking uniquely to individuals, though they were read in the congregation of many.

The seeker who studies the sacred texts from ages past around the world will discover the uniqueness of each one, arisen from its place in the world and through their cultural lens. All of them, while limited by words and language, probe deep into the depths of the understanding of God and His Spirit and this wondrous world we live in. Yet while through the limitations of space, time, culture, and language, we sense the boundless Divine One communicating to ours spirits. And in these sacred texts are found jewels of universal truths. The full recognition of these truths as universal, not merely tribal, regional, or national ideas, views, or realities, may have come in the peoples minds after some generations of reflection. Hindsight is so much clearer in seeing God's handiwork through the ages.

Seek it out, search it diligently, the universal truths found in sacred texts from ages past and in this text. Discover these truths from your own heart, which is connected to the Spirit of God who leads His children to discover truth. Let God be your ultimate teacher through the sacred texts you study and through the human religious teachers placed in your life. God sends teachers in our lives, from which we learn so much and deeply respect.

The Spirit of God takes us to a depth beyond the words on the surface. The words are like a medium or conveyor to the depth of truth and mysteries of God which go beyond words.

Blessed are those who revere their Scriptures. There are some traditions whose sacred texts have become so holy and elevated that it appears as if they worship the book. For those who do not have this tradition of revering your Scriptures, to you, it may appear that they make the sacred book or Scroll into an idol. Let God be the judge of this, since human judgment is so flawed, not seeing into the heart of people what only God can see. For God alone sees and knows what is in the hearts and minds of all His children (c.f. Ps. 139:1-6; Prov. 5:21; Quran 2:284). Though it appears that many of them are worshiping a book, for many of them, the book is really a symbol and a window to their true devotion and worship of the one Supreme God. These do not do it in ignorance of God who alone deserves all worship, but these are tangible windows of devotion to the invisible God. On the surface of appearances through human eyes, there seems to be such a variety of worship and religious expressions among theists, but there is more spiritual unity there than we can see, for each is worshipping the same yet in different ways. God be praised for His Word and truths communicated to humankind.

Do we peoples of faiths of Scriptures not prefer the written word of God over the oral? Where is the oral word of God, you ask? Were not many of the sacred words in ancient times oral before they were written, words of knowledge, wisdom, praise? It is believed that most of the traditions that wrote their Scriptures in ancient times contained portions that were oral, existing for some time before they were written, such as the Song of Deborah in the book of Judges (ch. 5), as many scholars believe. But some will say, "These accounts along the rest of Scriptures have now been written for perhaps 3000 years or even more. They have been memorialized in Scripture. It is in this form that God has been communicating His Word to use as long as we have been alive." O persons of faith, do not cut short the means by which God can speak. Is He not the Eternal One? If He spoke orally through His messengers then, even in ancient times or in the days of the Prophet Muhammad in the 7th cent. CE, can He not speak orally in any age, generation, through any prophet, messenger, or sage or teacher that He chooses? O beloved traditionalists! You are zealous for God, but in your religiosity, you could fall into the danger of denying the power of God. Do not use your religion for the purpose of controlling religious practitioners or God. Let God's living Word speak sacred knowledge through both Scriptures and oral words when God may so lead an earthen vessel by His Spirit.

Knowledge

O disciples and peoples of faith, you know how important knowledge is to life. Without knowledge, we are not human. And you know that there are all kinds of knowledge which all falls within one of the two realms, the mundane or the metaphysical, the material or the spiritual, the earthly or the heavenly.

In ancient days before the world got so complex, people mostly understood knowledge, couched in sacred lore, and mostly sprinkled with superstition. But God's Spirit sent points of Light to break into the predominately superstitious ways of animism.

When writing was invented, when the class of scribes and priests came on the scene, sacred lore first took on a high new magical level. But in time, many educated humans were enlightened and cast aside the magical notions of sacred texts, leaving the magical formulas to the few.16 Through the centuries and millennia, there have been a few pockets of cult people maintaining a magical practice of sacred texts even into the Common Era, such as Taoists and Kabbalists, each with their respective texts (Hopfe and Woodward, pp.191, 269).

Coming to the modern era, in the post-"Enlightenment" of rationalism, people has focused on the practical, learning the knowledge of many subjects: grammar, geography, science, math, history, and humanities to live a life in the real world.

Most importantly, of eternal consequence, is Divine knowledge. This knowledge alone directly assists us in reaching the goal of a blissful eternity with God. It is not knowledge alone, as you know, observant disciple, that leads to blissful eternity, Because God alone is the Divine One, when we speak of this knowledge, we speak broadly of the knowledge of God. The "knowledge of God," in turn, has a few distinct kinds. The first is the knowledge about the nature and character of God. The second is about the deeds and actions of God, which includes the revelations sent upon the Earth, in as much as some people and to what degree they believe they were direct revelations. And then, from the sacred Scriptures, we get much knowledge on many things, some of earthly matters but only known through the Scriptures, such as the occurrence of the talking donkey in Torah book of Numbers 22:30.

By faith, we know that God is the origin of the knowledge of Himself. This knowledge eternally existed in Himself, but none else knew because there were no other creatures in the universe. As heard or read in the Narrative elsewhere, God desired to share Himself with others by creating creatures, beginning with the heavenly beings. The moment they were created, they had instant knowledge of God and also the knowledge of themselves, both their self-awareness and the knowledge of their holiness.

For us humans, our knowledge is imperfect and more limited by our earthly creaturely body of senses. But God loves us just as we are. Speaking from our human perspective, we gain knowledge through life after coming out of the womb. Interesting, pre-natal babies seem to response and have some awareness of their mothers and themselves.

Knowledge, I submit to you, is one of the greatest gifts God has given us. Without the gift of knowledge and the ability to communicate these complex thoughts, we are basically animals. The greatest gifts God gave humans is knowledge, wisdom, and faith, and I submit to you that faith is the greatest.

From most ancient of days all the way up the verge of the modern era, sages, mystics, priests, intellectuals, early scientists had a unified sense between the physical realm and the spiritual realm. These two realms were so intricately connected. The Divine touches upon the human realm naturally. Sacred lore developed in all the cultures that produced religious traditions. Priests especially, from the Vedic priests to the ancient Egyptian priests to the Hebrew priests were the possessors of this special knowledge that the common people did not have, which gave them great power (that is, perceived power), even at times competing with the royal power when they each served different functions that should not have to compete with each other. These ancient priesthoods were able to maintain this control for centuries, but the world was gradually changing, developing toward the global age. In the development of the global age with international commerce by land and by sea, merchants learned to read and write. And universities developed. Knowledge was no longer just in the hands of the rulers and priests; it became democratized. Societies were developing, and advanced through the ages.

But while the written knowledge was viewed as conveying special power, let us not forget about the power of oral knowledge. So much knowledge and wisdom was conveyed orally. Sages for centuries told lore orally into the hear of listeners, some of whom no doubt were peasants and commoners, as well as rulers and aristocrats. And some were gifted with much wisdom and must have imparted some of their wisdom orally before audiences. The wisdom of Solomon is a prime example. While some of it was addressed to "my son," he no doubt spoke some of these golden nuggets of wisdom before audiences of his entourage, concubines, priests, and other peoples gathered at his court next to the temple in Jerusalem. His fame spread far, all the way down to where Yemen is today. The Queen of Sheba hears of his wisdom and comes all the way up the Jerusalem (1 Kings ch. 10:1-7). While Sheba heard Solomon's wisdom among her royal entourage and Solomon's entourage, we can imagine that some of this wisdom trickled down to the common people, since news and information most often spread by word of mouth in ancient times. But Solomon's wisdom was written down and preserved for posterity. For generations to come, Jewish worshippers, common people, priests, etc. gathering in synagogues would hear and learn of some of this wisdom, in light of the Torah.

Divine Wisdom

O peoples of faith and enlightened disciples, we come to another blessed teaching. Divine wisdom is of heavenly origin; it is pure. While we understand that sacred Scriptures have been penned on earth by men led by the Holy Spirit (c.f. 2 Pet. 1:21), it could be said that divine wisdom floats down from heaven to our souls, causing our spirits and hearts to melt before the awesomeness of God's faithfulness, mercy and love.

Divine wisdom is eternal, existing before anything in Heaven or Creation was ever made. Our earthly finite human minds cannot comprehend how divine wisdom can be eternal when God created and established this universe by His divine wisdom. But great Scriptures of the past declare God's wisdom and His word to be eternal. This is a mystery we cannot grasp, and this leads us to worship.

Divine wisdom is nothing less than a window from our soul directly to God. It is no wonder that many mystics through the ages became so ecstatic in their devotion on the divine wisdom that they wanted to shed this earthen body. But God has not raptured us yet. We find ourselves still in the earthen body. While in this state, we continue to need the divine wisdom, for without it, we are lost; within it, we are hopeless. And God continues to provide it.

Divine and Earthly, Worldly Wisdom

O discerning disciples, know that the heavenly is a model for the earthly. God has always intended the heavenly to be an inspiration to us on earth, but we people really tend to mess things up. But God, who is love, never gives up on us and continues to give us His wisdom by many means, by Scriptures, by signs, and by fellow human beings. In our state, we see the divine wisdom, which is heavenly, as pure, whereas the earthly wisdom is imperfect. But every day and night God reminds us of the heavenly. All we have to do is to look up to the day sky and the night sky and see God's heavenly wisdom, for us who have this faith.

God has also created us as sensual creatures, and so we can compare not only divine wisdom but earthly wisdom like a lush garden with fruit of all kinds ready for the picking to satisfy hungry souls. Its words are like honey on the lips. It is like the most soothing music in the ears. Its sound has gone forth from palaces, royal courtyards, sacred temples, stately gardens, flowing fountains and markets in all the worlds centers of great cultures from the East to the West.

The two main realms determines the two main kinds of wisdom, namely, the heavenly metaphysical, and the earthly, temporal. Spiritual wisdom bridges both these major realms, since God in heaven is the epitome of the spiritual, but yet He has also created humans as spiritual. The heavenly is the former and greater.

God has made us as earthlings, and therefore we do need earthly wisdom. Religion is for this life, but it carries us into eternity, by God's grace. So likewise in this life, we receive the heavenly and the earthly, and together they carry us into the blessed eternal life. There is the earthly wisdom which by itself is morally neutral. But there is much earthly wisdom which is moral, such as the wisdom that parents and grandparents pass on to their children, and religious teachers teach to their pupils. The heavenly is not only the model but sacred Scriptures, reflecting the heavenly, is a standard for the moral aspects of earthly wisdom. Blessed are all who listen and meditate on the abundance of wisdom of the Scriptures past, much of which includes earthly wisdom.

O disciples, we learn the distinction between the heavenly and earthly wisdom every day through the circumstances of life and through study. Simply put, the earthly wisdom helps us directly for things for earthly life, from mechanical issues to relational and people issues. In seeking divine wisdom while in this life, we should not ignore or discard the earthly wisdom, for a day may come that you may need it. We live in a material world in which we often need to apply our knowledge (wisdom) in fixing problems. There is some wisdom which could be life and death situations if we don't follow wisdom, such as running our cars and Planes without engine oil.

Beside the distinction between the heavenly and the earthly, there is also the distinction of the earthly godly and the worldly which is the earthly ungodly. The term "worldly wisdom" could be used in the positive sense, such as practical knowledge of conducting, for example, business affairs to lead to profitability yet with honesty and integrity. But in this teaching, "worldly" is used to connote the "ways of the world that do not acknowledge God and at times may even oppose God. In this sense, there is nothing that the worldly can offer peoples of faith that can compare to the godly wisdom, especially the divine wisdom that transforms us into lovers of God.

God is still the ultimate Source for the light of compassion in them and in thousands; and God can manifest points of light wherever His chooses.

So also, wisdom is needed for this life, but divine wisdom which is heavenly spiritual outlives every human earthly life and continues to exist in the heavenly realm. In distinction, the earthly wisdom is for life in the temporal, earthly existence, and is often very practical. Regarding the enduring heavenly wisdom, our earthly minds cannot penetrate, and when we do enter the glory state of the incorruptible, we still will not be able to exhaust or completely comprehend all the mysteries of divine wisdom. It is so much higher than worldly wisdom. In much distinction, the earthly wisdom mostly deals with people's relationships to each other and human behavior, and these things we can understand much easier, and much of this wisdom is common sense. The categories of the earthly wisdom may be defined as: wisdom for international affairs, wisdom for national affairs/ state politics, wisdom for work/business affairs, wisdom for learning/education/school, wisdom for the social realm (includes community and neighborhood relations), to wisdom for inter-personal relations (from lovers to family members to friends to neighbors to strangers). The wisdom of ancient Scriptures so filled will many golden nuggets but did not attempt to express its wisdom in these distinct categories if in Aristotelian fashion, and therefore does lack some clarity as to which realms and categories each word of wisdom is mostly addressing, and therefore it is up to the interpreter to figure out. Wisdom in these Scriptures makes truth clearer, expounding and explaining and applying, delivering clarity for contemporary souls.

Truth

O searchers of truth, I need not feed you Truth in the form of milk which a baby craves, for God has made our souls so to crave it. Here, I impart solid food. Truth is simple enough for a young child to essentially understand it, and yet so profound that genius' cannot penetrate it; ten thousand meditations cannot exhaust it. It is impenetrable by our fleshly minds, but through God's Spirit, He makes mysteries known. Thanks be to God!

From ancient times to the present, peoples everywhere perceived Truth to be higher, outside themselves, that is, universal, and a unified realty. Here we are talking about Truth in the grand scale which includes Truth from the heavenly realm. But, O discerning ones, even as you know the division of the heavenly realm and the earthly realm in regard to knowledge and wisdom, so too you know this in regard to Truth. There are eternal objective universal truths from the heavenly realm such as the truth of God, divine wisdom, His creation of the universe, and everlasting virtues. And there are truths of the earthly realm such as the family, ethnicity, and nation of our birth. These are temporal truths, not eternal.

From ancient times to the present, Truth comes to us through the following means: through Scriptures, which includes special revelation, through contemplation, through studies, through the dialectic of dialogue (c.f. Plato's Socrates dialogues), through experience, and through natural revelation. For us peoples of faith in God as Source, human reason is best understood as a facility to our grasping truth, not a source of truth. To make human reason the source of truth is one step toward an anthrocentric belief system instead of a God-centered (theocentric) belief system. The Hebrew Scriptures declares, "The entirety of your Word [O God] is truth" (Ps. 119:160). Praise be to God!

The truths that are universal, whether of the heavenly or earthly realms, are beyond the auspices of fallible human science. To try to prove a universal truth using human science is like trying to digest a good book using a fork, knife, and spoon. The dawning of God's truths upon an individual human soul and mind is a spiritual, not merely a neuro-physiologically phenomenon.

In this world among human societies, because they include many and various faith traditions and they include essentially the two categories of believers and unbelievers, there are controversies on earth such as the "Absolutism verses Relativism." Below, I give a teaching specifically on this topic. Suffice to say here that many of us believers grasp absolute universal truths for ourselves while recognizing some on this planet in human societies do not believe so.

Some pose the question, "What is Truth" There are many kinds of voices that can ask this question, from the range of believers in their sincere and passionate pursuit of truth to skeptics and down to the scoffers. This question is forever preserved in Scripture by Pontius Pilate while he was trying Jesus the Messiah (Jn. 18:38). In this scriptural context, the Christian answer is clear, given earlier by John, that Jesus Christ is "the Way, the Truth, and the Life (Jn. 14:6).

Those who do not believe in the absolutes and universal truths think that we who do are intolerant and fanatics. Do not confirm their own suspicious by being argumentative or obstinate in your own belief toward them, but rather, keep pointing them to the heavenly, for the heavenly is a model for the earthly. But some of these will never believe, no matter how clear God makes it to them. Some are destined for eternal darkness.

O hungry disciples, continue to search the depths of truths. Blessed Jesus said, "Seek, and you shall find" (Matt. 7:8). Discover your world of understanding opening. Find some things that were mysteries to you, now comprehended, though their depth is impenetrable.

Science

You also know, O observant ones, that science literally means "knowledge" from its Latin base. Moreover, the great religious scholars in the Middle Ages, Maimonides (Jewish), Thomas Aquinas (Christian), and Averroes (Muslim), all understood that God created this world and therefore there is essentially no conflict between science and faith. But science is the human pursuit of the knowledge of the visible and material world. Science has produced some revolutionary and paradigm-shifting theories, such as gravity, the laws of motion, other laws of physics, laws of conservation, etc. The ones investigating to gain the knowledge are all human beings. And all humans are flawed. Therefore, all science including all scientific experiments are potentially flawed, likewise scientific theories because the theorists too are human that each have their limited knowledge, ability, and bias.

God has given an innate curiosity to some souls, to investigate and learn about this planet Earth. Some of these are people of faith, some of whom become scientists. So much can be learned about the Earth, solar system, Space, and the universe through science. But all scientists run up against a big wall. Science does not answer the biggest questions that stirs in human hearts, like "Why are we here? What is our purpose in life? How do I fit into this overall big picture? Who made everything in the world and universe? We could use the word "truth" also to scientific laws and principles such as the fact of gravity and the speed of light speed limit in the universe. But we still reserve it for the ultimate things. And revelation from God's Spirit provides those lights to humankind, giving answers to the ultimate things as well as moral standards and wisdom for daily living.

There is such a thing as "true science," that which is in full accord with the nature of science, including investigation, and also in accord with God's Spirit. It operates with the "mind of God," that is, premised in belief in God works with this in mind, and with some revelation in mind, and yet maintains human reason.

Corrupted science is the fact of science by people, earthlings. Some, who are atheistic, have made science their God. They along with anti-Judeo-Christian humanists point out how the Christian Church squelched the true scientific work of Galileo, declaring him a heretic after he discovered the sun is at the center of our solar system, not the Earth (Boorstin pp. 381, 385). It is true that the Roman Catholic Church was resistant to change, and that their earthocentric view which they held onto was not the truth as science has discovered.

Theology and revelation will always be superior and higher than human science, because they deal with the enduring heavenly truths, whereas the earthly is temporal, temporary, and corrupt. Human science will fade away in the new heavens and the new Earth. But the true divine science will continue in eternity.

Despite flawed science in the human realm, we live in a great age, the age of Space exploration. Those theories that could have been flawed must have worked, because we used them to send the first human astronauts to the moon and back. That was an unprecedented triumph of exploration and science for humankind.

Peoples of faith may believe that God is allowing human beings to gain this knowledge which has so rapidly advanced culture technologically in the last 100 or so years. We can praise God for the wonders of the Earth and the wonders of the heavens being discovered, and for these human accomplishments. By faith we know that God is the real Source of all knowledge. And God is holy, righteous, just, good, and moral, and would only want humankind to use all this knowledge and technology for good moral purpose, and the betterment of humankind.

There has come one technology to humankind in the 20th cent. that has put such a fearful sobriety into our souls, and that was the invention of the atomic bomb and later nuclear bomb, which can destroy such a large area. This knowledge shocked the souls of millions at the thought for the first time in history, we are capable of killing off the human race in short time in a nuclear war.

With every new technology that human beings have discovered, it is used for both good and bad, from the wheel of the late Stone Age to nano-technology and genetics. Human science evidences the good and the bad, some who want to use it for good purposes, such as stem cell research to bring healing to people, and the "mad scientists" who want to genetically tamper with nature and end up possibly creating a monster.

Every generation desperately needs moral guidance in all things including science, to rightly use all knowledge for good and not evil. We could cite example after example where science was used for evil. I will use just this one, one of the greatest horrors: the Nazi regime led by the diabolical Hitler, utilizing the latest scientific and medical knowledge to exterminate millions of Jews, gypsies, and the insane. Peoples of faith should encourage their children to pursuit careers in science so they can make a positive faith and moral difference as well as have a meaningful career.

Good verses Evil

We come to the truths of good and evil, O peoples of faith and discerning disciples. Great is God and great is His goodness! "His lovingkindness is everlasting (Ps. 136).

There have been noteworthy teachings on these universal truths by sages through the ages. And indeed, whole books have been written on this topic. We need not trace all these discussions, but simply punctuate these truths for this current age and to discern pure revelation and various human interpretations, and sift through superstition.

The first truth we come to on this topic is that God is good, only good; there is no evil aspect to God or evil "side" of God. The Hebrew Scriptures of the past clearly witness that in God no evil is found, nor is there any imperfect thing in His Heaven (cf. 2 Sam. 22:31; Ps. 18:30; Ps. 50:2, etc.). It is a miracle for any Scripture to be passed down through time without being corrupted. The reality of the matter, it only takes one human hand, literally, to enter corruption into a sacred text. By doing so, with one stroke of the pen, one can and corrupt pure teachings of messengers who have since gone. This appears to be the case with the Zoroastrian Scriptures, the Avesta. The blessed Zoroaster, who received and communicated to his peoples the truth of the one God Ahura Mazda. But it appears that after his life was gone from the earth, the sacred Zoroastrian Scriptures were corrupted by later scribes, possibly sanctioned by the current Persian rulers long after Zoroaster was gone. It is likely that in this stage we find a dualism of God enter in the texts, in which one side is good, beneficent, and the other is evil. And this evil and dark side of God became the lord of demons and this lord's name: Shaitin, the Persian equivalent of Satan (Hopfe and Woodward 239). In other words, Satan was the dark side of God. While we do find the introduction of "Satan" in the Hebrew Scriptures, with his intriguing cameo appearance in the first chapter of the book of Job, the Hebrew Scriptures are otherwise consistent in the revelation that God is only good and only holiness is found in Heaven (with the exception perhaps of this passage in Job ch. 1).

The second truth we come to is that evil is not the absence of good; it is an intentional force. It is a force, action, mindset, meditation, and will in real beings, earthly and spiritual. It is not something that floats "out there" in space. "Evil," is only an abstract concept unless or until it manifests in some in some word or action by a being.

The next truths is on the source of evil and the spiritual problem of evil in relation to the holy God. The Bible essentially places it on Satan, the Devil. This is the conclusion of a composite of narratives prophecies from Genesis to Isaiah, to Daniel, to the Gospel of Luke, to the final book of Revelation. Here is a summary of these text references:

Gen. 3, Isaiah 14: 12-15; Daniel, Lk. 10:17; and Rev. 12:4a, 12:9. Some believers hold to a literal view of these and other Scripture passages, and other believers hold to a metaphorical. Whether literal or metaphorical, they ring with truth for each believer. Evil as a spiritual problem among people begins with succumbing to the Tempter, the Serpent, in the Garden of Eden (Gen. 3). The book of Genesis does not explain to use the origin of the Serpent-Devil-Satan. If we jump ahead into the New Testament, the blessed Jesus unveils one of the clearest scriptural prophetic verses on Satan's origin. When his 70 or 72 apostles came back joyfully, reported that even the demons "were subject to us in Your name" (Lk. 10:17 NASB). Jesus replies, "I was watching Satan fall from heaven like lightning" (Lk. 10:18). This verse is so revealing and yet at the same time it leads us to several more questions but which Scripture does not answer. Despite this, many Christians, in light of also Is. 14:12-15 text, interpret that there was a great rebellion in Heaven led by Lucifer, the Devil, Satan, and a third of them left their heavenly estate and came down to inhabit Earth and the dark underworld. There is a wealth of prophetic and apocalyptic passage in the Old Testament/ Hebrew Scriptures which are in the backdrop of many of Jesus' teachings, with many allusions to the book of Isaiah and the book of Daniel. After all, the Hebrew Scriptures was Jesus' Bible as well as the Bible for the earliest Christians. Jesus' crystallizes these prophecies into one fresh prophecy. The "fall from heaven" in Jesus' declaration ties it with Isaiah 14:12-15, which has the equivalent phrase "fallen from heaven." The context of Isaiah's prophecy is that it is an oracle against the king of Babylon to whom the Jews were subjected to when they went into Babylonian exile. An historical interpretation is a valid one. This interpretation applies verses 12-15 to the king of Babylon. This historical interpretation of Is. 14:12-15 makes sense when we go to the book of Daniel. There, we find king Nebuchadnezzar trying to get the Jewish people to fall down before his great image. Instead, the Jewish monotheistic answer via Isaiah is, "No! you Nebuchadnezzar are the one who is going to fall, and so great will be your fall because you lifted yourself up to heaven." This contrast of "falls" is one of the many word-plays in the Hebrew Scriptures. But with Scriptures, especially prophetic scriptures, there can be more than one layer of and level of meanings. While Satan is not mentioned by name, Lucifer is in the text as in "son of the morning," its meaning, as some translations translate verse 12. Besides the historical interpretation, which in this case should be the literal interpretation, an alternative is a metaphorical-spiritual one. In one sense, the prophet uses the historical figure as the symbol and window into the spiritual meaning. A closely related metaphorical-spiritual interpretation is to specifically apply the "son of the morning" to Satan.

Another clear New Testament prophecy is found in the last book of the Bible, Revelation which prophetically unveils that the tail of the great red dragon "swept away a third of the stars of heaven and threw them to the earth (Rev. 12:4a NASB). This prophetic book associates the dragon with Satan (Rev. 12:9). And the Bible often associates stars with angels, especially the book of Revelation. This would lead us to believe that one third of all the angels left Heaven at some undisclosed time, and its implied they are under Satan's dominion. The literal interpretation of this text would mean to interpret the " third" literally. While Scripture does not tell us specifically the total number of angels God created, the term "myriads" is used in Revelation, which could mean a million. Say there is one million angels. One third is 333,333. Why would 333,333 holy angels want to leave their heavenly habitation with God to live in a wicked environment with Satan? This number I find untenable. A metaphorical interpretation seems more fitting. A metaphorical interpretation does not deny the scriptural truth, it just views the word "third" as a metaphor. For more insight into the meaning of a "third," we go back to the Hebrew Scriptures. Here, we find an abundant number of references for a "third" especially noteworthy in the prophetic such as Daniel which Jesus referred or alluded to. How many times a day did Daniel pray? Three times. How much of Belshazzar's kingdom did he promise to the man who could interpret his dream? A third (Dan. 5:7). There are several other examples of "thirds", but one more I will cite is the Hosea's "He will revive us after two days; He will raise us up on the third day" (Hos. 6:2). Together, these references reflect that a "third" was a fairly common thought-pattern for the Hebrew people. The full associative meaning of this metaphor may be lost. The truths of Scriptures surrounds and goes beyond our fallible interpretations whether they be literal or metaphorical.

These Scriptures gives the Judeo-Christian answer to the source of evil. From the cosmic perspective, Satan is the source. This is not to excuse our own individual behavior. These Scriptures also define the spiritual problem of evil, and proclaims the good news that God, in His goodness, is victorious over all evil, and gives this victory to all believers. Life is to be lived under God's goodness. It is also in this life where sometimes we feel the weight of the struggle of good and evil, sometimes caught right in the middle. God's words gives people hope to overcome.

Islam's Quranic Scriptures also has several reference of Satan (Iblis) and depicts Satan in much the same way, an arch spiritual foe, enemy and resister of God and the true faith. But this was not the case for the Arab peoples before Muhammad's revelations. The Quran and Islamic scholars refer to the time before the revelations as "the time of ignorance"[17]. The Arab peoples were mostly animists, people who believed that nature was full of spirits all around, some who were good and some who were bad. Jinn were these spirits, which are also mentioned in the Quran. Muhammad, in fact, upon receiving his first revelation, was terrified, believing it was a Jinn who appeared to him the cave on Mt. Hira outside of Mecca. He was so frightened that he straightway went back to his house wanting to hid from the Jinn (Lings, p. 45). But more importantly for Islam is the belief in one God whom they also believe to be the all compassionate, gracious, and merciful one.

Zoroaster, who lived back perhaps around Moses day or even before, laid down a strong ethical religion of good thoughts, good words, and good deeds, of which God knows all things and judges all souls in the end accordingly to determine one's destiny.

The biblical and other sacred Scriptures uplift and praise the goodness of God. He is the source of all good. All good flows from Him. Overcome evil with good, the apostle Paul exhorted (Rom. 12:21). Good conquers evil and wins the victories and we will triumph on the side of good in eternal bliss. Goodness is not just an abstraction of the mind. It is real, intentional. And goodness exists on the two planes, the heavenly divine realm, and the earthly, temporal, realm. God has intended the pure goodness of Heaven to mirror it down to Earth; the heavenly is meant to be a model of the earthly. From the hearts of millions of people have dawned the truth that God is good. God desires goodness to permeate our minds, hearts, and souls.

O learned disciples, we have pondered the truths of good and evil in the heavenly, spiritual and earthly planes. May the light of God's goodness and righteousness be magnified upon you to make a difference in this world.

Righteousness

O peoples of faith who desire all the good that God has for us, we come to this foundational teaching on righteousness. The light of righteousness was held high in the age of faith. But secularists in this secular age look back to the age of faith as an age that held people in superstitious religion. But the truth is, secularists are gladly getting rid of the eternal truths, including righteousness, that God enlightened humankind through revelation. Let the flame of righteousness be held up high once again, proudly, like a thousand Olympic torches. Let us wave the banner of righteousness from the religious houses and steps of national and state capitols around the world, and proclaim it. Let us not let this developing dark secular age stamp it out.

O good people of God, let us understand how important and significant this foundational teaching is. First, the source of all righteousness is Divine, God's righteousness. It is integrally a part of God's character, one facet on the diamond of His character which includes truth, justice, holiness, and perfect character. God is eternal. Therefore, it is eternal righteousness. And most importantly from our perspective, it makes all the difference whether we are granted to live in eternal glory or not. The gift of eternal life in Heaven and Paradise is dependent on God's mercy and grace. It is also dependent on His imputed righteousness on our souls after the great Judgment, when our souls are purified of sins. Without His imputed righteousness, we would not be allowed to enter the glory of Heaven. The angels would have to escort us instead to the place of eternal darkness. But God does not want us to be deceived to think that we can live like a heathen through life, and then at the end, completely confess all our sins before God, expecting Him to forgive. God's righteousness is not just some far away reality in Heaven. God has and continues to desire that it dwells on Earth through His human lights, empowered by His Spirit. He desires that we walk by faith in His righteousness, being lights of His truth in a darkened world. Living in God's righteousness also reflect our having a relationship with the living God. O, therefore, may we come to love this word, like all the words of God. The psalmist declares, "Oh, how I love your law!" (Ps. 119:97). May the truths of righteousness through God's word, highlighted in this teaching, be firmly planted in our souls and bear fruit like mighty oak trees in this world.

The first truth we come to is that God is righteous and the source of all righteousness (Ps. 119:137). The second great truth is that God's "righteousness is an everlasting righteousness (Ps. 119:142). But the first time we encounter the word righteousness in the Bible, the Hebrew Scriptures/Old Testament in particular, is in the first book: Genesis. The passage reads, "And he [Abram] believed in God, and He [God] accounted it to him for righteousness" (Gen. 15:6). Because this is such a seminal verse, let is briefly put it into context. This was the third time God spoke or appeared to Abram (Abraham). And each time God give Abram an amazing promise. Each one was not a different promise but like a musical string building up like a crescendo. The first one was remarkable and seminal, in ch. 12, the call of Abram passage. God promises to "make his name great...I will bless those who bless you...and in you all the families of the earth shall be blessed" (Gen. 12:2b, 3a, c). Then the next time God speaks, it was "after Lot had separated from him" (Gen. 13:14a). And seeing the land of Canaan which is where God led him, God said, "I will make your descendents as the dust of the earth..." (Gen. 13:16). Then, at a time in which Abram was afraid he had no heir and therefore no descendants, which implies he had not yet believed or grasped the first two promises yet, we are told, "…the word of God came to Abram in a vision, saying,' I am your shield, your exceedingly great reward'" (Gen. 15:1). Then God proceeds to prophesy that Abram's heir will come from his own body (vs. 4), and God continued, "Look now toward heaven, and count the stars if you are able to number them…so shall your descendents be" (vs. 5). This then leads us to the seminal verse, ""And he [Abram] believed in God, and He [God] accounted it to him for righteousness" (vs. 6). The third time God's wonderful promise came, he grasped it, it stuck, and he believed. But what is this that "it was accounted to him for righteousness"? This is God's gracious act. The Law of Moses came perhaps 400-800 years after Abrajam. The apostle Paul articulates this for the Christian Gospel in distinction to Judaism, stating that the Law which came after the Abrahamic promises did not nullify the promises, but rather the promise coming first, is superior (Gal. 3:8, 15-18). Those Christianity and Judaism grew apart, thanks be to God that we are unified in the one eternal blessed Kingdom of God.

The Kingdom of God

O dear friends of God who desire a destiny of eternity in God's glory, many of us have come to spiritually discern that God's heavenly kingdom is from everlasting to everlasting.

How diverse has God's Kingdom been manifested on Earth, from great temples, basilicas, and cathedrals, to house churches, mosques, sanghas (Buddhist monastic communities), and outdoor sanctuaries. And how diverse are the peoples of the Earth whose faiths embody the Kingdom! Diverse are its expressions, O earthly saints, according to the various traditions.

I highlight one tradition and extrapolate a spiritual significance unto a universal and global outreach. The prophetic portions of the biblical tradition elevate the earthly kingdom of Israel to a spiritual kingdom, even to the theological significance of the Kingdom of God on Earth.18 As highlighted elsewhere, people, even people of faith imperfectly, even sometimes with a fleshly mind, interpret their own tradition's Scriptures. Yes, ancient Israel was a real, imperfect, insecure nation in ancient days. But the prophetic words lifts it up to spiritual and eschatological meaning. Yet some still want to interpret

"Israel" according to the flesh, that it is according to physical descendency. This latter point is fine for merely earthly kingdoms and states like modern Israel. But God's Kingdom is spiritual and heavenly, though it exists on Earth imperfectly through the light of revelation. So, if you are willing to receive, the spiritual kingdom of Israel is a metaphor for the spiritual Kingdom of God on Earth that reaches out around the Earth to all God's peoples. Is not God one, and this is but one Earth, and that there is one spiritual Kingdom of God? Do you, beloved enlightened friends, see a spiritual nobility in this? Or is the name "Israel" a name to which you find it hard to connect? I have good news for you my beloved friend. Your glory to come is not dependent on perfectly accepting each one of these teachings. For all our knowledge in this earthly realm is imperfect. We trust in God to carry us into His eternal glorious Kingdom in His time.

Let us never confuse an earthly kingdom with God's Kingdom, no matter how powerful it is or how splendid its palaces, nor matter how religious it seems to be. Power corrupts people, and as the truism continues, and "absolute power corrupts absolutely." Human kingdoms are necessarily concerned with national and regional security, safety of its citizens, provisions of needs especially food (trade), and the general health of its society and social needs. But the spiritual Kingdom of God is completely and perfectly concerned with human souls, their being led to the knowledge of God more intimately than natural revelation, their being enlightened in many truths, and their being peoples of God, possessors of salvation and hope of eternal glory in Heaven.

Peoples of God

O peoples of faith, peoples of God, disciples on the path of a relationship with God: You may be well familiar that there are at least some traditions, whose Scriptures, each revealed to a specific people in a specific culture and at a specific time, speak of them being God's people. The natural inclination of an "outsider" is it interpret this in an exclusive way, leading them to feel like an outsider. Is this not a refection of the natural human interpretation with our limitations and imperfections? If we, in faith, have ascented to the truth that God made all people and desires all people to be in His blessing and live in blessedness for eternity, then any of those covenants of the former sacred Scriptures were not intended to be exclusive, although in their cultural context, they were for the most part, focusing in on themselves. But even in these Scriptures, great lights of God's truth shines out. The biblical tradition is such a great illustration of this. When these Scriptures are read and interpreted by the aid of the Spirit, we see a reaching out to many others. It was never meant to be according to the flesh. The flesh cannot achieve spiritual goals. *Salvation has never been by race. Its always been by grace.* Leaving aside the theological debate for now regarding the role of human works in salvation, this teaching focuses on the defining as the peoples of God. In the ancient Semitic and Hebrew cultures and other ancient cultures, getting in covenant with and having a covenantal relationship with God was the most common expression, and important.

But we live in a global age. Our horizons have been expanded out to encompass the whole Earth, like on a space craft in orbit looking down on the whole of the Earth. From the position of faith that God made all things, created the heavens and the Earth, and that He created all living things including all human people (by the God-given ability to reproduce) and created their souls, and that He is a benevolent God who desires all to know Him, then it does look like each of the religious traditions did not have the whole truth and they each see through their culturally limited lens. None of them are wrong but all are limited and see only a portion of the whole picture. But through them all come wonderful points of light, revealed thoughts. From one, the apostle Paul proclaimed that God "desires all to be saved and to come to the knowledge of the truth (1 Tim. 2:4 NKJV). The Bible and other Scriptures teach that God created all races, and desires that peoples from all races come to know Him. Perhaps God's word through Abram, "… through your seed, all the families of the earth will be blessed" (Gen. 12:3c) is one of the greatest unfulfilled prophecies of all time. Perhaps this is one of the main reasons that God has not ushered in the End and the great Transformation of souls yet, to continue to bring His blessings to people around the world. The Gen. 12:3 prophecy infers that God desires that all tribes and peoples on Earth to be peoples of God.

But humans, with sin and corruptions raising out of their earthly natures, have even used religion, such as their religion, to deny that another people of another faith are not people of God. This is a great sin. Generally speaking, no human soul can tell another people that they are not the people of God. The Spirit of God can move prophets to warn specific individuals of their sin, including those in great sin or wickedness. While souls are still in their earthly vessel, repentance is still possible. Peoples of faith, all who believe in God, should accept all peoples as creatures of God, those who recognize the one Supreme God and those who do not. Those who do not still deserve equal respect and dignity. And we could still see the light of God in them: such wisdom, intellect, devotion, etc. are all from God. True love leads us to see various peoples of humanity, all peoples, as objects of God's love. The teaching on the Peoples of God is not for mere head knowledge, but it is to help us to see that we should love all people, truly taking the Golden Rule seriously.

The teaching on the peoples of God also leads us to a related teaching on priesthoods.

Priesthoods and the Order of Melchizedek

O searcher of truth, prime yourself for discovering many truths of priesthoods. Did not God communicate at times His word through priests and did they not preserve the sacred writings from ages past? They were not merely the pawns of the king or ruler nor were they Marxists who wanted to control the masses. Most of them were pious men and women who devoted themselves to God and faithfully served in their office. Praise be to God for all the faithful priests who have served faithfully throughout the ages. If God did speak in ancient times not only through sages and prophets, but also priests (in fact some priests were sages), can not the Eternal God do the same today? But many peoples of faith in our age have come to have a negative view of priests, either from some reported abuses, or personal experiences of poor ministry, or because their tradition has a negative view of them. The purposes of this teaching is to give an historical and spiritual account of priesthoods, and show their positive aspects. In the process, some "timeless" truths may be discovered that is applicable for every generation, for those who will receive.

And now truth seeker, listen to me, a truth-gatherer for the 21st century, as I impart understanding of priesthoods, beginning with an historical survey.

In ancient days, it was common for developing religions to establish priesthoods to function for several purposes as human societies developed, such as the Sumerians in ancient Mesopotamia in the 3rd millennium BCE. The places where they arose corresponded to where temples or ziggurats were built. The establishment of the sacred precincts birthed the institution of priesthoods. They were basically the representatives of God or gods on Earth. They were the very channels through which God spoke, and so they were the intelligentsia who penned the sacred lore, and determined rites and rituals (Oppenheim pp. 230-231). All this was important in maintaining order, especially in the realm of religion, in society. We could not envision this ancient society nor that of ancient Egypt without their priesthoods. They were a powerful class. So too in ancient India. The Vedic priesthood of Brahmins was the 2nd most powerful class in Indian society all the way up to Gautama Buddha's day who may have been the first to oppose the priesthood (Hopfe and Woodward p. 139).

In the history of real priesthoods on Earth, they cover the whole gamut from pure piety and devotion to politicizing. We find both the good and the bad. After a track record of over a hundreds of years on Earth, some people developed a distrust for them, some for good reason. And this has been carried forward through the millennia all the way into the 21st century. Some even opposed priesthoods for various religious, social, and political reasons, most of whom were keenly aware of corruption within, including the Buddha (see below). There is that truism: "power corrupts." Most priesthoods became powerful, and corruption came in. History unveils wealth and opulence, politics, and even murder in sacred precincts.

In ancient Mesopotamia, they controlled the wealth of the city. The poor basically remained poor and the royalty got most of the wealth, and this was done in the name of their gods. We can find or surmise on occasion some priests plotting to overthrow rulers, and perhaps even kill princes. This was most likely the case in ancient Egypt when Akhenaten declared Aten as the one God who alone is to be worshipped, which threatened the livelihood and even survival of the Amun priesthood and caused much instability in the country (Fletcher pp. 52, 87 and Osman, p. 162).

Coming to the Common Era, the first new religion on the scene, Christianity, continues the legacy of the Israelite priesthood of God but at a new spiritual height and with the christological viewpoint. This priesthood was no longer determined according to the flesh, ancestry, being of the tribe of Levi, but for all believers in God though the Messiah, the priesthood of all believers. This Scriptural basis they looked to in Exodus 19:6, "[God speaking through Moses] and you [all] shall be to Me a kingdom of priests and a holy nation" (NKJV) The apostle Peter in the 1st cent. CE writing to the believers in mainly Anatolia, some of them who had to be Gentiles, wrote, "But you are a chosen generation, a royal priesthood, a holy nation…" (1 Pet. 2:9a NKJV). Peter surely seems to be speaking in spiritual terms, not referring to an actual order, religious class. There is such a theological richness in the Biblical tradition which also includes the mysterious order of Melchizedek, that I have a teaching below just on this order, in detail. During the first three centuries of Christianity, there were pastors and elders, overseers (bishops), teachers, and apostles. But there was not an order of priests, properly understood. But after Christianity gets established and institutionalized, and develop strong traditions in their new holy cities such as Rome and Constantinople, priesthoods get established on these heels. And wealth and opulence comes into the Church, and seeds of corruption were wafting from the seat of Peter to the Mediterranean seas.

The next major world religion to arrive on the scene in the Common Era was Islam in the 7th cent. *The Holy Quran* only has two references to "priests" and none on "priesthoods," based on its index, if its index is complete. They occur only two verses apart, and the first one is clearly talking about Christian priests speaking negatively that Christians seem to be offering worship to their priests and to Christ instead of God (9:31 p. 508). The next reference is even more emphatically negative, "O ye who believe [speaking to Muslims]! There are indeed many among the priests and anchorites, who in falsehood devour the wealth of men and hinder (them) from the Way of Allah" (9:34 p. 509). If these two references alone was it, it may suffice to have discouraged the earliest Muslims to establish a priesthood. But there is a cultural reason as well. The Arab culture was nomadic to semi-nomadic which is not conducive to priesthoods since they require an established stationary sacred place. Priesthoods were not a custom for Arabs.

Advancing forward all the way to the 19th century in Persia, the Baha'i Faith emerges out of Shi'a Islam (Hopfe and Woodward, p. 14-2). Baha'ullah, the founder of the newest Faith, continued forward the general non-priesthood practice from Islam. The unique Babi and Baha'i experience seals this non-priesthood belief and practice as founded by the sacred writings of Baha'ullah. First we should understand that while Islam did not have a priesthood, they did have clergy. And the clergy of the Shi'a sect of Islam have a special power as viewed by the Shi'a people. They believe, for example that the Shah's word is the word of God. Both the Bab and Baha'is were not only persecuted by the Muslim rulers, but they were also opposed by the Muslim clergy, Shi'a and Sunni. They both were personally oppressed. This definitely had an effect on Baha'ullah, influencing his anti-priesthood perspective carefully detected in his writings. In his *Lawh-I-Aqdas* (Holy Tablet), which in part is speaking to Christians, in one passage, he speaks directly to Christian priests, writing, "O concourse of priests! Leave the bells, and come forth, then from your churches. It behoveth you…the Lord is come in His great glory" (Tablets of Baha'ullah p. 13). What he is saying is that he, Baha'ullah, is the Second Coming of Jesus Christ and you need not look for another. I am He (ibid. p. 11). Leave your churches and follow me. His Tablet's index cites these pages as well (pp. 10, 238, 258). There is another passage in this volume of his sacred writing that his followers are not to confess their sins to any other, which includes priests. The function of priests to hear followers confess their sins and bestow forgiveness has been a Christian practice, particularly among Catholic and Orthodox churches, the latter of which had a small presence in Persia. It is based upon some key New Testament Scriptures including its foundation of Christ giving the spiritual keys to Peter (Matt. 16:19). I have heard some Christians say essentially the same thing. "I don't need a priest to confess my sins to. I go straight to God." So what was Baha'ullah's concern of priesthoods? Was there a distrust and disdain for priesthoods? Was it a natural progression of the Quranic verse cited above? Was it religious-cultural, that is, not a practice in Islam? Was Baha'ullah keenly aware of corruption in priesthoods, including the Brahmins in ancient India? Baha'ullah, raised in a ruling family no doubt received a good education which included the reading of the Hindu as well as Muslim literature. It may have been all of these.

Whatever his specific reason, Baha'ullah did not have a positive view of priesthoods.

In this world, there is both good and bad. When we consider this fact and the fact that virtually all priesthoods in human history got intricately involved with the temporal politics of its nations, we should not be surprised to find some bad in them as well as good, from ancient Egypt, to the Hasmonean dynasty Jewish priesthood in Jerusalem, to the Roman Catholic priesthood. When the German monk Martin Luther took his first trip to Rome in the early 16th century, he was nearly shocked to find some immorality among the clergy in Rome, and some abuses such as flippantly speaking through the words of the sacred mass (Bainton pp.37-38). The rule of celibacy for RCC priests combined with planting seeds of sensuality through art depicting nudes within sacred houses of God during the Renaissance were no doubt factors in producing bad fruit centuries later, even manifesting in priest pedophilia in the 20th and 21st century, but in no way excusing these shameful acts. Despite these scandals, the RCC priesthood remains firm, a testament to the strength of its institution.

Generally, the number of religious traditions which have priesthoods seemed to have diminished some in the Common Era. The destruction of the Jewish priesthood and Temple in 70 CE signifies a fundamental change. If we were to rely solely on the book of Hebrews to determine whether Christianity would pick up the baton of priesthoods, we would surely think not. But priesthoods are more than about performing animal sacrifices. From ancient times to the present, they have served as mediators of prayer, on behalf of the peoples. This alone is a very sacred and special work. They have served as the professions of religious rites for all times, ancient to the modern era. In the Common Era, priesthoods continue with no bloody sacrifices; instead, they receive offerings of tangibles such as money and food by the peoples, and lead the peoples in spiritual offerings of thanks, praise, and worship of God.

O eager disciples to learn, we have not yet penetrated all the truths of priesthoods. Take a moment to rest the mind before we re-engage and ponder some more truths, starting with some basics.

The two fundamental spiritual dynamics of priesthoods are two movements. The first is the movement of God to people, through which the priests assist and intermediate. This is the sacramental movement. And the second is the flow from the people to God, through which the priests also assist. This is the sacrificial, such as prayers and offerings. These two dynamics are going on all the time, and even simultaneously, in active priesthoods, by faith or course since God most often remains invisible to our eyes For example, when a priest is bestowing a blessing, say, at the conclusion of a ceremony, the people by faith believe God is bestowing it through the mere mortal human who is also touched by sin.

The next truth we should ponder is this. If God did ordain certain priesthoods in the past, and if He did not abolish all of them, then there should be some legitimate priesthood(s) living on even today in the 21st century. Is it possible for human societies to abolish priesthoods, but not God for His peoples on Earth? Yes, but this alone does not prove God ordains any priesthood to continue into the 21st cent. A diligent study should be made by the Scriptures of your choice to determine this. The statement above began with two "ifs," and here is where we must dive in deeper.

Allow me, beloved ones, to delve into the Scriptures dearest to me and those I'm most familiar, the Bible, and highlight two main priesthoods from these and what their states may be in the 21st century.

The two main biblical priesthoods were the Levitical and the Melchizedekian. The Levitical priesthood was tied to a tribe of Levi and to their cultic center with its sacrificial system, and it was not permanent, as in "forever," based on the whole of the Bible (the Christian Scriptures), but abolished through Messiah who was the perfect sacrifice that all Old Testament sacrifices foreshadowed, according to the author of Hebrews (c.f. chs. 6, 7, & 8). The second is the mysterious order of Melchizedek which is only mentioned two times in the whole Tanak/Old Testament, but then spoken of in such grandeur nine times in the book of Hebrews in the New Testament. The "order" of Melchizedek is actually mentioned only one time in the Old Testament. The archetypal passage of Melchizedek's only appearance in the Torah/Pentateuch, Genesis 14:18-20, mentions him as a "priest."

The priest implies an order, but by definition, an order usually needs more than one priest to be called an order, and Melchizedek could have been a "solo" priest. But the Psalmist of Psalm 110 writes in such a significant and Messianic sense, elevating the first mention of the order of Melchizedek to biblical proportions carried eschatologically, way beyond the constraints of the Torah, when writing, "You are a priest forever, according to the order of Melchizedek" (Ps. 110:4b NKJV). Now to whom is this psalmist referring? The best answer is verse 1: "The LORD said to my Lord" (NKJV), which still leaves us to ponder the meaning of this mysterious verse. In the Hebrew, LORD is the tetragrammaton "YHWH, God's personal name. (BHS p. 1194). The mystery of this verse is that "my lord," (Adonai) is usually used for God but can be used for rulers or kings. It does not make sense that God is speaking to Himself. And this very question was posed by Jesus to the Pharisees in His day in Jerusalem, knowing they did not have an answer. Jesus begins the discussion with the question, "What do you think about the Christ? Whose son is He? (Matt. 22:42 NKJV). The Pharisees answered, "The son of David" (vs. 42). Then Jesus said to them, "How then does David in the Spirit call Him 'Lord,' saying 'The LORD said to my Lord...'" (vs. 44). Jesus the Christ puts the Messianic and the christological meaning to Ps. 110:1, which is the person directly connected to Ps. 110:4. This passage from Matthew's Gospel alone, tied to Ps. 110:1-4, leads the Christian interpreter to understand that Jesus is both the Christ, which is the intention Jesus was aiming for, and that the Christ is "a priest forever according to the order of Melchizedek."

Up until this point in the biblical record, Melchizedek is only mentioned twice (Gen. 14:18 and Ps. 110:4), and then alluded to in Matt. 22. Then toward the end of the Bible, the order of Melchizedek is referenced no less than nine times in the book of Hebrews. They all point to Jesus Christ as the sole one who can make a legitimate claim to the order of Melchizedek. Verse by verse, chapter by chapter, the author of Hebrews demonstrates Jesus Christ as fulfilling the Old Testament and greater and superior to it and to the angels, and it is in praise to Him.

In summarizing the biblical tradition, God defined a holy priesthood through the Levites, based on his covenantal relationship with His people Israel, and much later psalmist prophesied of a Messianic figure order of Melchizedek who will sit at the right hand of God, which the New Testament clearly presents as Christ Jesus, fulfilling the Old Testament. The Levitical priesthood had served its purpose.

This teaching would not be complete without mentioning a priesthood or two in the modern age that also believes it is a part of the order of Melchizedek. The Mormons believe that their priesthood is a part of the order of Melchizedek. There also may be other modern religious groups or cults that claim connection with or a part of this order. Historically, however, there is no evidence whatsoever of an actual order of Melchizedek existing in biblical times nor all through the 2000 plus years of the Common Era. It is easy to make a claim of something, but much harder to demonstrate it. Moreover, the point of the author of Hebrews is to give worship to Christ. Any other claims made on this order only detracts from the worship and praise of Christ. Moreover, learned ones should consider the motivation of these modern or cultic groups to making this claim to the prized biblical order of Melchizedek to give credence and authority to their religious system.

In conclusion, God is the God of order. All human beings who ascent to God, are in some way touched or inspired by order both cosmic and temporal, and some have creatively established religious orders through which we can catch glimpses of paradise or heaven, shadows or types of heaven to come. There has been both good and bad in priesthoods throughout history because human beings are prone to corruption. Because God is good,

God has only done good things through priesthoods. One of the special accomplishments that priests in religious orders have done is they have been the penmen to write sacred Scriptures. This is such a holy honor thing, to in effect, minister the word of God to people, or at least sacred texts that inspire people to the Divine, and to lead people to thank, praise, and love God. Historically, priests have and continue to function as worship leaders. They have officiated at religious festivals. And they have produced hundreds of sacred teachers and preachers for God's people, men and women. God can continue to do great things through priesthoods. But trust needs re-building. Integrity, and Scriptural grounding and legitimacy needs to be maintained. There is always need for good religious leaders. Priests are a viable office for leadership in religious communities for those who sense a calling to this ministry. Not all peoples of faith today feel the need for priests at all in carrying out their faith. They believe that they have direct access to God. They too are blessed peoples of faith who should equally carry out their faith in freedom. Christians have a tradition of directly bestowing the great blessing of the forgiveness of sin from Christ, through the agent of the priest. Entering a priesthood should be voluntary. It is spiritually noble and honorable for men dedicating their lives to God through the priesthood who see the Church as their bride. But celibacy is not the natural gift of most men, nor even most priests. Priests should be allowed to marry, which means that the vow of celibacy not be mandated for all, but a free choice of those who wish to fully dedicate themselves. May all peoples of faith be blessed through their ministers and come to God's house.

The House of God

O disciples and peoples of faith, living stones in the habitation of God's holy places, we come to this blessed teaching on the House of God. The beauty of the concept of the House of

God is that it harmonizes our basic need for shelter with the Transcendent Divine.

God has placed in humans such a strong spiritual desire for the transcendence. Certain human beings from ancient times have had such inspiring spiritual experiences that propelled them to want to enshrine it. We certainly see this on the mount on Transfiguration, when once Peter saw Moses and Elijah talking with Jesus, he said, "Lord, let us make here three tabernacles: one for You, one for Moses, and one for Elijah" (Matt. 17:4). Houses for God, temples, shrines, are as old as the oldest cities and towns. From most ancient times, the various temples, houses of God, that were built, were special meeting places with God. The common peoples were welcome to place offerings and say their prayers. In some places, priests were established to maintain them. Its unclear, though, whether the original impetus to build them was more out of the community's desire to be closer to God or more from a leader-visionary- sage or prophet who moved for their building. Archeologists have pieced together some things of their history, but these ancient temples lacking survived texts or documents keeps silent on this point. But the main point is clear: the houses of God are places where people have drawn closer to God, meet Him, offer offerings and prayers, and commune with God.

From the various shrines for various deities and to God Almighty built in ancient times, in Mesopotamia, Canaan, Egypt, Arabia, Anatolia, China, and Japan, many of them came to signify "The House of God." Collectively, the Spirit of God is communicating the truth of the need of humans to dwell closer to God. The feeling of distance from God has been a systemic spiritual problem for mankind for thousands of years. The remedy is to build a structure called a "house" in a locale dedicated to God or a deity.

The prophets of the blessed past called their peoples to meet God of their faith each in their appointed consecrated places which became sacred places, each in their own homelands of origin in their time.

The great Hebrew prophet Isaiah wrote, "Now it shall come to pass in the latter days that the mountain of the YHWH (God's) house shall be established on the top of the mountains, and shall be exalted above the hills, and all nations shall flow to it. Many people shall come and say, 'Come, and let us go up to the mountain of the LORD.... (Isaiah 2:2-3a NKJV)

God foresaw our day, our global age, and a growing movement of global faith peoples. God has brought a new age as prophesied through holy Jesus who proclaimed, "neither on this mountain [Gerizim/Ebal in Samaria] nor in Jerusalem [Mt. Zion] will they worship Me but in spirit and truth they shall worship Me" (John 4:21, 23 NKJV). This speaks of *no central* place on earth globally where human beings meet God and worship Him. There is no geographic point of latitude or longitude, but speaks of the spiritual Zion of longevity, the sacred meeting place of the Divine and human soul, wherever their bodies are physically, locally. John, Jesus' close disciple believed to be the author of this Gospel, and it is believed that John wrote it between 90-95 AD (CE), which puts it perhaps 20 or more years after the destruction of the Temple in Jerusalem, which gave ample time for the blessed apostle to contemplate and theologize over the new meaning and re-interpretation of the faith in light of the upheaval event of the Temple's destruction. This passage clearly marks a total re-orientation of the faith from its former focal point of Jerusalem to outward, throughout the world, there, here, and everywhere.

The believers of Judaism have the Wailing Wall, the Christians have the Holy Sepulchre, the Muslims have the Ka'aba in Mecca, the Baha'is have the Shrine of the Bab (International Shrine), but the prophetic Scripture from John 4:21, 23 looks to a new day when peoples of faith are not obligatorily bound to attend one specific spot on the earth for the sacred meeting of God, worship, and prayer. Religions create rituals, requirements, and obligations. But the Spirit of God creates a spiritual holy habitation of the Divine with people of faith, through their hearts and spirits. The cry for God in the human soul is still outward, externally, and so it is fitting to have external visible spaces. After all, we are still in the body and our body has to be somewhere at all times, until our souls permanently depart from it.

King Solomon also had a clear vision and understanding that no earthly temple can truly house the God of Heaven and Earth. At the dedication of the first Jerusalem Temple, Solomon prayed, "But will God indeed dwell on the earth? Behold heaven and the heaven of heavens cannot contain You. How much less this temple which I have built!" (I Kings 8:27 NKJV) And yet, we know historically just how splendid that Solomonic temple was (c.f. 1 Kgs. 6:20-22; Hag. 2:3), but architecturally, it was not unique (Mazar p. 377)

O peoples of faith globally, is there not diversity among you? Are there not unique traditions and customs that have become a part of the cultural fabric of humanity? Do we therefore need to try to force a visible unity and make a bridge of impossibility in trying to establish a central sacred place on Earth for all God's people? Wisdom, I say, would lead the wise to see that this would only lead to further conflict, arguments and disputes as to whose country it should be located in. It is much better to understand these prophecies spiritually, including that of Isaiah ch. 2. Peoples of faith should be free to visit the places of sacred pilgrimage in their own tradition, but also visit sacred places of other traditions too. The vision for the future is that all the sacred houses and sites of pilgrimages around the world not only get a flow of pilgrims in their own tradition but many visitors of other faiths, in cultural exchange and mutual support in the love of God and fellow human beings. This suggests a positive mutual global faith awareness.

Global Faith

O disciples and all peoples of faith, globally, you know at the outset that when we speak of "global faith," we are not speaking of one religious tradition; it is a collective concept standing for many families of faith traditions which all have a universal outlook. These families of faith traditions can in turn be sub-divided into many religious denominations and organizations. The expression "global faith" is like from an "eagles" perspective, or more fitting, from the perspective of the international space station in Earth's orbit looking down, and figuratively seeing faith on Earth below in its many and various traditions.

These Scriptures have no purpose, goal, or desire to unite the religions or faith traditions in the world into one, creating one global religion or religious institution. These Scriptures are apolitical, spiritually-minded and focused. This is clearly defined this way because otherwise many would understand "global faith" in some unifying way. Respect is given to each of the traditions. And we are cognizant of the popular Christian understanding of specific End Times prophecies regarding the Antichrist taking up his seat which has been understood to imply a one world system and government established. This is certainly not the aim of these Scriptures. These Scriptures are light, bringing truth to humankind, centered on God, His holiness and goodness, and shunning all works of darkness. While believers believe God will bring true prophecies to pass, few are looking forward to the tribulations to come which has been prophesied.

As we gain in greater understanding of the faith traditions around the globe, the Spirit of God leads us to greater mutual respect for each other, and even developing sensitivities towards peoples of various beliefs. Next, we will define faith.

Faith Defined

We should first define faith. In essence, it is the inclination and capacity to believe in that which is beyond the physical senses, to ultimate reality, and ultimately, God. It involves the mind, heart, and soul. I believe that the entity of faith and the residence of it in our beings is unique, and special, not just simply our thoughts, views, or opinions of the mind, or our gut feelings. I think it is a mystery, a gift from God to humankind.[19]

Faith has a beginning and end, in a person's life and in the history of humanity. Faith first begun on Earth with the first person who believed. According to the Bible, Adam was the first man. Faith will end on Earth when God ushers in the Consummation of the Ages, and re-makes heaven and Earth. The beginning point of faith in the individual is, naturally, when a person begins to believe. And while our souls are made to live forever, in Paradise/Heaven, we will see God and the angels and will no longer be in the state of faith. The state of faith ends when we are changed from the corruptible to the incorruptible, from the mortal to the immortal (1 Cor. 15:54).

Is there a distinction between faith and true faith? Many religious persons, scholars and non-scholars, do make a distinction. For some, the main difference is between intellectual faith and heart-faith. For others, it may be more a matter of degree. The word "true" itself is used in at least two different senses. The one sense is as the adjective of truth. The other sense connotes a "pureness." Peoples of faith have the freedom to define terms in their words, and yet isn't it a mystery and wonder that so many spiritual humans on the planet end up deriving at very similar truths?

The Life and Gift of Faith

O gifted disciples and peoples of faith, from wherein is the seat of faith in an individual, and from wherein does it arise? Does faith not arise from within the soul, heart, and mind? If God looks to us to see faith, the faith directed toward Him, as being most pleasing, and if this faith is a necessary factor for us to be received into Paradise and Heaven, then it is quintessential. If it is also viewed as a gift of God, then faith is one of the greatest gifts we can have. It ultimately comes from God, and its object is God. If any created creature, heavenly or earthly, expected the object of our faith to be directed toward them, this would be sheer egotism and narcissism. But God is God, not a creature, and He is worthy of all faith.

Every soul God has created, I suggest, has been created with a capacity to believe. The capacity is like a empty container that needs to be filled with good content. When we are born, the container is not completely empty, since there is the aspect of us created in God's image, that there is perhaps a shimmer of inclination toward God, for many souls, but this is a mystery, that some are more receptive than others. (See the teaching "Born to Sin or Not, Submitted or Not" below.) Historical Christianity and Islam differ significantly on this point). Then from the child's infancy to its growing up, all or any faith aspects it is fed by parents and organized religious instruction, in whatever tradition or traditions, is the content that is put in the container of faith. The child's precious mind, heart and soul, latches unto that which it has been fed. So there is some truth, as many have observed, that if one is raised a Jew, they are probably a Jew in adulthood. If one is raised a Christian, they are probably a Christian in adulthood. And if one is raised a Muslim, they are probably a Muslim in adulthood. But we also know the complexities of life and human beings. Some people do turn away from the faith that they were raised in. But of these who do turn away which typically happens in adolescence, a portion of them return back later in life to the same faith tradition.

Faith has to be nurtured. It is not automatic. Children receive the content which is imparted to them by their parents and through any religious education they receive. Parents of faith should nurture their children's souls from the time they come out of the womb, speaking and singing softly the words of God, saying prayers to God, etc.

Sometimes faith comes to children not because of such clear presentations but despite muddled mediations of the word. The Spirit is the continual assist to lead God's children to faith, and ultimately Heaven.

Faith is for this life in the body. Once we by God's grace are changed into the glorious body and brought into Paradise and Heaven, our faith will be completed. Will we still need faith in Heaven? Here is a mystery that other prophets and apostles have only given us clues. We will be glorified, and we will see God and the angels. Therefore, we will no longer need faith in the sense on this earth where God remains invisible to us. But in the sense of faith that leads to adoration and worship, we will be overflowing without ceasing, with this expression of faith while living in glorious Paradise.

Faith and Religion

O blessed disciples with faith unto eternal life, we have already established the high value of faith, pure faith out of the heart and soul, and we have established, that when we speak of faith for the sake of these teachings, we are often referring to the actual faith in an individual, their heart, mind, and soul. This is the faith, rising within an individual person, that clings to notion of God, the word of God, the belief in a merciful God, and which latches onto the promises of God. Faith is a precious thing. If it leads us to our eternal places in glory, then it is more valuable than gold and silver. In these teachings, when I address you as "disciples and peoples of faith," the word "faith" here is used in both the sense of the individuals who individually possess faith and also in a collective cross-creedal sense.

O disciples who are exercising your faith, faith is a living dynamic disposition of the heart, mind, and soul in a human being, and religion is the worldly structure of faith, with rules and regulations, human made rituals and customs. In essence, faith is God-born in the human soul, and religion is human-made. Now there are many specific religions on the Earth, each with a distinct belief system with a set of rituals.

In distinction to faith, we have this word "religion" that is used so commonly and sometimes carelessly, lacking clarity. Many people in our age have been enlightened to the truth that religion is earthly, essentially man-made. The human sense of religion does not save. God saves individual souls when God sees faith and the soul's inclination toward Him. The common use of the term "religion" is that it is of the earthly realm. It resides among humans. "Religion" often refers to human-made systems of beliefs and practices, and the organizations and institutions which are formed as a result. The beliefs may be inspired. Some contain direct words of God through prophets in their Scriptures. But the religion is a human structure which includes a community of leaders and followers and social structures. We could suppose that there is religion in Heaven—all the angels adoring and worshipping God. We could call this Heaven's religion. But virtually all the time, the term "religion" is used for the earthly realm. From our human perspective, religion is fashioned by human beings, some aspects of which includes Divine inspiration and God-honoring customs and practices mixed with human-manufactured rituals and social constructs being lived out on the human plane. In short, we could say that faith is Spirit-wrought and religion is human taught.

And now, O studious learners of faith, let us return back to the term "faith." There is another meaning for which it is being used in this contemporary age, most notably in the last two decades. "Faith" is now being used synonymously with "religion." Journalists picked up on it and so now it is commonly used in this sense. So when someone asks "What faith are you?" They are asking what religion or religious tradition do you hold to. It is understandable that this term "faith" came to be used in this sense. In the broad perspective of the field of religion in distinction to other fields, anthropology, archaeology, information technology, etc. it would be said that to hold to a religion "takes faith," meaning there is no hard or empirical evidence to support it. The things of God and His words to humankind takes faith to believe, for they are from the heavenly realm. Religion deals primarily with the invisible things." God is invisible to our eyes, and our faith is invisible. And virtually all religions, unless one is talking about, say, the "religion of sports," holds to some assertions that cannot be verified tangibly and scientifically. It takes faith. So in this sense, it is acceptable to use the term "faith" synonymously with "religion," but with caution. It also creates some confusion. If we already have the term "religion" why not continue to use it for "religion"? Part of the confusion is that it sets up a false assumption that all the religions deal equally with "faith" in the first sense above: a high value in individual faith that is essential for salvation. For most of the religions, in fact, faith is not the most significant thing: it is keeping the law or morals, meditating intensely, or properly performing certain rituals a certain number of times for so long. Christianity, of all the religions, appears to be unique in having a fundamental emphasis on faith in their Savior that will lead them to Heaven.[20]

Even if we agree that religion does not save, we can consider that, humanly speaking, religion is necessary. It is the mark of a religious person, in whatever particular form it manifests. And faith, let us say, is absolutely necessary. Without faith, what hope can we have? Faith and religion, therefore, are both necessary. Both should be imparted naturally to young people, by instruction, by modeling, and by example, not by force. We should not stop with imparting the basics of your faith tradition, what your religion teaches. We ourselves should strive for spiritual maturity in faith and then lead our children to the same. One important but perennial difficult distinction is separating faith from one's religious institution or organization. We cannot emphasize enough that our faith is in God, not human beings nor even in the religion or the human leaders that represent it. When leaders fall or organizations fail its own people, many believers become disillusioned. This can simply be avoided by telling our children: "Our faith is in God. We are so thankful to be in a religion that teaches and preaches us this, but our faith is not in them, but in God." In reality, we know that we are in this temporal world with fallible people and fallible religious institutions and organizations. Blessed are those who have faith and in whom faith is found on the Earth (c.f. Lk. 18:8), and blessed are the souls of all the faithful.

Earth is imperfect, tainted by the corruption within humanity, and this reality should lead us to seek the pure and true religion.

Pure and True Religion

O disciples who yearn for the pure and true ideals of religion, we have just distinguished faith from religion. Now when we speak of "pure" and "true religion" the words "pure" and "true" are ideals. They lift the meaning of religion to a higher level that the mere human plane, to the ideal and spiritual plane. To comprehend this teaching, one should put on their ideals hat. In this teaching, the meaning of "pure" and "true" are related. But let us talk about "pure" religion first.

If religion is in the impure human realm as we just stated above, how can it be pure? Is it not the impure nature of human beings that makes religion impure in reality? We can talk about "pure religion" because it is an ideal, and the ability to think in the realm of ideals is a gift from God. It is not mere human abstract fabrications, but it is through this realm and the faculty to reach to this realm which is one important way that God communicates to us.

Religion at its best is pure faith and pure deeds of love, compassion, and kindness. The apostle James writes it this way: "Pure and undefiled religion before God and the Father is this: to visit orphans and widows in trouble, to keep oneself unspotted from the world" (James 1:27). This should be an inspiring verse. But what about showing compassion on the crippled, poor, and destitute? What about visiting the sick and dying? James captures a part of the essence of pure religion but he obviously did not intend to state a comprehensive list of selfless actions that evidences pure religion flowing out of a believer. But after going through all the teachings of Jesus in the New Testament Gospels, and then also the Pauline epistles, I would expect the one New Testament verse speaking on what "pure religion" is to be something like this: "Pure religion is to believe in Him whom God has sent, keeping yourself away from idols, keeping yourself morally and sexually pure, having relations only with your spouse, having compassion on the sick, frail, weak, crippled, elderly, orphaned, weak, and distraught, caring for those in the household of faith, having hospitality to strangers, and giving charitably.

Now let is turn to "true religion." In the first sense, as an ideal, "true religion" is closely related to "pure" religion, near synonyms. In this ideal sense, it touches upon both the spiritual and human realms at the same time. It is the human who is thinking the thought, but the thought is in the spiritual realm. Can your mind grasp this?

The second sense of "true religion" is that which we are all familiar with, and may even hold to it, believing that one's own religion is the "true religion" and that the other religions have it wrong or are even false. This meaning to "true religion" of course is a much different sense than a synonym of "pure religion." There are not only historically millions, but probably billions of religious peoples through the ages who have considered their own religion the "true religion," understood exclusively, whether Hindus, Buddhists, Jews, Christians, or Muslims. Virtually each religion believes that it is a "true" religion. And many religions, particularly the monotheistic religions, have viewed their religion alone as the "true religion," exclusively, and all other religions as false. A careful study reveals that as each of the religions developed their distinctions, then this view developed afterwards. But when the religion was first founded, the founder saw his new-found faith as part of succession of prophets, and predecessor religions. This is certainly true for both Christianity and Islam. The prophet Muhammad viewed the new Islamic faith as a continuation of the true religion from Abraham, Moses, and Jesus (e.g. Quran 2:125-136). But the foundational passages in the Quran are problematic in its disagreements and contentions with the biblical Scriptures.

It is for this reason among several related reasons that this Scripture was birthed, to help bridge the differences of understanding and model a way of peace. If it accomplishes only this, it will have achieved a noble goal.

Many people in this age have come to see that it is not all black and white when it comes to truth and religion. Each religion will have degrees of truth and divine inspiration and certain amounts of added human rites, rituals, and structures. Many people have come to believe that no one religion possesses the full truth. In other words, there is some truth that can be found in every religion, though some have paths distinctly different than another. Some of them share some universal truths and some of them have exchanged concepts with each other through the centuries. Human beings have continued to be enlightened through the ages. We, in the 21st century, standing in hindsight, have the blessing and privilege to be able to learn from all the past ages and from all the religious traditions, if we are willing to study, to find similar or different expressions of related truths already held. Various religions can assist humankind on their journey of spiritual nobility.

But as many also know, the attitude of "my religion is the true religion" has been a real cause for religious conflict in the world. It is not just the raw emotion that has led religions to get people into great conflicts. It is when people put themselves behind the politicized power of their religion-this has fueled the ugliness of conflict as much as if not more so than raw human emotion.

A thesis I assert here is that all the previous blessed Scriptures in the past were used in a corrupted sense when they were politicized. The texts themselves for the most part were not changed (although cases that they were: Cyrus the Great apparently politicized the Zoroastrian Scriptures). It was their use and interpretation of by religious but imperfect people for politicizing power that reflects corruption, based on the premise of divine Scriptures being pure, reflecting God and is intended for spiritual nurture of souls, not for political gain. But in reality, all religions have been used for political gain by temporal powers and factions.

In this next teaching, we continue to delve into faith and religious traditions' distinctions and light.

Faith and Religious Traditions Part I

O devoted disciples of various traditions, we have contemplated how fundamentally important faith is for our spiritual journey toward eternity. Now is there faith without any religious tradition?

Have not all people throughout the ages that have had faith, received it through a religious tradition? It can come through a mentor's teachings or non-organized tradition, but for most all of us, it has come to us through an organized tradition. Faith has been instilled in most all of us through being imbedded in a cultural way, through a specific religious tradition.

We are very aware how personal faith can be to so many individuals. Since faith and religious traditions are such close companions, it does not seem strange to use that religious traditions have come to be so dear and sacred to human beings as well.

Enlightened peoples of God, in this first of two teachings on Faith and Religious traditions, I highlight the different types of traditions. This is a fundamental because the word "tradition" is used for several different things. Therefore, I break them down for you here in these categories or types: traditions of rites, traditions of customs, traditions of thoughts, stories, ideas, Scripture traditions, and traditions of commentaries on Scripture. This list I just gave is a more humanistic or anthropocentric approach. Now, O believers in God, let's see this list one more time but from a theocentric perspective, since all things begin with God: Scripture traditions, traditions of commentaries on Scripture, traditions of thoughts, stories, ideas, traditions of rites, and traditions of customs. Some of these categories need no explanation. But briefly, traditions of rites are prescribed forms, one type of ritual. And where does oral tradition fall in the list? There are different kinds of oral tradition, some of which is commentaries on Scripture, additional prophetic mandates, and additional material on the sayings or actions of a prophet or holy teacher. As important as oral tradition has become to schools within the great Abrahamic faiths, it may be considered its own category.

Religion can be divided into two categories: beliefs and practices. All rituals fall in the practice category.

The truth is, tradition has a powerful grip on the human souls, for those who have become so accustomed to it and come under its spell. So powerful in fact is tradition that it can override sacred Scriptures or common sense faith! Human tradition can win out to the revelation of God. Many examples could be cited, but I will highlight just a few. In Judaism, the pious view of the Hebrew language of the Torah being so holy that it is believed to have fallen from Heaven. In Christianity, Jesus' view of the Jewish tradition of elders was confrontational to the tradition, evidenced in Mark 7:3-7 and Matt. 15:6b. Also, the required vow of celibacy for Roman Catholic priests is not a scriptural command. For Islam, the pious view of the Quranic Arabic being so holy, believed to be the heavenly language of God, is a tradition that goes beyond the Quran.

It is true that we humans can tenaciously hold on to our traditions. If we are not properly and fully educated in our faith, we may believe that all our traditions are divine, that they have fallen from Heaven to us. But in reality, a significant portion of all non-scriptural traditions, such as customs and some oral traditions, are human-made. An honest approach by religious leaders and people is to honestly acknowledge and teach these distinctions, and itemize those traditions that are not directly from God's word.

As I say in another teaching, rituals do not require faith. They are performance orientated. But stating this alone is an incomplete picture. There is often an internal drive propelling the ritual, and for many people of faith historically, it is to get right with God by some means, prayers and other rituals. Presumably, the priest or leader who may be leading the ritual has personal faith and wants to believe that his or her actions will have some efficacious and positive spiritual benefit upon the people. In regard to the action traditions, they are distinct from faith itself. It is hoped that all action traditions are God pleasing, but religion is known for producing erroneous traditions that seem to have more of a purpose of control than to liberally dispense spiritual blessings on the people.

Religious peoples, the laity and the ordained alike, can both be watchdogs of their religion to keep it steered in the true path, as they collectively define it. They may find some traditions that are not supported by their Scriptures or may be questionable. There may even be a couple superstitions found. May the Spirit of God move freely to unify the people in heart and mind. God is for order, stability, and peace. God does not create chaos. If there are major changes discovered that should be made, do so slowly, caringly, and properly, not secretly. The whole body should be informed of the changes to be made. Approach in love. We are creatures of habit that do not like change.

O faithful ones, are you faithful to God as you understand through your faith tradition, or are you merely faithful or loyal to your faith tradition? If you are faithful only to your tradition, this may not be anymore than religiosity, and you may not in fact know God for yourself. God is inviting you, bidding you, to come to know Him for Himself, and not merely through the speckled camera lens that any religion can provide. He wants you to have a relationship with Him. It is awesome to think that we humans can have a relationship with the living God of the universe! But when we feel we have achieved this, we first should recognize it is itself a gift of God's grace, allowed by His Spirit, not something we could achieve, thereby being humble, not boastful, prideful, or arrogant.

There are many people of faith on Earth that for them, religion is basically a duty, and a brief amount of time set aside weekly to fulfill. It helps them to feel better, in this tough world of trying to make it. And it is good to feel better. God wants to help us, knowing the struggles of temporal life. But it is all too easy to keep God at a distance in our own lives, not allowing

His Spirit to really come in and take charge. It is often a fearful thought for men, the idea of someone else taking charge. Men are to open up and see God as their Father, the perfect model. And God is looking for us to trust Him who alone is unfailing. The only disappointment we should ever get from God is Him NOT sending us to Hell, which we deserve, but this should not disappoint us, but be a tremendous relief.

Since we will all answer to the God of the universe on that Day of Judgment, much safer it is to know God, to follow Him in your heart and life, than merely have a religion. Religion is for humanity on earth, but actual faith is for human souls on the path to a blessed eternity. Relationship with God is considerably better than simply "I have a religion." Having a relationship with God goes beyond the confines of control of a religious tradition, system, institution, or organization.

Light and clarity are yours in regard to richly understanding of faith and religious traditions. We have one more teaching on faith and religious traditions which will bring even more clarity and truth.

Faith and Religious Traditions Part II

Now dear disciples, let us briefly highlight the faith traditions in the world. They can be simplified into three basic belief systems in this world. The three belief systems can in turn actually be simplified into two: theistic and non-theistic (the latter not to be confused with atheism which for the purposes of this book is not considered a "faith" belief system). The non-theistic religions are defined as religions because they have distinct belief systems, they have an ultimate goal of a state beyond the earthly life in the body, and they possess a set of rituals and beliefs about the rituals. These belief systems may acknowledge a God or some deity or deities, but the focus of these religions are on the individual's own efforts to escape the trap of the body or to see all temporal sensory knowledge as an illusion, namely Jainism and Buddhism. Then the theistic religions are divided in two. They both have belief in God or gods, one or many. Then, of those who emphasis a belief in "God," there are basically two conceptions of "God." Both of these hold to the ultimate, supremacy, and eternity of God, the Source of all, but one sees God as a personal Being, where the other lesser so, or explicitly as impersonal.

O disciples and peoples of faith, as we probe deeper and search for a fuller understanding of the truth, we should know what our presumptions are, and always keep them in mind. For example, the monotheistic viewpoint has the presumption that God made everything in the universe. This presumption leads those of this view to consistently ask the "Who" question. If God did not make the universe, who did? It doesn't make sense that the universe came about by chance. And what about noble truths such as mercy, compassion, love, righteousness, and justice? Can a thing have created these? The non-theistic religions that nobly speak of some of these truths are without the Who, namely God. How could these things have come from the Divine Source if the Divine Source does not exist? These concepts themselves make no sense unless there is a mind. Without a mind of God, man really becomes the deity and center of the universe. But Buddhists and Jains will have a different perspective and assessment on this.

All these characteristics that have inspired goodness, righteousness, and noble character upon the Earth through the ages in human civilization, yes, also wisdom, honor, mercy, compassion, loyalty. Are these all not personal characteristics? How can a mere thing possess and lead human beings to a good spiritual path? For the monotheist, it does not make sense to take away the person-ness of God.

There is a very well established theistic belief system but de-emphasizes the personhood of God, explicitly teaches the impersonality of God. This is classic Hinduism's teaching on Brahman, is more or less equivalent of "God."

But the de-personalizing of God is not limited to Hinduism. Even the strict monotheistic religion of Islam, avoids emphasizing the person-ness of God. Part of this is a distinct Islamic theological tradition that did not go through the debates on the personhood (Lat. *persona*) of God as Christianity did at the first Christian Ecumenical Councils. But there also appears to be a fear of falling into idolatry through the personification of God, a fear of leading to image making, and thus worshiping the things in nature in place of God. Could one be a danger, though, of deifying God? The concern may be to make God out to something He is not. But if God is not a person-Being, then what is He? How can God not be a person-Being if God has a mind, a will, and a heart that can love and also feel disappointment over His creatures when they commit great sin? The fear appears to a concern of bringing God more down to our level, to fashion Him more into OUR image? A valid concern is to maintain the transcendence of God. Judaism, Christianity, and Islam have all thoroughly maintained the transcendence, "other-worldliness" of God, beyond our human-ness, the Eternal Creator Being who is Sovereign of the universe. Christianity among them has done well in maintaining both the transcendence and the personhood of God.

Dear astute disciples and peoples of faith, take these thoughts to help lead you to what you believe to be true. Each person is to seek for the truth and distinguish for him or herself including the spiritual value of merit.

Religion and Merit

I need not teach you, O faithful ones, how religious peoples are. Human beings have been very religious from most ancient times, through millennia, all the way to the 21st century. Having already above elucidated at length on faith and religion, you probably already have a good idea what I will be teaching on this topic of religion and merit.

Spiritual merit to an individual soul, which is usually perceived or felt merit, since spiritual things are not like tangible awards, comes through both faith and religion. It is human reasoning that leads to ask valid questions such as this one: if there is merit, who is the one who gives the merit?

As I studied various religions, I was particularly fascinated over the merit concept in the non-theistic religion of Buddhism for which there are millions of followers. If this religion is not "God-focused," where does the merit come from if it not from God, as monotheistic faiths hold? From where does their sense of merit come from, in their own perspective? Hundreds of thousands if not millions believe they get merit from visiting certain holy sites and temples and performing certain rituals and prayers and giving offerings. If they don't belief God in Heaven is giving them the merit, who then is? "Who" may be the wrong question to ask for a non-theistic religion, but "what" may be a better question. Do they themselves have a distinct understanding in their minds as to the source of spiritual merit? If it is unclear to themselves, it is less clearer for a monotheist wanting to understand how they understand this. This very thing fascinated me. And I explain it this way: that this desire and need they feel to earn merit arises from their souls. It itself reflects a facet of that universal truth of God making humans to yearn for the Divine, although some souls are raised in religious traditions without the belief in God. This reveals the universal truth of humankind's deep desire to find favor with the Power of the universe, understood differently according to the religious tradition they learned (whether that Power is God, deities, or buddhas). Many raised in a Buddhist tradition are not instilled in the theistic way, but the yearning to be in good favor (through merit) and at peace with the Source of the Universe still strongly seeps out in their religious practices, because of the religious nature in which God has created humanity.

There will always be uncertainty for the human soul from merit through religion, that is, through our rituals for following instructions from a minister. We can never be sure we have done enough to please God and be squarely in His favor. Then there is the merit through faith, faith in God's promises, such as desiring to bless all the families of the Earth. This kind of merit is really blessing. The term "merit" is really from mankind's wisdom, not generally from Scriptural revelation, at least not the Biblical Scriptures. Merit is also a good human motivator toward spiritual benefits. It requires sheer faith because most often the nature of the received nature is simply perceived in the souls of the practitioners. The merit or blessing through faith is more sure than merit through religion. And I will show you yet a greater, the greatest merit. This is the merit of God's forgiveness and grace that He bestows on those who believe and repent. This is the only sure merit that opens up the eternal Kingdom of bliss for human souls.

From Ritual and Religion to Relationship

O persons of faith, whether you have received much education in school, or educated mostly by the school of experience, you have come to an awareness of the importance of ritual in human life. And now I will teach for greater understanding on this. Humans, including religious peoples do not need to be inspired by revelation from God to have rituals but God has put within the fabric of their soul the sense of the sacred (Eliade p. 11) Rituals have been a part of the fabric of human culture from the old stone age. As religions were birthed, they could hardly been practiced without ritual. Once religions developed, religion become the queen of rituals among the spheres of human life. Sacred texts did guide in spelling out specific rituals to perform, as yet in ancient times when magic still had a stronghold on human minds.[21]

All religions have rituals. Even for full-time mystics in their devotional life will go through rituals in their day and night engaging and disengaging in their meditations, prayers, study, and contemplation.

Rituals are good, serving many purposes for human beings, but there is yet a higher way I show you: a living relationship with God. To think that we could have a personal relationship with God almighty in one sense may sound presumptuous, even a bit arrogant. But for the peoples of faith who believe that God, Creator of the universe, personally knows each one of us, and desires to have a relationship with each one of us-this is an awesome thing. To develop and nurture a relationship with God does not mean you have to disregard any rituals of your religion, unless you are enlightened to any of them actually being a hindrance or unenlightening. We may conclude that the purest religion we could practice is one that draws us into a personal relationship with God. This may be in the assembly of fellow believers or in your private chambers. Many mystics are drawn into such a deep relationship with God, more so deeply than most normal or average peoples ever achieve. Some of them speak in terms of a "relationship" with God. Others use other thought patterns to describe it, or believe that their relationship or experience goes so deep beyond which words can describe.

O you who are spiritual, do not look down on the one who attends to their religion as like a duty or obligation that certainly seems void of a relationship with God. There are different types of souls. They just may be spiritually immature. And then there is the type that knows they do it just for the ritual, human classic religion devoid of the Spirit. Did you come to your relationship automatically? Were you not guided? All souls need to be guided, instructed, and encouraged to reach this goal, a part of our becoming spiritually mature. Love these ones who have not arrived yet. You could help guide them or inspire them by the example of your life in speech and deed. And who knows but the mystery of God, one of those days when they are in their ritual duty, the Spirit of God could come to them making their day of spiritual encounter.

Blessed are all the peoples of faith who come into a relationship with God.

From Head Knowledge to Heart Experience

Another truth that has reverberated in the hearts of many people of various faiths in our generation, is an awareness of the journey of faith to be from head knowledge to heart knowledge. And when we say, "heart knowledge," we do not speak of some feely-good dream-wish state, but a reality in the depth of ours souls, at the existential level, that leads us to believe and confess with certainty: "I know that I know. I can't explain it, but I know the truth from within the core of my being. It is not merely head knowledge. It flows out of a much deeper level which the Spirit of God assists us with. God desires for the divine knowledge and faith to not be merely in our head but also in our heart, so He sends the Spirit to assist us. Preachers can preach that our journey needs to go from our head to our heart, they can preach and preach it, but it is the Spirit that enables us to take this journey. And when we go on this journey, it leads us into a closer relationship with God which pleases Him.

O wise disciple, do not be unwise, like the student in haste studying for a test, and only trying to memorize the test answers and not actually learning the material in the book itself. Do not devalue the head knowledge. It is still important. And we need to pour ourselves into learning much head knowledge about the faith and the Scriptures and their historical, cultural, political, social, and religious contexts. By the aid of the Spirit, as we seek God's guidance, as we study the Scriptures, moments of insight come, like divine sparks, and moments in which the Holy Spirit puts the word into our hearts. Those are most blessed and sacred moments. If we got only one of those moments after spending 100 hours studying the Scriptures, it would be worth it.

It is normal for all of us in reading Scripture to feel like it is head knowledge. We can feel distant, so far removed from that time and place, such as when the prophets of old lived. And it may seem like stories, but the full reality of those texts do not sink in. We can only imagine what Jeremiah went through, such as being thrown in a pit. We can only imagine what Ezekiel saw when he writes, "I was…by the river Chebar, the heavens were opened and I saw visions of God" (Ezek. 1:1b). The Scriptural writers describe events that we were not present at, nor were we with the prophets when they had their experiences. But what we do know by faith is that the same Spirit that revealed to the prophets of old continues in this world and is with His believers. Do not, therefore, fret over the hurdle of from head knowledge of Scriptures into heart knowledge. As you seek God, His Spirit will open your mind and open your heart. But people of faith, the same Spirit that revealed to the prophets of old continues to work in the world, even today, and works through living Scriptures, even these. It is better to seek the living God than to seek an experience. Seek God and He will bring an experience of His living word to your soul according to His gracious will and divine providence. Faith and reason can be companions.

Faith and Reason

O dear disciples thirsty and hungry for truth and Faith in heart and mind, our teachings on faith would not be complete without relating faith to reason, human reason. Human reason is a faculty of our thought processes in our minds, but because we are body, mind, and spirit-soul, yet one person, so each of these are connected. Yet we may at times experience a tug in opposite directions in us at the same time: our heart leading us to believe one thing, but our mind leading us to think and believe something different. At other times, we may feel such a harmony between our mind and our heart. A crucial factor in this is what we feed the mind. If an adolescent becomes an atheist but was not raised an atheist, most likely it is because they feed themselves or were fed from some source material from an atheistic perspective.

Faith and reason are distinguished in regard to their primary seat. For reasoning, it is in the mind, and for faith, it is primarily in the heart and soul but faith includes the mind too. For people of faith, human reason and faith are generally not intrinsically diametrically opposed. Atheists and agnostics or secularists generally have a different view on this, lifting human reasoning up to supreme level, and seeing faith as archaic, childish, or superstitious. But for the people of faith, there is often harmony between faith and reason. For example, many people of faith in the Creator God consider it more reasonable to believe God created the universe than everything forming by chance over a period of billions of years. When one speaks of human reason, we can further sub-divide into two senses. In the one sense, it is unenlightened by God. In the other sense, it includes a mind enlightened by some truths of God, through, for example, Scriptures. Debates on faith and reason have been going on for years among religious peoples, scholars, and scientists, but perhaps often without distinguishing these two kinds of reasons and therefore lacking the clarity these subjects deserve. One will speak of reason as unaided by faith or revelation and another will speak of it as aided by faith and revelation. When the terms are clearly defined, light also comes to the people in discussion. The human ability to define the terms is itself a part of God's gift of reason.

O praise be to God for reason which He has given us, but greater still is faith, one of the greatest gifts of our infallible God, the key to a blessed eternity.

Infallibility

O peoples of faith, we come to the teaching of infallibility. This teaching is mostly in regard to the teaching of the infallibility of a high office, and at the end of this teaching, we will turn briefly to the teaching of the infallibility of holy Scriptures, held by a few traditions, since we have already addressed Scriptures.

There are at least two religious traditions which holds to infallibility of their highest religious seat and office. Because an "office" is a position of leadership, if this teaching did not address leadership, it would be an inadequate teaching.

So we begin broadly with leaders by asking these questions. Is leadership not important for all things religious, ecclesiastical, and political on Earth? It is indeed. In the words of my leadership "guru" and mentor, John Maxwell, "Everything rises and falls with leadership." The second question to ponder is this: has God not used leaders throughout history, including the many found in the biblical record but even in post-biblical times? I would say "yes indeed." The biblical record is full of men and women (yes women too like on the early Israelite judges Deborah, c.f. Judges chs. 4-5).

My first goal for you in the lesson of infallibility of the high office is first to develop a sense of appreciation for any leaders that God can use, to appreciate the great responsibility of souls under their spiritual care, and all the good that they can do. But the second goal balances the first: to develop a sense of the wisdom of caution from assigning such great power of infallibility to one man via the office, knowing the corrupt inclination of all human beings. As said before dear beloved believers, my main goal in these teachings is not to indoctrinate you, but to guide you in your search for the truth.

Now we come specifically to the doctrine of infallibility of high offices. Two religious traditions in particular, along with their institutions which hold to this doctrine, are historic, very well established and have millions of adherents. Therefore, we ought to have care in this discourse, ever mindful of real souls, over a billion in fact, and not to go down the wrong path of harboring negative thoughts of the peoples who hold to these religious traditions. We should approach this and all teachings with respect even if we do not hold to the doctrine of infallibility, for the sake of the love of our fellow human beings of different cultures and traditions.

First, I simply define infallibility and secondly, I will state what the doctrine of infallibility is for these traditions. Infallibility literally means without error. What these two main traditions which holds regarding the doctrine of infallibility teach is this: their chief religious leader is infallible. They do not teach that their whole religious organization is infallible, only chief spiritual leader. There is a difference between the two religious traditions on this point of infallibility. For one, their view is that their high leader appears to be infallible at all times, even when not speaking publicly. The other tradition holds that their high leader is infallible when he makes official statements.

In your search for truth, I strongly suggest study their own sacred Scriptures first, and see whether their Scriptures do indeed state their chief leader is infallible. I will give you a preview: their Scriptures do not (their doctrines of infallibility of their chief spiritual leader came latter in part, it appears, to preserve their institution). What you may find is that the chief leader's position is not even mentioned in the sacred Scriptures at all, but was a position, the tradition developed after their Scriptures were compiled. These religions do have additional traditions than what are in their Scriptures, including their claim of "Oral Tradition." Therefore I suggest to, secondly, consult these additional traditions (for example, the Hadith for Islam). In your search, you can frame your search with this question: "Is this teaching of the infallibility of this religious office from God, or is it of human origin? Once you have done your own study, prayerfully, guided by the Spirit, conclude what you believe to be the truth on this matter.

I will share with you a few more thoughts, but this I do cautiously. O how I wish that we all could be blissfully innocent and pure in faith. But through knowledge and the Spirit's guiding, our spiritual eyes become open, and we see more truth. Sometimes we may discover that something in our own tradition, we thought was from Heaven, the word of God to us humans, but then only to discover that it is a human-made tradition. O, do not let your core faith in God be shaken. Build your faith on the solid Rock of God. It alone is unshakable. Be careful not to put trust beyond human capabilities to any human being, no matter how charismatic a leader may be. With caution I state this, because my desire is to strengthen the faith of the peoples of the world, not to discredit any faith tradition. But what if the truth is that within some religion traditions are teachings that are not from God but from human beings? It is not angst that compels me to bring clarity to this topic, but perhaps the Holy Spirit to guide you, truth-seekers, to discover greater truth.

Discover the historical truth in this that both of the two religious traditions to which I state below, developed their doctrine of infallibility of their chief spiritual leader in Medieval times in which most people were commoners subject to the powers that be. The power of faith and religion was wrapped up in the power of the state. Most people accepted these powers and few questioned them. But that age is past. The democratization of knowledge has come to the world.

In this age, we feel we have the power to question authorities and academia teaches us critical thinking including to question presumptions and assumptions. God has gifted us humans which such a wonderful mind. But most blessed are the thoughts that lead to the praise of God and pure faith in the Divine. God is the greatest authority in the universe and has modeled this in the earthly, placing authorities on Earth. We should respect authorities, even if one such high religious authority, held to be infallible, you hold to be a human doctrine. Moreover, we should pray for all of our leaders both religious and political. And we should let them know that we pray for them and wish God's blessing.

And yet, O truth-seekers, this attitude of the heart and mind just expressed above should be balanced with the caution of our revering high religious leaders to fall into the error of a human cult, taking the true worship off God and placing it upon the high office or the man who occupies the office. We should admit the truth that we human beings have a weakness when it comes to strong charismatic leaders that rise on the Earth. There have been many gifted and charismatic leaders in the Catholic popes and Shi'a Islamic Iranian Ayatollahas throughout the last several centuries. The much good they have done, are they not written in Heaven's book? But at the same time, granting them infallible spiritual status conveys an unparalleled power that in theory is above dictators, emperors, and other earthly sovereign rulers. It could be noted that "Ayatollah" means "voice" or "word of God." Ponder the affect this has in the minds of the pious followers of this tradition, and the power that he could wield over the people and their nation. We should simply ask, can any human being be given such a power and NOT succumb to any corruption? Are we not all touched by it? For pious souls, they see that God gives a special dispensation of grace to them in office. For others, it is a step toward deifying them. They are mortal human beings like you and me. And if they are infallible, most would not believe they were infallible as a teenager or adolescent. So some very special and rare power had to have come to them and transform their nature by the time they came into their office. And by definition, It only takes one error to make someone fallible. Infallibility means absolutely without error.

In searching for the truth, consider not only the religious authority but also the political authority the leaders in these special offices have had, to wield influence among peoples in the world, especially the faithful of their traditions. Regarding the truism that power corrupts and absolute power corrupts absolutely, could it be as much that its' scrutiny actually brings to the surface corruption that was already in the human being rather than the new power making corrupt a person who before was not corrupt. But the new-found power gives opportunity for great good but can also pull corruption out of a soul like sweat from pores on a hot day. Consider also the claim of infallibility as not merely giving such great power and authority to one man in such a high office, but its function to give legitimacy and power to the whole religious system and institution of their respective traditions, and thus also the political power it combines with creating a super powerhouse. Moreover, it may be a truism that most political powers use religion for their advantage. But search and remember all the good that such leaders have done in these long-established traditions, and be respectfully mindful of the long history of these institutions producing many faithful people, many saints, and doing much good and charity. As peoples of faith, we need to always be mindfully aware that we are to see with our spiritual eyes as much or more so than our earthly eyes. Earthly eyes can only see the temporal, political, people physically. But spiritual eyes sees the work of God on Earth through His Holy Spirit, grace where the world wants gives edicts, forceful words, and punishment. God's kingdom is other-worldly. These high religious offices are sandwiched right in the middle of these two kingdoms, the spiritual and earthly. And there is continual tension and often conflicts between these two kingdoms.

We are in the post-Protestant Reformation age which opened the door to question ecclesiastical authorities. Martin Luther, the 16th cent. German theologian and leader of the Protestant Reformation, when he was asked to recant all his writing before the Diet of Worms, spoke with conviction, "I do not accept the authority of popes and councils, for they have contradicted each other—my conscious is captive to the Word of God...." (Bainton p. 144). Luther's point of the first half of this quote is that institutions can err just as human beings do. Luther did not accept the infallibility of the pope. Later, he did accept the authority of the papacy but on the basis only as an earthly, not a divinely established institution. So as to not mislead you, Luther was not an anti-authority radical. In his *Small Catechism,* he taught that we should have respect for those in authority. The second half of Luther's quote above deals with the interesting and "modern" appeal to his conscience instead of being an obedient monk before his religious authorities (in the Roman Catholic Church). This appeal was bold and a rare thing in his day. But this appealing to one's own conscious was not unique to Luther; it is echoed on other pages of history from the Middle Ages to the modern age. Voices, like Luther's, through time, have opened doors for people and society to question authority, religious traditions, and institutions. Each voice is a link in a chain of thoughts and values of appeals to individual conscience, freedom and the right of individual souls to search and determine truth. The call to individuals to "independently search for the truth," which implies individually and freely, is one of the tenants of the Baha'i Faith.

Lastly, I give a brief few thoughts on the belief in the infallibility of sacred Scriptures. It is a blessed and pious thing to believe that one's Scriptures are not only inspired by God but also infallible. This works for many souls. But many others see the truth of the human origin of the books and compilations of the Scriptures while even holding to the belief in God's inspiration at the same time, and moreover, find scribal errors in the copying of them. This should not at all destroy or diminish faith, except for the few who really believe their holy books fell from Heaven. If there is a holy book that breathed through and through with Divine truth, and true prophetic voice, but contains only one mistake, such as one biblical author citing another but incorrectly cited the source, that Scripture would technically be fallible, not infallible.[22] Sacred Scriptures, whether the Torah, the Bible, The Avesta, the Quran, or the Adi Granth leads its readers to believe that there is only one infallible: God.

Praise be to God for His faithfulness, trustworthiness, and infallibility. And may all peoples of faith respect their leaders, be obedient, and be lovingly possessed with the truth and come to love the religious body where they are a part.

Oneness of the Body of Faith

O heavenly desirous disciples, you are also being enlightened about ideals in religion, but that they are not merely intellectual nor even just a moral exercise, but they are also vehicles through which the Spirit communicates to people. Religion leads and inspires people to good and noble ideas, concepts, and spiritual truths. One such ideal is oneness in the body of faith, within each tradition. In your study of world religions, you have already learned the reality of a broken world, each of these religions evidencing a fragmenting before they were even fully developed, speaking from an historical perspective. While as yet not out of their adolescence, factions and splits developed, increasing the difficulty of expressing the oneness of their faith-tradition to the world: Jainism, Buddhism, Judaism, Christianity, Islam, etc. Every tradition has its conservatives and liberals, its literalists and metaphoricists, its fundamentalists and its mythicists, with most of them being moderates in between.

In light of previously considering the unity of reality, we can perceive or ascertain by faith that sages, prophets, and apostles in past ages may have tapped into that same source of the unity of reality, which is the Source, and Spirit of knowledge, wisdom, and revelation. And does not the Spirit of God reveal to us that He does desire His faith bodies on Earth to express oneness in heart and mind? O, may there be abundant diversity within and between the faith communities, in dress, in music, in ritual, and dance, but may we exude with one heart and mind! The Psalmist declared, "Behold how good and pleasant it is when the brethren dwell together in unity" (Ps. 133:1 NKJV). And in Christ's great high priestly prayer, He prayed, "I pray for them…those whom You have given Me, that they may be one as We are…I do not pray for those alone, but also those who will believe in Me through their word; that they all may be one, as You Father, are in Me an I in You, that they also may be one in Us…that they may be one as We are one…" (Jn. 17:9a, 11c, 21a, 22b NKJV).

Consider this truth, O beautiful disciples, that the ideal of and God's desire for oneness of His bodies of faith on earth, flows out of the reality of His ones. The biblical passages mentioned just above are theologically connected to the clear confession that Moses led the ancient Israelites to speak out, "Here, O Israel: The LORD our God, the Lord is one!" (Deut. 6:4 NKJV).

If indeed God desires for His peoples on earth to live in peace, which we have ascented to, then blessed are they that work toward peace. The apostle Paul, in his articulated Christian theology, speaks of the work of Christ this way: "For He Himself is our peace who made both [Jews and Gentiles] one, and has broken down the middle wall of division" (Eph. 2:14 NKJV). The prophet Muhammad saw the faith revealed to him as bringing together Arabs and Jews, such as in his mystical vision to Jerusalem, where he claimed he "met Abraham, Moses, and Jesus, had led a delegation of prophets in prayer" before God (Brown, p. 59).

Worship and Meditation

O disciples and fellow people of faith everywhere, you no doubt understand the importance of worship and meditation toward ultimate spiritual goals. Along with offerings and prayers, worship and meditation are among the most basic and important religious activities, making this another foundational teaching. Because we are approaching this from a global perspective, we are discussing many faith traditions which will be different perhaps than your own. It is possible to maintain the integrity of your own faith tradition while at the same time building respect for others of different traditions.

In ancient times, worship and meditation, that is, contemplation, were intricately connected, one flowing into the other; for example, an ancient human pondering the stars on a clear night sky and leading him to prostrate before the sacred sense of the Divine Source.

Moving forward thousands of years to our time, after several religious traditions have fully developed and ran their courses, we could see the world as spiritually divided somewhere basically in half: those who worship God and those who meditate with a non-monotheist worldview, leading them not to worship God but achieve some other goal, whether to achieve Nirvana, as is case for Buddhism, or to find the Divinity within you, as is the case for New Age meditation, heavily influenced by a form of Hinduism. The God-worship view essentially leads the human believing soul to look up to the heavens and outside themselves

(Lat. Corem Deo). The New Age view seems nearly the opposite: looking inside one's soul to find the Divinity. This is the beginning of these divergent paths which get more divergent as one studies to understand in more depth the concepts and beliefs of both these two main views. But we should ever be mindful of the commonality, such that we are all fellow humans who deserve mutual respect and love (Golden Rule) from each other. The awareness of this global spiritual division should not lead to any divisive attitude, but rather an opportunity to respect and love other human beings who are different than ourselves or hold to quite different traditions. There is a parallel global division which falls not quite on the same line but similar. One view is God as a Personal Being; the other view of God as an Impersonal Being. As a teacher of Religion, I do not assume that all people use the word "God" in the same way. In learning about another person's faith who is different than yours, ask them. Most people are glad to share their faith when they have a willing ear and sense the person carries a mutual non-judgmental attitude.

For the worshippers of the personal God, there is no other way. God is worthy of all worship; not only that, He expects worship. Because God is God alone. Beginning in ancient times, teachers and priests did arise whose teachings and writings articulated a faith in one person, Supreme God worthy of worship and which created religious systems which developed and has been carried forward to the 21st century numbering well over two billion adherents. A weekly worship gathering arose from traditions of this view, but God is worthy of worship everyday. He cannot be worshipped, thanked, and praised enough for all He has done.

On the other side is a very different set of traditions. The focus is seeking the ultimate goal of permanent extinction, Nirvana, or to find the Divinity within you. Meditation is the main practice which can take place everyday. Beginning in ancient times, teachers and priests did arise whose teachings and writings birthed quite distinct religious systems which developed and has been carried forward also to the 21st century, which offers the world an alternative to the worship of God. There is well over one billion adherents of this view.

The majority of adherents on both sides of this divide are adults, and adults already have their beliefs formed, and they will most likely not change much through life, at least not in most people. On this global field, we may invoke the Pauline principle here, "Let each one be fully persuaded in their minds (Rom. 14:5). The context of Paul's statement was in regard to holding certain days of the week as sacred, such as which day is the Sabbath day applied now to the much larger context.

The biblical God-worshipping Scriptures speaks of the knowledge of God going out to the whole Earth in a prophetic sense. This in part propelled missionaries of the biblical tradition to go all around the world. And a great impact as been made. Yet non-God-worshipping traditions are strong in some places on the Earth where the biblical tradition has never had a strong impact. While their may be cultural, social, and political factors to this reality besides spiritual factors, I have become convinced that there will always be a certain number of people all Earth, in every generation, who willfully do not chose God (in other words, they were consciously made aware of God, but they elect not to follow God). And faith cannot be forced. I have concluded then that we should keep loving and praying for them.

The first sense of "meditate" is to think, which includes contemplation. Every religious tradition, indeed, every religious person hopefully engages in this kind of meditation at least occasionally if not regularly. And so "worship" and "meditation" should not be pitted against each other as in "worship or mediation?" But enlightened ones come to learn that both Buddhist and New Age meditations are specific methods and techniques based on beliefs, some of which are not only quite distinct from but perhaps even dialectically opposed to the personal God worshipping traditions. In regard to the latter, many find truth is this that they can worship the God of the universe and meditate all they desire with their heart, mind, and soul, as the biblical Scriptures models.

People of faith everywhere should have the freedom to believe as they choose, and to practice their religious tradition in freedom. In this 21st century, we have become more aware than ever of the many faith traditions in existence on Earth on which we co-habitat, and accepting this fact (level one tolerance), should lead us to strive for mutual respect, cordially relations, understanding, and peace with our neighbors, co-workers, community members. May this be a workable guide for us in the 21st century, maintaining one's on faith-tradition footing while also having mutual respect for all others and recognize diversity of faiths globally.

Diversity in Communal Worship

Abundant is the diversity in communal worship, O peoples of faith, that we can observe if we were to visit various places of worship. The movements and gestures of people and clergy or priests are many: hands reaching out, hands folded, heads bowed, heads looking up, standing, kneeling, and sitting. In many places, all the people are basically expected to follow the same movements together. Some are more exact in the unison movements than others. And on the other end of the spectrum of diversity, we have worshipers who are gathered together more informally, and each worships in their own way and is allowed in the Spirit to be guided so. Some are full of ceremony and rites, others are plain, not written, but guided by the Spirit. Great indeed is the diversity in communal worship on Earth.

"A religion that likes all its practicing believers to go through the same exact rituals in unison, all going through the motions in unison, though they may claim divine sanction to the ritual, we discerning disciples know the truth that it really reflects a ritual of human origin, for God is interested in His peoples worshiping Him in truth, in the Spirit, in the heart and soul which only God can see. Those unison rituals of human origin no doubt led modern socialist philosophers to see the controlling aspect religion has on the masses, leading Karl Marx to pen the now famous line from his *Communist Manifesto*, "religion is the opium of the people". The truth found in biblical Scriptures and known within the souls of many is that God looks on the inside of our hearts and our intentions. The externals are circumstantial. Humans look at what can be seen externally through the eyes, but God knows the hearts and minds of all souls (see the teachings on Pure and True Religion above). Believers, even in the context of communal worship, should have the freedom to worship God in the quiet of their hearts and souls, and not be controlled by the religion with rules that they all have to bow down, kneel, sit, or stand together at the exact same time. Earthly religion in reality does reflect a controlling aspect at times. (see the teaching on Pure and True Religion above).

On the positive aspect, all the worshippers gathered, doing the exact same movements at the same time, in human eyes, expresses a unity of faith, if indeed they all believe the same. But the nature of ritual is that ritual does not require belief at all, just motion or speaking some words from the lips. The true unity is the unity of belief, heart, soul, and purpose (See teaching on Oneness of the Body of Faith).

We human beings are comfortable with the custom is which we were raised, generally, or the one we become accustomed to. The dynamic of Divine worship is that it is supposed to all focus on God. But in reality, human beings, yes, common peoples of faith, get focused on the particular rituals. We are sensual creatures. Sometimes we may enjoy looking around to see other people worshipping, experiencing God in their own way. This too is good. The Spirit can show us things, teach us new things. There comes times when we should close our eyes to focus just on God. Blessed is the diversity and the freedom the peoples of faith have in communal worship. Blessed are all who submit to God, where the submitting is in the heart, through true faith, not determined by outward rituals. And blessed are all who are enlightened to the truth the God is interested in more than just a submitted people, as if God is a taskmaster, but those who freely follow and love Him, once enlightened by His mercy, grace, and love.

Love

O beloved peoples of faith, both sacred Scriptures and mystics have revealed to us the truth that love is the greatest spiritual path, the path to the love of God. There are few sacred Scriptures of the past that have said it so clear and succinct as the apostle John: "…for God is love" (1 Jn. 4:8b). The Scriptures speak of the pure love for God. The Greek word the New Testament uses, including this key verse of 1 John 4:8, is agape (Nestle-Aland, p. 622). Agape love is the purist, selfless, and unconditional love. It is not conditioned on meeting certain expectations. We can see why that when fervent disciples of God taste the pure love of God, nothing on earth compares. The intense devotion to God becomes more joyful than any earthly pleasure. It is usually only mystics who ecstatically experience the intense devotion of the love of God, but would to God that we all experience this at least one time in our lives, all believers, for it is the very foretaste of Heaven, better than any earthly pleasure. We can love God in our daily lives, work and play, school and choirs, day and night. God's mercy and love is enduring. It will be there for us when we awake in the morning. Most of us don't feel the need to pray long hours of the night. But blessed are all men and women who receive the love of God and who love God.

Male and Female, Yin and Yang

O disciples, men and women of faith, we come to the truth of male and female. Nature does testify, and it is plain to all, that embedded in virtually all creatures is male and female. By God's design it is so, for reproduction at the biological level.

But as you know, God has created us human beings not only as the crown of creation, but as spiritual creatures. And He has knit in our souls the need for companionship, in a similar way that God desired to have companionship in this universe, thus creating angels and humans.

From the beginning even to now, God has intended the two genders to be complementary, in essentially the same way and truth as expressed in yin and yang by ancient Chinese philosophers. In this understanding of nature, there cannot be yin without yang, and there cannot be yang without yin. Now yang is the male, warm, light, dry forces of the universe and yin is the female, cool, dark, damp forces of the universe (Hopfe and Woodward p. 182). The Bible/Hebrew Scriptures/Torah's Creation account says "... male and female He created them" (Gen. 1:27b) and then blessed them (vs. 28). When man and woman were brought together, they were meant for companionship and harmonizing and having children.

God never intended there to be strife, competition, or battle between the sexes. These have resulted from sin. The strife, conflict, and competition between the human sexes is complex, some stemming from our base natures to survive, and all stemming from our spiritual corruption within our beings. At a spiritual level, the voices of discontentment over one or the other gender in society is a symptom of all of these: sin, corruption, and rejection of God's word.

O how wonderful are the gifts that God has given to both males and females! To the woman He gave nurturing and caring skills more so than man. And He gave woman the gift of being the child bearer to bring new human life into the world. This is so sacred. Life is sacred from beginning to end, but we human beings feel that sacredness most at times of new life and times of death of a loved one. To man God gave the greater strength in taking dominion of the Earth, in building homes, chopping down trees, making tools, in hunting. And to man God gave the seed, the sperm and the organ in which to implant in the woman to bring new human life in due season. To both woman and man God gave intelligence to think, to solve earthly problems, to socialize, and to contemplate the wonders of life and the mysteries of the universe. God be praised for all these gifts to male and female including their unique gifts.

But what should we say, O believing women and men, in regard to the Scriptures which were written from a male perspective, out of a patriarchal culture? Is it not best for us to see this as through their cultural lens, which was paternalistic. Is it not best to see that God's Spirit was communicating divine truths, but these men had a cultural lens which all too often viewed themselves as superior to women. To benefit ourselves spiritually, we must look beyond the cultural lens, through the sacred texts, to get to the truths God's Spirit is communicating, just as we do with all metaphors. Many of us have come to the truth that God is technically neither male nor female, but not all of faith have come to this yet since the sacred word of God as our "Father" is so ingrained in their souls.

There are many traditions of interpretations including Midrashes and legends, whether of Jewish origin or not, that may be of interesting reading, but of little help to our faith.

We should exercise caution in regarding these old or modern scholarly interpretations which treat the sacred text like going to the theater to watch a secular movie, or interpretations by some scholars who want us to find conflict and strive, battle between the sexes on many of its pages.

Nobel Peace Laureate Elie Wiesel, in his book: *Messengers of God: Biblical Portraits and Legends*, speaks at length on Adam and Eve. He comments on the Midrash's comments on these biblical portraits more so than the biblical texts themselves. In the story of Adam and Eve eating the forbidden fruit, he relates that Eve gave Adam the fruit: "He probably did not know where the fruit had come from" (Wiesel p. 24). He goes on, "How could he trust anyone again? His own wife deceived him, perhaps even doomed him…" (ibid p. 25). But Midrashes, legends, tales, and myths often seem to muddle or obscure the truth and are therefore of little help when it comes to faith, though they are interesting reading. Its our fallible focus on human foibles that is the problem whether the interpreter is an average layperson or a biblical scholar, instead of interpreting Scripture spiritually, wrought by the Spirit of God in minds and hearts who have welcomed Him in. You, blessed man or woman of faith, determine truth for yourself as you search truth Scriptures.

By the Spirit, we see the positives of all the gifts that God has given to us believers.

Many peoples in the 21st century have outlived the Genesis story of the fall into sin. They find it too simple, and smacks of a pro-male position firmly rooted in Hebrew-Semitic culture. The Scriptures of this book, as was said in the Introduction, is not meant to replace any of the Scriptures of past origin. But it does retell the Creation story and "cleans up" those cultural criticisms to bring a fresh story for today's world where the value of equality has been established in the many parts of the world.

Beloved people of faith, this truth of God-created male and female, intended as complements and harmoniousness, is a key to blessing and happiness that can help transform the planet to a more content and happy place. When children grow up never hearing their father or mother say negative things about men or women, this will make a difference in their life, even if the predominate popular culture through television portrays the negativity and competitive aspects. Godly parents being good role models will make a world of difference for their children.

Finally, there is nothing wrong with having love in your heart for companions of both the opposite and same gender. But God has intended sexual relations with the opposite sex, as nature itself unveils. The former apostolic age was more harsh, even condemnatory, on those who practiced homosexuality. Many people of faith hold to the belief in the unwavering will, laws, and principles of God, that they do not bend with society. Society is more sensitive on these issues more than ever, and it may be wise for peoples of faith to also develop more sensitivity, being caring in our approach, letting the Scriptures speak, motivated by pure (agape) love as people for whom God also loves. We should be reminded that Jesus Christ even acknowledged "eunuchs who were born thus from [their] mother's wombs" (Matt. 19:12). This reveals a truth that most likely since ancient times there have been a certain number of boys/men who had feminine tendencies and traits (presumably more female hormones) and likewise girls/women who had masculine tendencies and traits (presumably more male hormones). Societies the past ages seemed to handle this better, had places, roles such as eunuchs. God has created male and female as the two genders. But we also learn from God's natural creation that there is so much variety. There is variety within the two genders, from macho men to feminine-inclining men, and vice versa. God, by the Golden Rule, calls us to love everyone. It does not mean to compromise your own standards as you know them from the sacred Scriptures of your tradition, but to have a greater understanding of the truths, and see from a bigger picture in God's diverse world. Praise God for male and female! The light of equality is shining in this age.

Spiritual Equality and Social Equality

O peoples of God, disciples of holy faiths, and seekers of truth, we come to the truth, if you can accept it, of spiritual equality and the modern human agenda of social equality. The foundations of understanding this teaching have been laid above, namely, the oneness and reality of God, the heavenly Kingdom, and Earthly kingdoms, Priesthoods, and the Abrahamic faiths. Because religion is people centered, and people are earthlings, we cannot stay in the heavenly spiritual realm in our thoughts for very long. We have to come back to the earthly realm. But this teaching begins in the heavenly spiritual realm and only the spiritually minded can grasp it.

Spiritual equality asserts that both man and woman are spiritually equal before God in regard to gender. It has taken humanity over a few thousand years for the light of this truth to come to many people. But this achievement has come with a great cost of many lives, especially in the modern era (Faizi p. 7).

The reality of spiritual equality is a heavenly reality, from God's perspective. It bespeaks a truth that God declares both human genders equal before Him. When does this happen for each soul and how did the light of this truth come historically through the ages? We could spend a couple hours on this wondrous truth, but below, we will cover the highlight points.

First, the heavenly spiritual equality needs to be clearly distinguished from the earthly human realm where human structures more often than not have social inequality in whatever society, culture, and nation. The amount of distinction between the heavenly reality of gender equality and the human social realm parallels the amount of difference that Heaven is from Earth, between the heavenly spiritual realm and the earthly realm. Second, we should distinguish the earthly spiritual realm from both the heavenly spiritual and the earthly visible realm. Because human beings are also spiritual by nature, we can talk about a spiritual realm on Earth, but this realm is imperfect and corrupted, compared to the perfect which is in Heaven.

Now having simply distinguished the heavenly spiritual from the earthly social, we have just taken a step that apparently most of the points of light in the past did not do or clearly make to their disciples, which in turn resulted in some conflict in the social realm. My thesis is that the failure to distinguish these two realms was one of the factors for conflict on Earth in regard to social changes. The light of spiritual equality whether heavenly or earthly, by points of lights, spiritual teachers and founders, had social ramifications in the earthly realm. The fact that it has been in this realm where conflict comes among peoples, including peoples of faith, in civilized societies. The predominate societies were paternalistic, male-dominated, with a status quo which we could say was the principal cause for the conflict. Also by nature, people do not like to change when it comes to customs. They had gotten accustomed to life with inequality between men and women for thousands of years. Then the points of light intruded into this scene teaching the nobility of equality of gender. Humans by nature interpreted the messages more carnally, earthly, than it perhaps intended, specifically, in a social way in society. But for the founders who were non-theistic, such as the Buddha (we will discuss more below) did not have the heavenly in their worldview. So their teaching aptly applied to the earthly spiritual and social realms. They apparently well intended their message of equality to apply to the earthly social realm as well as in the achieving of their religion's ultimate goal. Their messages were then perhaps deliberately not clear on this distinction of the heavenly spiritual and the earthly realm, because they did have the heavenly framework or thought pattern. Or more accurately, their message of equality did apply to the human social realm but only to those who became a Jain, a Buddhist, a Babi, or Baha'i. But as these religions developed and got more powerful by the sheer numbers in their movement, others in society outside their groups felt the status quo threatened and some stirred up trouble. A great trouble there was, even a great tribulation, such as the Persian Muslim power's persecution of Babis in the 19th century, killing thousands of them (Faizi p. 7).

Even though neither founder of Jainism or Buddhism (Mahavira and Gautama respectively) established theistic religious systems. But they certainly deserve to be among in the hall of great points of light that paved the way to both spiritual and social equality. Those who hold to the monotheistic view distinguish the spiritual equality from the social equality in the human realm to the degree of the difference between God and humans. Some have summarized one of the main messages of the Bible as "God is God and we (humans) are not. If God in Heaven says that both genders are spiritually equal, including the Judgment of souls, this would be a spiritual reality that nothing on Earth could change, even if 100% of all souls and societies were unaware of this truth.

One of the clearest expressions of the truth of the spiritual equality of the genders before God for all time, I submit, was the apostle Paul's word to the Galatians: "...for there is neither male nor female; for you all are one in Christ Jesus (Gal. 3:28b NKJV). From the context of the rest of Paul's writings, he certainly was not trying to lessen or obliterate the differences of the genders physically nor was he writing about social equality in the human realm. He was speaking of the heavenly spiritual realm: before God. But most of the other religions appear more focused on the social realm.

It is not until the 19th and 20th centuries that social equality rises, after thousands of years of human history of predominate patriarchal societies. The Baha'i Faith comes into the scene in the 19th century like a harbinger of the modern movement. Though many in the West are still unfamiliar with this religion, it appears to have actually been a driving force behind the equality and equal rights movements even in America. It is hailed as the most modern of all the world religions not merely for its being born in the modern age, but for its strong teachings of equality of humanity, of races and genders. There is no question of this religion's teaching on social equality. But the spiritual principle behind it also implies the equality of the genders before God in Heaven.

This, dear men and women of faith, introduces the teaching of spiritual equality and its social ramifications. Now we take this brief pause before going into a little more depth into this great topic.

In brief review, let us highlight the perceived truth of spiritual equality. What matters not nearly as much is what humans say on this matter. What matters much more is what God says on this issue. There is of course disagreements among the peoples of faith globally, all depending on what their source Scriptures they are using. If it turns out in truth that God's perspective is that both genders are equal before Him, then His word is final. How could any of us dispute God?

Now we expound on the heavenly spiritual equality with these following three aspects: 1) when God looks down on Earth from His Heaven, He sees both genders as equal, 2) When God judges each soul in the Judgment, gender is not a factor as if God has a bias for one sex or another, and 3) a spiritual equality among people in the human but invisible realm, separate from social equality.

If we probe a little more, we should relate this too and consider the nature of God in regard to gender. In my teachings to you and in this Scripture, I have elucidated on the genderless of God, or also the both-genders God, but that for convention, I often refer to God in the third person masculine singular pronoun "Him," not because God's sex is male, but "It" in English is so impersonal. "Brahman" in Hinduism, which is in the neuter case, is closer to the truth of God's actual nature of neither male nor female. And yet it is appropriate to often think of God in the masculine form because the progenitor role "He" had in the universe is a masculine role. But there are also feminine aspects to God's Creation which may in turn reflect aspects to His nature. The ancient Chinese teaching was the two predominate forces of nature, yin and yang, in which one is female and the other male, and there is a little yin in yang, and a little yang in yin is applied to the forces of nature (Hopfe and Woodward pp. 182-183). The Hebrew prophets were embedded in a rather strong paternalistic culture. Therefore, God is always referred to in the masculine sense.

Moving on from the nature of God itself back to our topic, let us briefly trace the history of the development of the light of equality. It appears that Gautama Buddha of the 6th or 5th century BCE may have been the first light to teach a sense of equality of the genders (Hopfe and Woodward p. 135). He departed from his polytheistic Hindu upbringing, and taught a new non-theistic way in which each needs to seek their own enlightenment, not by the aid of gods, but through their own seeking, meditating, Eightfold Path, and that both genders could find the same enlightenment (Hopfe and Woodward p. 137).

It would be 400-500 years later before we would get such a clear light in the 1st cent. CE as expressed by the apostle Paul to the Galatians: "...for there is neither male nor female; for you all are one in Christ Jesus (Gal. 3:28b NKJV). This spiritual equality stands in distinction to the general physical inequality of men and women which Peter references, also in the New Testament Scriptures (c.f. I Pet. 3:7). Where did the apostle Paul get this light? Was there another influence? If trying to understand this culturally, it is baffling, since Paul was thoroughly of the Hebrew paternalistic culture, a Hebrew of Hebrews, a Pharisee of Pharisees (c.f. Phil 3:5; Acts 23:6). But points of light received special insight, even revelation, which is certainly the best way to understand the origin of this key verse. The significance of this wondrous statement by the thirteenth apostle of Jesus Christ revealing the spiritual equality of genders is a word that has much potential of peace in the hearts of men and women through these last ages.

We now move forward from the 1st cent. to the 7th cent. CE, to the time of the prophet Muhammad. Coming to the great faith of Islam, we find that Muhammad significantly raised the status of women in Arabian culture, relatively. Women in pre-Islamic Arabia were very poorly treated. There was even the practice of burying unwanted female infants alive in the sand. The Quran expressly forbad this cruel practice (Brown p. 26). Moreover, Muhammad limited the number of women one man can marry to four (Hopfe and Woodard p. 359). But Muhammad, the Quran, and Islam stopped well short of the light of equality of men and women, both or either spiritually and especially in society. Islamic culture has always been a strongly male-dominate culture.

But through the Middle Ages into the modern era, the strongest light of equality rising slowing like a bright star seems to have been the word from Christ's apostle Paul which was embedded in the Christian faith which spread all through the West. In contrast, the very strong paternalistic Arab-based Islamic culture remained in its Quranic culture which was being left behind in regard to the advancement of equality of the genders. Islam has never espoused equality of the genders.

Oddly, it is out of Shi'a Islam in 19th century Persia that the Babi movement and the Baha'i Faith arises. Ali Muhammad of Persia, the forerunner to Baha'ullah of the Baha'i Faith, called himself the "Gate of Faith," the Bab." The Bab advocated sweeping religious and social reforms, such as raising the status of women" (Hopfe and Woodward p. WC14-2). The Baha'i Faith which arises out of the Babi movement proclaimed one of their fundamental teachings, that all of the past religions are manifestations from the same Source, God. Baha'ullah affirmed and advanced the social reform the Bab began, bringing it to a new level of teaching the equality of men and women and that there is one human family and one human race. Therefore, he taught the unity of mankind in *one* social order (The Gleanings, p. xi).

Now in the early twenty-first century, society has made much advancement toward equality of the genders in this temporal realm. The Baha'i Faith has been one of the main drives of this social movement. In hindsight, we see that the dramatic social changes caused social upheaval in the heyday of change. Could these great social changes have come peacefully and gradually? Because of the nature of human beings, I do not think that the conflict could have been avoided. There may have been less conflict and upheavals in this moving toward social equality if the points of light had taught the distinction of the heavenly from the human social, and emphasized the heavenly spiritual equality for some time, allowing human beings more slowly to ascent to the truth. But the points of light seem to come on the scene abruptly. But when would there have been a good time? The powers may have felt less threatened and the status quo society not challenged if the points of light emphasized the spiritual reality. If they allowed this truth to sink into the souls of many people, beginning with their followers, for a few hundred years or more, to give more time for humanity to then become receptive of the application of the spiritual truth to the social human realm instead of driving humanity forward too fast. There still would have been much resistance and some conflict, but not as much. Many lives could have been spared. But the loss of many lives of religious faithful, martyrs, their blood was viewed as fueling their cause (Faizi p. 10).

Dear noble peoples of faith, we have just covered about 2,500 years of religious history, briefly, in regard to this important topic of spiritual and social equality. Let us summarize. For many in our age, the idea of the spiritual equality of the genders is viewed as a truth. This truth stands or falls on God's view on this matter, which people ascent to mostly through the Scriptures of their own faith tradition and partly from the internal spiritual sense. But there are some major sacred Scriptures, such as the Quran, where this principle is absent. Islam unquestionably historically has been a male dominating culture, and shows no signs of changing. The temporal social realm of equality is distinct from the spiritual realm of equality before God. The social is determined by the cultures in question. The West has led the way the way of equality of the genders in the social realm. Fundamentalist Islam has been opposed to this, seeing this western trend as ungodly. But the truth of the spiritual equality, which affects the temporal realm, has enlightened millions of souls in our age. Several points of light have come through the ages: Buddha, Jesus, the apostle Paul, Muhammad, the Bab, and Baha'ullah. Most of these, however, did not clearly distinguish between spiritual and social equality, which was a contributing factor, I submit, to the conflict in the ensuing social changes. Social equality is a noble human pursuit. The spiritual piety of most people in their own traditions may interpret their own sacred Scriptures on this point spiritually. But most of these traditions have also to some extent applied them socially, at least within their religious communities. The Baha'i Faith certainly stands out as a clear leader through the ages in applying this truth to the social realm. There is no uncertainty about it: the Baha'is teach the *social* equality of all humanity.

This brings us to focus specifically on the topic of social equality. And we should ask this probing question: Of all the sacred Scriptures throughout the ages, have there been any before the Baha'i Scriptures of the 19th century that specifically taught the social equality of humankind as a revealed spiritual, and perhaps Divine truth? As stated above, the points of light themselves appear not to have clearly distinguished. As for as I know, I am not aware that any of the sacred texts before clearly did teach that social equality for humanity was a religious truth, until we get to the writings of Baha'ullah in the 19th century. And of course, if we are Baha'i, we accept this as a spiritual and religious truth that all human beings should be socially equal. The implication of this is the obliteration of the social classes, unless the Baha'is mean it only in spiritual terms. But the social realm is not primarily a spiritual realm. It is a social reality in real human societies. It would be different if Baha'is said that in the Baha'i community everyone is equal socially. But Baha'is clearly apply their belief to the whole world, the global vision spoken by the Bab and confirmed in Baha'ullah's writing. For example, in an excerpt of Baha'ullah's writing, it reads, "The world's equilibrium hath been upset through the vibrating influence of this most great, this new World Order. Mankind's ordered life has been revolutionized through the agency of this unique, this wondrous system—the like of which mortal eyes have never witnessed (Faizi p. 121). This passage not only speaks to the Baha'i belief is human social equality for all but also reveals a world order, apparently a code-word for a one-world government, which Baha'is are working on.

In contrast, in other religious traditions, most notably Hinduism, the classes are not just a social fact of society, they have divine sanction by their ancient sacred texts, namely, the Vedas and the Law of Manu (Rig Veda p. 31; Hopfe and Woodward pp. 90-93). In this belief system, the social, economic, and occupational classes in Hindu society were divinely sanctioned. Therefore, the Baha'i revelation in the 19th century directly counters this. In Baha'ullah's mind and his son Abdul-Baha, these Hindu notions may have been among his list of "superstitions" (Hopfe and Woodward p.14-4)

I present some cautions in regard to the push for social equality, not to be confused with social justice, as though it has Divine support. As stated above, striving for a social equality is a noble pursuit. The Baha'i Faith, it could be said, more than any other faith on Earth, has pursued the spiritually noble principles of a one world, one humanity, and equality for all. We may even all agree that striving for social equality in all human societies is a noble pursuit. But is it God's design? For example, that men and women should get equal pay for performing the same job-this indeed is noble. But it is entirely unrealistic and against nature to try to fit all human beings in the same social class. The fact has always been from the beginning of humanity to the 21st century that not all humans are equal. Some are more capable than others. Some are leaders; most are followers. Some are well suited to be clergy, doctors, lawyers, politicians, bureaucrats, administrators, teachers, and others are well suited to be merchants, tradesmen, craftsmen, artists, park technicians, street cleaners, and janitors. The first aspect is that this teaching works to obliterate the fundamental teaching of diversity in God's creation. Indeed, there is one God who created one Earth, but He created such a magnificent diversity on Earth reflecting His incomprehensive knowledge, design, and wonders. In all the history of humankind, all the lights upon the Earth, I am not aware of any of them, prophets or sages, that taught the obliterating the differences until we come to the Bab and Baha'ullah in the 19th century. The truth of God's diversity applies to the human species. God created all kinds of races, and put human beings in tribes around the Earth which in turn developed their own languages and cultures. God be praised for the beautiful diversity of humankind!

Truth-seekers are courageous in probing tough questions, even if it prospectively means that a particular thesis, principle, or notion held by a particular religious tradition be deemed not from God's revelation, but of human origin.

When Baha'is teach, "one human race," which is one of their fundamental beliefs, it is meant both spiritually and temporally. Indeed, the spiritual meaning of it is a noble teaching, and even with its practical social application to human societies on Earth. But some have a concern with the literal meaning an application, which logically leads to the conclusion to obliterate the actual racial differences when taken to the full extent to the point. And even if most Baha'is do not understand it to this extent, the literal meaning of it still runs counter to the diversity of all Creation as designed and intended by God for living creatures on Earth including humankind.

What informs Baha'is beliefs most is not the Bible which teaches diversity in the creation, but beginning with the foundation of the Quran, the rising above the Quranic foundation came the very progressive "one human race" teaching begun with the Bab, elevated by Baha'ullah, and sealed by Shoghi Effendi before the world. The social application to this belief in equality of genders, races, classes in human society is a very noble goal. It was too big of a pill for Muslims to swallow, though. This most recent and most modern noble Baha'i faith gave the offering of social equality to the modern world, and our generation will pass this baton and be carried far into the future so long as lights remain. Baha'ullah did write (trans. by Shoghi Effendi) of the "intangible bonds of unity" (Gleanings p. xii).

To teach that the genders should be equal is one thing, but to each that all social classes should be equal too (or class obliteration) is another thing. As much as we may like to have paradise on Earth, we cannot expect society to confirm to our pious heavenly ideals. There have always been those who have more than others in societies, going back to the hunter-gatherer days of early humans. Some are more industrious and more gifted at becoming prosperous than others. One of the major positives of having different classes from the rich to the poor is it creates opportunity for generosity of the prosperous to be charitable or serve those in greater need. If everyone was of the same exact economic status, no one could help another person charitably or financially, for that would create an imbalance which would become taboo in this non-reality society. It can only exist in ideas, dreams, and wishful writing on paper. But societies are imperfect, and so there is the negative of many wealthy persons tending to look down at the lower classes, harbor attitudes of entitlement, and worse, rigging financial systems so that the wealthy get more wealthy, taking even more money from those who have little to begin with.

My conclusion is that no system on Earth will ever be perfect until God creates the new heavens and the new Earth, and life will dramatically change after that. Striving for a social equality, rightly defined, is a noble pursuit. From another angle, the Baha'i system may be grouped with the select few groups in the modern age, along with many Adventists, who are trying to make a paradise on Earth. I don't think it is a coincidence, if fact, that Adventism started in America at about the same time as the Babi and Baha'i movement began in Iran. While there was minimal communication between America and Persia in the mid-1800's, there may have been some influence going on, at least the exchanging of ideas through the news media.

O all blessed peoples of faith. I commend this teaching to you as truth-seekers. May this teaching have served you light of knowledge with clarity understanding, to help in gathering truth, although from one of many imperfect vessels. My understanding is not perfect. This teaching is not the final word on this topic. We all are in progress spiritually as individuals and society as a whole. By faith, we know that God has set us all on a blessed journey to eternity.

Life in the Body: Spiritual and Physical Natures

O beautiful disciples and peoples of faith according to the spirit, I need not teach you the truth of reality of ourselves, our existence, our consciousness, and the fact of life in a body while on our earthly journey. There may be a few people in recent decades of this modern era who have gone so far as to even question our existence. For most of us, this is unreasonable and even approaches insanity. We know certainly that according to our physical nature, our earthen vessel, our mortal tabernacle, we are creatures of bone, *besar* (Heb. flesh), blood and breath, beating heart, flowing blood, the wind of life, and various necessary organs for the body. What surgeon has ever cut into a human and found a body with no blood? Our bodies require water to drink and food to eat without which we will physically die. And who in sound mind could deny we have consciousness, awareness of ourselves and the things around us? Even animals, even insects, have an awareness. This makes sense in the natural sense for survival, and also in the sense from the position of belief that all was created by God.

And I need not teach you the elementary things, such as the truth that our bodies are our temporary shells, our containers through the earthly journey, until we step into eternity. This you already know.

Let us explore a little more deeper in the reality that we have both a spirit and soul. God created us with soul and spirit in a body, a harmony of three as for as making one being. But it does not mean that there are never conflicts between our spirit and our flesh. Our flesh is selfish, always wanting its way, wants to be pampered, and seeks pleasure. Our spirit and soul can give into this, but our moral conscience often sounds the alarm and tells us to stop, saying, "that's wrong."

To be human includes having impulses. But as moral and spiritual creatures we must tame and control our impulses, appetites, and passions.

There are plenty of scholars who teach that the concept of human spirit is a vestige of the animistic belief going back to very ancient times, which believed that spirits were all around in nature. But also going back to ancient times, intelligent human beings, the first philosophers, deeply thought about the cosmos, life, and the nature of human beings. They discerned the human soul in their deep inquisitive search. Some of them no doubt sensed and felt a connection between their souls and the all-encompassing power of the universe, the Source. Ancient Greek philosophers talked about the human soul in distinction to the body of flesh, and believed it was more enduring than the mortal body (e.g. Plato, Stumpf, p. 55, 63).

A mystery and truth is that with and from our spirit and soul within, we sense beyond our five senses. We can contemplate the Transcendence and we can ponder the mysteries. From this seat of inquiry, we can intuit. And from this seat, we may be inspired to thank, praise, adore and worship the Transcendence. The seat of belief within us seems to be intricately connected to the seat of the metaphysical sense.

Every generation has its naturalists and materialists, considering our natures merely physical, and the soul a part of our breath. Once we die, that's it; we stop existing, they believe. But for us in faith, let us say:

For the body God did create five senses. And God gave humans a sixth sense: the spiritual sense. With the spiritual sense, we discern a reality beyond the body we feel connected to the Divine, the life Source of the universe, we worship God, and we intuit.

After accepting the fact of life in the body, we come to the varieties of beliefs on religious views of the body. They can be reduced to essentially three views paralleling "loose, moderate, and extreme." The range of views through the history of the developed religions have varied from a high view of the body to a strong negative view of the body. The strong negative view led to the practice of asceticism (extreme self-denial) which is found in most traditions. Few have emphasized the pampering of the body. All the faiths considered "noble faiths" view the body of flesh as at least inferior to the spirit, if not bad or outright evil, and all therefore have the ultimate goal of deliverance out of, or salvation from the body to a better state, whether Paradise, Heaven, or Nirvana. Within each tradition there is usually this range from those who are average normal people, some who are affluent and have wealth and adore themselves to those who practice extreme asceticism. In that all these noble faiths have the goal to get out of the body, they share this in common.

The fact that there has always been a variety of "paths" within each tradition, from normal lives of attachment to things to volunteer extreme asceticism is not due to the specific religious tradition as much as it is due to one's piety preference. And one's piety preference and the sense of the Calling of God may change through life. One in his early 20's may feel that call to follow a mystic full-time, but after 5 years be led back to a normal life, get a job, have a family. And another may live a normal life and work a career job for 30 years, but when retired, feels the Call of God and devotes himself full-time as an ascetic. The same for women. Some of the most famous women in history were especially devoted to God either as a mystic or prophetess but the degree to which they served or felt that Call may not have been static through life). If, therefore, the specific "path" one chooses is mostly motivated by the inner Calling of God's Spirit and one's personal piety and not the established religion, these decisions should be freely made by each person, and they should be free to change their minds later on. Parents, be sensitive to this. So many parents have this notion or vision of what their son and daughter should be in life, only to find out sometimes by heartbreaks that you are kicking up against God's bricks. God may have other plans for that soul. You do not own the soul. The son or daughter came out of your bodies according to the flesh, but the person is a gift from God, and God is the Creator of all souls, and plans destinies for each of His children. Be in tune to the Spirit by carefully observing the gifts that God has given him or her, and form your vision of career mostly on the gifts evident. But this is faulty since some gifts are not discovered until adulthood.

Most people of religion around the world are normal. They want to live normal lives, not practicing the ascetic lifestyle. But if you know one who is feeling that Call to follow that path, do not discourage them. God may be calling them because it is a step in their earthly journey. It may only be for a season, not life-long.

We live in an age that is more health-conscious than ever. There is nothing wrong with taking good care of your body. In fact, many people of faith consider this an important principle. We have been made with a body, and it is a temple for God's Spirit; therefore, we should take care of it. This ethic of body care is strong today. In this body that God gave us, we also experience some good things in life. Enjoy the things that God has placed on this Earth for enjoyment: the sights of beautiful sunsets, mountains, landscapes, the pleasures from the taste of foods and sweets, the aromas of flowers, and the pleasure of intercourse in mutual and proper relationship. Perhaps indeed God created these things as pleasurable to us humans to balance the pains and griefs that He knew earthly life would bring, by His design.

The noble faiths have inspired pious ones to get in full pursuit of achieving the ultimate goal of permanent release from the body, without suicide. But they have also inspired noble hearts manifesting good deeds, charity, selfless acts, lives of serving others, including feeding the hungry and having compassion on the poor, the sick, the destitute, etc. Their faith, for the most part, did not lead them to turn away from the problems of the world, of which problems of the body are a focal point of the experience of maladies. But the image of the classic Buddha with his eyes closed could be viewed as closing one's eyes from the problems of the world, life in the body, and while looking so peaceful, it basically is compassionless, ignoring peoples problems. The Buddha taught that attachment to life is what has caused these problems in the first place, and the way to escape from life is meditation leading to enlightenment and leading to Nirvana (Hopfe and Woodward pp. 139-140). The historical teachings of Gautama Buddha, who lived in the 6th or 5th cent. BCE (same time as the end of the Old Testament period), did not emphasize compassion. But the now established Hebrew Scriptures was a clear shining light of compassion. The Hebrew Scriptures are rich in use of three terms: *hesad* (lovingkindness, mercy), *hamal* (compassion, pity), and *racham* (compassion, mercy) (Strong's Concordance). The Buddhist emphasis on compassion appears to have come on the scene very much later, as in the last 50 years or so, in part due to the knowledge of other traditions the Judeo-Christian and ethical monotheistic traditions having the light of compassion well established, and after Buddhism came to the West.

O blessed peoples of faith, know that humans have been learning from each other for thousands of years, and religious traditions have shared and learned from each other as their peoples or cultures engaged, discoursed, and exchanged. The religions which we call the "noble religions" have never been static. Each and all have been growing and maturing. Overall, humanity is supposed to be on a path of spiritual maturity. All the noble traditions now sincerely desire to assist fellow human beings in meeting their ultimate spiritual goals, with pure ideals and good intentions, with a good moral grounding. They desire to have at least compassion on the poor and needy if not help them.

When we dig deeper into the distinction between the monotheistic traditions and the Buddhist tradition, we do find a quite different view of the body and the world, and the ultimate goal. It is so distinct that it should be evident to an ordinary reader. The Buddhist tradition, Gautama taught that knowledge humans gain through the senses is illusory. This teaching essentially reduces our very lives to an illusion which fundamentally different than the worldview of a personal God who created all things and people. This idea itself was not invented by Buddha, but it was found in the Upanishads of the Vedas that had been in existence for perhaps even more than 500 years before Gautama. Gautama did uniquely teach that the ultimate goal is the extinguishing of desire, lust, craving, the cause for pain and attachment to live. The permanent extinguishing of desire, cravings, and lust is Nirvana (Hopfe and Woodward, p. 140).

Blessed are all souls who strive to live in peace, and the freedom to live their religion.

The Bible, on the other hand, the Judeo-Christian monotheistic Scriptures, gave a different reason for the cause of pain and suffering (elsewhere in this Scripture find a the prophetic word on pain and suffering). The sacred narrative in Genesis, back to Adam and Eve in the Garden of Eden (Gen. ch. 3), conveys or at least suggests that pain entered the world through sin, the sin of Adam and Eve eating the forbidden fruit. This has functioned as this tradition's answer to this fundamental problem of mortal life for well over 3000 years (as well as pain and suffering). There have been a range of interpretations of the stories in the Bible, especially these of "mythical" proportion, from the literalists to the figurativists, the fundamentalists to the liberalists.

We realistically recognize the life in a human body of bone flesh, and blood, and know its mortality. By faith, we know its our temporary earthly tent until we, by God's power, transforms us into glorious spiritual bodies when we enter Paradise and Heaven.

We join with the hundreds of thousands of saints before us in the mystery of life in this shell, an earthen house for our soul, to carry us through this life and our earthly journey's end to the door of eternal glory.

Brothers and sisters, does it matter what we do in our body? Does what we do in the body affect our spiritual life? Will not God indeed judge us by our thoughts, words, and deeds while in this body? There is, therefore, a direct correlation. What we do in the body certainly matters. All the ethical traditions presume this.

There are yet other mysteries we still do not understand while we are here in the earthly body. If you hold to this tradition or at least consider this for the sake of argument. The New Testament Scriptures speaks of Jesus Christ's body raising from the dead a few days after crucified, into a glorious body, and He appeared to His disciples on a number of occasions. Then after 40 days, ascended into Heaven to reign with God the Father (c.f. Acts 1:9). Did Jesus' glorified body have blood? Most Christians, greatly influenced by the Christian communion ritual in which they believe Jesus gives them His blood to drink, certainly believe so. But God is Spirit, and Heaven is a spiritual plane altogether different from the Earth and physical universe. There is no need of blood in the heavenly bodies, neither in the angels nor in Jesus' ascended body. But He communicated this words to His disciples who were in the human body, in human terms they could understand. Blood is necessary for bodies in this material world, but in the dimension above, the immaterial, they need not blood.

The mystery is that blood, in the moment of transformation and glorification, will instantly dry up like dust.

God loves us as we are, knowing the reality of the life in bodies He has given. We have the perfect freedom to experience balanced lives: balancing the physical requirements and the spiritual engagements. God has given us time on Earth, the daily/ nightly and weekly cycles for eating, bathing, grooming, having sex, taking care of children, working, earning money, buying, shopping, learning, educating, training, and praying, meditating, studying Scriptures, worshiping, attending religious gatherings, fellowshipping, socializing. These are the many activities of life in the body, and we need not feel guilty of the pleasures experienced within God's will and design, with no injury to ourselves or others and within the parameters for moral human behavior in the form that we have received. Human life in the body, orientated spiritually, is a tapestry of engagements of mundane and spiritual, temporal and metaphysical activities. For the soul that experiences the true love of God and spiritual ecstasy, not even the most pleasurable sex in the body compares, as some mystics may testify. The greatest glory of life in the body is the intense sustained worship and adoration of God and mystical communion. But most human souls through at least a significant portion of their lives do not have the leisure or spiritual maturity for this. Here we monotheists can learn from our Indian Hindu brothers and sisters. For centuries, it was a custom, even to this day, that when a man retires and his children now have children (his grandchildren) he devotes himself full-time to God. But in Western society, most who retire essentially continue to serve themselves, and enjoy their families including grandchildren. The enjoyment of these things in retirement is also a gift from God. But God welcomes those into a deeper relationship with Him through mystical devotion. The mystery of mystical devotion while in the mortal fallible body parallels our eternal soul in us in the mortal body, and mirrors also the reality of the two main realms: material and immaterial, the temporal and the eternal.

Finally, brothers and sisters, to complete this discussion fully of life in the body, we should ponder toward the end of life, a journey that we must all take, except those that God calls home even earlier. Why is it, fellow humans, that after working all through life to gain all this knowledge, skill, and ability to the point that we can really make a difference, be experts or at least advisers in our field, and we basically get all our life issues worked out, that then our health goes down and it may be time to die or at least the employers want to get rid of all these seasoned ones to make room for the younger ones? It is then that we should be at our best in knowledge, skill, in producing, in advising, but life is going down because we are on the back side of life approaching our mortality. This does not make complete sense except that God is preparing us for the step into the glorious eternity.

In these days, people are living longer than usual, some with 20 or even 30 years in retirement in good health. Praise be to God for the health and ability to enjoy retirement. But let us not live for ourselves alone, but make a difference in other peoples lives too. It is so honorable to love and spend time with grandchildren and great grandchildren. But there are bigger issues for which God may have prepared such ones, using the knowledge and experience they have, to make a difference, such as in a third world country with very little water, food, health care, etc. If God has us still on Earth, perhaps we have not finished our purpose in life. If you were unable to do what you really wanted to do during your working years, the drive that God's Spirit placed in you, then retirement is the time to do it. Let us not depart the body without accomplishing that which the Lord God has placed us here to do. Let us live for others, guided by the Spirit of God, and make a real difference in this world. The soul that departs the body exhausted from holy work unto God even to their final

days, set apart for God's purposes and Kingdom on Earth, is a
blessed soul indeed and will have rewards in Heaven. Blessed are
those who conquer the body and depart it.

Conquering the Body of Flesh and
Balancing Body and Spirit

Having established the truth of life in the body, dear disciples, we
come to the reality of spiritually conquering it.

Lord Jesus said, "Flesh gives birth to flesh, but spirit gives
birth to spirit. God has created us in this dichotomy of both
flesh and spirit, at odds with each other, not constantly at battle
with each other. The uncomfortableness that so many people feel
and experience itself unveils the truth that our body is not our
permanent home. Our spirit, through earthly life, moves closer to
its journey into glorious eternity. The truth of the spirit/soul God
created in people living for eternity has dawned upon millions or
billions of souls through the ages. And our physical bodies, the
Creator beautifully and wondrously made. How wondrous are all
its systems, so intricate and complex it is incomprehensible, its
millions of nerves and billions of cells. As our earthly container,
it is while in this body that our spiritual strivings and battles are
done. We must control and sometimes battle with our cravings,
desires, lusts, especially when they are motivating us toward
selfishness, immorality, or even evil. These cravings arising from
the body of flesh including a fleshly mind which distracts us and
pulls us away from a fuller spiritual life. A life in the body needs
food for sustenance, rest, sleep, and other nurture and care, not
like the angels. Some pious and devout ones attempt to attain to
the spiritual heavenly realm while as yet in the body, and some
believe they have arrived, though not yet shed the mortal body.
Some have claimed to have conquered this life.[23] The day of
Transformation will come, as the former Testament prophesied,

when our corruptible [nature] will take on the incorruptible, when the mortal takes on immortality (c.f. I Cor. 15:54) and we will be much more like the angels and live in glorious habitation forever.

Strive to find the balance, O souls. While our flesh pulls us down, can entice us to sin by its lust, balance with your spiritual knowledge of truth that God made us including our bodies beautiful, and it was not His intent that we should be at war with our flesh always. God knew of the struggles that we would experience in the body of flesh, and deeply cares for us, but humanity did succumb to corruption and even knowledge that comes to people comes through a corrupted fleshly mind, that when light comes, it corrupts the light, not letting it shine, and where there is positive energy, focuses on the negative energy instead. The truth is that humans are corrupt and one of the clear evidences of this is the great negativity that exists in people.

So what was the source for human corruption, and where did it come from? You no doubt know the ancient sacred story of Adam and Eve falling into sin. You may understand this story literally or metaphorically. It expresses a truth that has not changed since at least the time the book of Genesis was penned, that humans are corrupt in relation to a perfect and holy God. It remains in part a mystery, buried deep in our ancestral minds the cause of human corruption. Some have settled on the evil spiritual source as the primary cause, and others, primarily fallen human will. In either case dear ones, do not blame your flesh for all the evils of the world. This does not lead to soundness of mind, as God desires spiritual and mental prosperity for His creatures on earth. And yet this should be balanced with the truth from Lord Jesus who taught that out of the heart comes evil thoughts, murders, adulteries, etc. (c.f. Matt. 15:19; 5:27-28). What did Jesus mean by "heart"? Did he mean it literally or figuratively? And what is the source of these wrongs? Is it the same heart that loves God and loves our family? Here, so far, we have spoken of the bi-fold reality and realm: spirit and flesh. But the apostle Paul expressed our human nature as body, soul, and spirit (I Thess. 5:23b) which may have been expressing a truth commonly held by not only Jews but Greeks too. To which of these, then, does the heart apply, as Jesus spoke and meant it? If it is understood in spiritual terms and not simply the physical organ in the body called the heart, then it teaches that our spirit (or soul) within us is also corrupt, as most understood, since those who are open to the truth realize that it is our will that often gets us into trouble, since we do not always will good. Therefore, when we seek salvation, forgiveness from God, and purification from sin, we pray it for our whole selves: body, soul, and spirit. This truth is expressed this way by the apostle Paul in this benediction prayer, "may your whole spirit, soul, and body be preserved blameless at the coming of the Lord Jesus Christ" (I Thess. 5:23b). This implies that all three divisions of human nature: body, soul, and spirit, fell in to the corruption of sin and needs redemption.

The good news is that God has saved humanity, and desires to apply His salvation to all three components of our beings, through faith, believing His Word.

Among the world of books and scholars, there has not been uniform definitions on the terms "soul" and "spirit," some understanding them nearly synonymous. While recognizing the apostle Paul's tripartite division, in this Scripture I use them as near synonyms. While the terms are used often in Scriptures, they often lack definitions because they presume the readers already know what they mean. But the full mysteries to life will not be known until we are glorified.

Back in Genesis ch. 1, it says that human beings were made in the "image of God" (Gen. 1:26-27). So which of these three, if we hold to these three as distinct, body, soul and spirit, does the "image of God apply to, to all three or two of the three? This is a good question, and different scholars will give different answers.

But it is a mystery because God did not explain in His word. I am inclined to thing that it is our spirit-soul most of all that was made in the image of God, the part of ourselves that is closest to the Divine. It mostly is the ability to ascent to truths such as holiness, goodness, righteousness, justice, and mercy that God has communicated to us through the Spirit to our spirits. Some will ask, if our spirit (or soul) is the component that was made in the image of God and is eternal, how could it get corrupted? The simple answer is that it is not a separate being from your soul and body. You are one being, and your being is corrupt, and therefore each division shares in the corruption. Wherever you go, your whole being is there. You cannot leave your home, planning to do something you know is not nice or good, and tell your spirit or soul to stay behind so as not to participate in your unkindness or wrong. It goes with you and participates in it with you. Individuals would only deceive themselves to think that they can engage in wrong or sin one day, and the following day be a pious religious person, thinking these two will not effect the other. They will, because it's the same one person.

Finally, brothers and sisters, in life when we are strong, we know how difficult it often is to conquer our flesh, our sinful desires. Because of our inclination to sin, we must always be on the guard all our days in the earthen body. But as we age, we get weaker and weaker to when we finally die. How then can we ever conquer the flesh? When we do grow old, and feel that we can no longer fight evil or sin. The spiritual lesson in this is that we ourselves, no matter how strong we are when we were younger, cannot conquer this ourselves. It is only by God's mercy and grace that He will carry us up to glory. This is the journey common to every human. It is humbling to grow old and die. God provides special dispensation of His grace to souls who know and pray to God. Blessed are the souls to go through journey with God. And how blessed It is for other souls, family members, ministers, and friends, to observe this journey when the person is at peace. This is what the Scripture verse means, "Precious in the sight of YHWH God is the death of His saints" (Ps. 116:15). Life is most sacred at the very beginning and very end, but many struggles lie in between.

Struggle

O brothers and sisters of faith, who know the struggle that comes with life, I sought the Lord in regard to universal struggle in life temporally and spiritually. Great and glorious is God who enlightens His servants with knowledge and wisdom. He did shed a glorious light of understanding, that I thought I had been transported into glory. But I was lying still, and I could hear my heart faintly beating, so I knew I was still in the body.

The Spirit enlightened me to two main planes of struggle for humanity. The first plane is the struggle embedded in the reality of human life that all humans experience. The struggles of life, getting our daily provisions such as food and water, clothing, supplies, keeping a home, adequate work and employment, health and medical care, the pain of child birth, the stresses of caring for family members, the grief over the loss of loved ones, etc. All these struggles are facts to human existence that all humans, including those who don't believe, experience.

Then there are the spiritual struggles of which people of faith are particularly conscious of and in tune with. God's Spirit did enlighten the understanding of my heart and mind to the types of struggles in the spiritual plane. The first kind of struggle is like growing pains. As we grow spiritually, there are growth pains as will. One of the focal points of struggle here is between two wills: our will and God's will which is like a parallel between the will of a child growing up and the will of their parents. We know that God's will is absolute, but even children of faith can still be stubborn or rebellious and want to do their own thing which turns out to be unwise. He lets people basically do what they want, but in the end, He will judge all souls for all their thoughts and deeds. As children struggle will their parents over whose will rules, so also in the spiritual level, we do the same with God. The second type of spiritual struggle is more mature than the first. It is a positive one of our earnestly seeking to know God's will, but God's will is often unclear in regard to specific things and circumstances in life.

For at least one faith tradition, there is the jihad struggle in battle and warfare with believers who fight for what they believe to be the cause of God.[24]

The final type of struggle is in our soul's final days, hours, seconds of life on Earth, to know whether we will make it into glorious Paradise or Heaven. God will lead all the faithful and all the truly repentant who call out to Him, to the glorious place or state.

O precious souls, it is not pleasant when God brings us through His caldron. Some of the things that happens to us in life is not by God's chastising hand. But there are times He chastises us. The author of Hebrews declared this spiritual truth: "For whom God loves, He chastises" (Heb. 12:6). Better is it for us to go through a temporary cauldron of God's chastisement in this life than to experience His displeasure at His Great Judgment. We see God's loving hand through the caldron He sends in this life, when we see the beautiful soul that He attempts to make us into. By the fire of the caldron, it removes the impurities and brings out the brilliance of some precious metals, silver and gold, through the radiance of our spirit. Rejoice! Knowing it is only for a little while. We are in the hands of a beautiful Master. All of our struggles will one day end.

Born to Sin or not to Sin, Submitted or Not Submitted

O disciples and peoples of faith, you are no doubt acquainted with your faith's beliefs and teachings regarding the state of human beings particularly when they first come into this world through the birth canal.

Do humans have inclination of sin, or even carry the seed of "original sin" when they are born or are they basically sinless till later actual sin comes, and do they naturally submit to God or not? These theological issues, since we are really talking about each human's spiritual condition in relation to God, have been discussed among these religions among themselves, each in their own tradition, for centuries, before ever really engaging between the different faith traditions. And each major faith tradition, namely Judaism, Christianity, and Islam developed their own distinctive doctrine on this in the Common Era where each one does not agree with the other.

What then is the truth of this matter? Which one is the truth? Listen to me, O searchers of truth, as I elucidate truth on this significant matter, incline your thoughts to my words.

You may already believe you know this truth on this matter, that tradition which you were taught, the tradition of your upbringing. For Judaism in the rabbinic age, there is a range of beliefs with the Orthodox view basically a sinners view to the Reformed view that humans are mostly good, but have the capability for evil too.[25]

For Christianity, relying upon a key verse in the Hebrew Scriptures, believed and taught original sin, that every human is born with original sin (c.f. Ps. 51:5; Rom. 5:12-15). Christianity also of course was not united and homogeneous in its views, where the view of original sin was emphasized more by Western historic and institutional Christianity, held also by the Eastern Orthodox but not emphasized as much.). Then, coming on the scene in the 7th cent., what Islam teaches is basically the opposite of the

Christian teaching, and Judaism's teaching falling somewhere in the middle. From this historical perspective, Islam departs from both its Jewish and Christian spiritual forefathers. Islam teaches that every soul born is born in a state naturally submitting to God. The way Muslims understand this word "submitting" is not simply referring to an action, but is the very state of a person's soul; so significant, theologically loaded is this term, that it is as important as the term "salvation" is to Christianity. "Submit" is the most important term, one may say for Muslims, as it is a form of the word "Islam." It is the most fundamental term. Moreover, Muslims teach that each human being therefore is naturally a Muslim (one submitted to God), but that they are raised in various other traditions, if raised in a non-Muslim home. The holy Quran makes Abraham a submitter of God (The Holy Quran 2:127-132).

Again, dear beloved one, you probably believe that which ever one of these teachings you hold, is the truth. And now, I show you a process of thought by the Spirit and reason for your pondering. God's Spirit is mighty in revelation, the giver of pure knowledge and wisdom, and the discerner of the corrupted ways of mankind, even the well-intended doctrines of religious leaders may be tainted by this world's imperfection. Who amongst us perfectly understands both God and humanity, the natures and states of the two? Consider these three faith traditions, each non-coincidentally developing their own teaching, separate, distinct, and even conflicting with the other traditions' views. From this broad scope, it definitely does not appear that the same Spirit revealed all three incongruent views, but the Spirit can reveal truth in all three, and also discerns the doctrines made by man, the revealer of human thoughts. Christianity and Islam's teaching on this is based to varying degrees on each of their Scriptures, but all the doctrines on Earth are imperfect, because our vessels which houses our minds are imperfect, and all human languages are imperfect. But the Spirit is a mighty revealer. Could it be that each one of these reflects an aspect of truth? Anyone who denies that virtually every human being has the tendency to sin and actual sin in their lives, like telling a lie, is deluded. Human beings have a corrupted aspect which arises evidentially in the adolescent years. The Biblical Scriptures most strongly express human corruption.26 But that is only part of the picture. By faith, we see a more whole picture with the other part of the picture being God. And what God says and does about the human dilemma makes all the difference. Human beings are redeemable, as the Bible in particularly declares.

The Jewish teaching (mainly in the Reformed branch) that people are mostly good or at least capable of mostly good ideally inspires more goodness by inspiring others and supports mankind's path of spiritual nobility. But it seems sorely inadequate to explain the horrors, atrocities, great sins of mankind on Earth. Herein we find popular humanistic doctrine, catering to humans, what makes humans feel good. Essentially, people do not like to be told they are sinners.

The Christian doctrine of Original Sin implies such a gravity to the point of depicting babies coming out of the birth canal as if balls of bundled sin. In this, we find aspects to the doctrine of mankind, from theologians and priests in the Middle Ages. And yet it reflects an aspect of truth held by billions of people on Earth: the fact that all human beings are imperfect compared to God's holiness and have some sin.

In regard to the Muslim doctrine of humans naturally born submitters to God, herein we can find at least this truth: the truth of the born-with-no-prejudice. The truth of the born-with-no prejudice has been discovered by millions through the ages. For centuries, parents of different cultures have observed that their children display no prejudice in playing with children different than them in race or culture. They just want to play with somebody else. It is their parents that teach them prejudice as their children grow up. It is when they hear their parents in the privacy of the home say things like, "We don't associate with those people because they are different" or for various specific reasons, children pick up on their parents and teachers attitudes the second they come out of the lips of the adults. If prejudice then is taught to children and young adults, what are they when human beings are born? Perhaps the truth is that humans are naturally non-prejudice. But does this mean they are sinless or born naturally submitted to God? It would be a huge jump in assumption. Does it not stand to be sensible that if every human being has sinned at least once (although most may admit they sin every day with imperfect thoughts, words, or deeds) that there has been something passed through the human seed to all humans. In the least, every human has the proclivity to sin from the very beginning. But babies, by nature of their infant stage in life, have not yet been given the opportunity to sin. But watch them grow- any parent will observe sin in them when they unreasonable refuse to do a chore or do any bad thing. Behaviorists of course would explain that "sin" is learned behavior. But I need not disclose to you, peoples of faith, even some of you who may work honorably as a psychologist, that so much of modern psychology is made up of human theories and teachings27 seems to be devoid of divine knowledge and wisdom. Now if virtually all humans show some imperfect obedience to their parents whom God has placed as their number one human authority, does it not reflect their imperfect, even sin state in regard to their spiritual relationship with God? How is it then that Muslims believe that all humans are born naturally submissive to God? It is an imperfect, man-made teaching extrapolated from the holy Quran. The Quran simply states that Abraham, his sons, and Jacob were submitters of God (*The Holy Quran* 2:132). It does not even detail that they were submitters of God from their first day of life, born naturally submissive. It is from Muslim piety, from Imams that produced the notion that not only Abraham and his sons but all humans are born naturally a submitter of God. This is a doctrine of man, not a revelation from God's Spirit of revelation.

So learned ones, we can find truth in all of these views from each of these three great Abrahamic faith traditions. At the same time, within these traditions we can distinguish or discern some human doctrines.

Time will fail us to recount all the supporting passages from the Scriptures of the past. In my discussion above, I had not yet highlighted the seminal foundation of the goodness and badness in humans from the Judeo-Christian perspective. It goes back to the beginning.

The Story of Adam and Eve in the Garden, which you are probably well familiar with, depicts them living in an innocent sinless state in the Garden of Eden, until in chapter three of Genesis, they eat of the forbidden fruit. Then sin is brought into the world. The Hebrew Scriptures from this point throughout convey a theology of sin that has been passed down through the physical "seed," that is human reproduction, to children, who in turn pass it on to their children, and the whole human race was infected by this. The apostle Paul, a theologian of the Hebrew Scriptures par excellence, picks up on this, confirms, clarifies, and strengthens this teaching, where he writes, "Through one man sin entered the world, and death through sin and thus spread to all men...nevertheless death reigned from Adam to .... (Rom. 5:14, 14a NKJV). The apostle Paul continues with articulating the Christian answer to the dilemma of sin, which namely is that God sent His Son Jesus to die on the Cross for the sins of the world.

Moral laws, such as the Ten Commandments, have been lifted up as clear standards by which we human beings can judge ourselves (besides God's perfect judgment) are mostly sinners, or a mixture of good and bad. In regard to the moral law and laws in general, it has been commonly spoken by many people in recent years, "Laws are made to be broken." It is foolish talk.

O peoples of faith, you know this world does not desire to serve or follow God. You know that many people reflect the "world," not the world in what God intended, but the world that humans have made by their corrupted ways. But wait! It doesn't have to be. This is still God's world. It is really us, how WE see the world. Persons of faith who have so been touched by the Spirit of God on a day, will tell you how their view of the world suddenly changed! If more people would be so touched by God, this world could be transformed. And then peoples views and attitudes would change from believing we are born to be bad to born to glorify God. It is not that God is too selective and limited in whom He moves upon to touch in this special way, but God, knowing all souls, must know how many would still reject Him.

As peoples of faith, we have an awesome responsibility in setting examples on living lives for God, morally upright, and instilling good thoughts and values of God, His word, Laws, wisdom, etc. to those in their lives and in their communities. Grievingly unfortunate is it when religious leaders fall, and their falling into gross sin is made public. This is a public embarrassment to their faith organization and to faith in general. Shame of persons of faith who just wait for their religious leaders to fall, giving no prayer support preceding their fall and/or when they fall, and then gossiping about it. God is very displeased with this behavior. This leads us to the teaching of good and evil and the freedom of the human will.

Good and Evil and Freedom of Will

O disciples and peoples of faith who desire good and spiritual freedom, we come to this foundational teaching on good and evil, and the freedom of the will. In your lifetime, you have been taught good and evil, right and wrong, and you who have come to know the freedom of will, at least from human experience, if not also religious instruction as well.

Let us begin with the age-old topic of good and evil, more ancient than when humans first began to write. Ancient peoples told oral stories which included struggles of good and evil, right and wrong. Some sages crafted an inspired morality, as if a beam of heaven's light came down to their mind as they spun their stories. The stories were of human life. But also stories of the gods were told. And then, the light of one Highest God who created all things in the heavens and Earth came to some human soul that history may not have recorded, since it was in the days of the oral stories before they were written down. And in time, God sent prophets, Zoroaster and Moses, to communicate the revelation of divine righteousness and justice and the demand for our alignment to it (for the Mosaic laws, see Ex. chs.19-24). These defined good and evil, based on the word of the divine law. But Moses and the early Hebrews were not the only ones with the sense of good and evil. Ancient peoples everywhere seemed to have a sense of good and evil to some degree or another. Some seemed to have more light than others who seemed to be more superstitious and animistic. And later lights that came, Buddha, Mahavira, Laotzu, Confucius, to name some well known ones, brought light to their cultures, defining good and evil and emphasizing the good. In the Hebrew tradition, later prophets (after Moses) came to clarity the light of God's instruction in the past. The Jews emphasized the Torah over the prophets. Then Jesus of Nazareth, the Christ, comes on the scene speaking with authority of the Torah as an incarnation of the Word of God. This light unveiled a spiritual truth that no matter how good we think we can keep the law externally, the human heart is corrupt. For example, to just look at a woman lustfully, one commits adultery in his heart (Matt. 5:28; see also Lk. 18:19).

Because of our nature of inclination to sin, we must always be on the guard all our days in the earthen body. We must continually commit ourselves to good. We must get goodness in us through the devotion and meditation on Scriptures.

Some question the existence of God or at least a truly caring God. If He is all-powerful and good and just, why does He allow evil to exist and wreak havoc by horrific events, such as genocides, random killings or the killing of innocent people. All religions have to wrestle with this reality and attempt to give answers to their people. No answer to this fundamental problem would be complete without speaking of the factor of the freedom of the human will.

Many humans have come to the understanding that God has created humans with a freedom of will to chose. It is gravely unfortunate that some choose to do evil. The Almighty God has the power to stop any and all evil from happening. It is a mystery why He did not prevent great tragedies such as the Holocaust. We attempt to come up with answers. There is no religion on Earth that has come up with the definitive answer to this great universal philosophical and religious problem. But many of us may conclude that God allows perpetuated evil on Earth because of a deep respect of the human will He created and gave to each human being. This answer is only a partial answer and falls short of offering comfort to anyone who has lost a loved one by a victim of crime or some horrid act or to friends of victims. But God can and does work good out of evil which is a wonder to behold in so many disasters and tragedies. We find people selflessly helping one another, neighbors and strangers. Together, we see the worst and best of humanity when observing good and evil on the Earth. May people of faith not turn away from God in times of deep pain, tragedy, or disaster. But even for those who do turn away, God does not turn away but continues to love those souls, like a great loving Shepherd, and continues to call those souls back to

Him when they are healed of their pain. God does not lose a single soul. We do see another benefit, though uncomfortable to say the least, for peoples of faith living in the world that has some evil as well as good. God's Spirit can purpose to strengthen our faith and our relationship with God, and build strength and character, and give us hope in the eternal life. If this life was Paradise, we would not have anything to look forward to in the hereafter. In this life on Earth, we are but pilgrims passing through.

O good people, the topic of the freedom of the will naturally flows out of the teaching of good and evil. It is surely an important component in the understanding of why God allows evil in the world. It may not completely resolve the mystery in our minds, but we know, that despite all of humankind's knowledge, we still are not like God in perfect knowledge.

Let us now lay a scriptural foundation supporting the truth in freedom of the human will. Beginning with the Hebrew Scriptures, there are clear passages which indicates that God's people have been given choices, namely to choose good or evil, to choose to live according to God's laws and receive blessings or chose not to live by God's law and receive curses. This is detailed in Deut. chapters. 27 and 28. And then two chapters later, the key clear verse: "I call heaven and earth as witnesses today against you, that I have set before you life and death, blessing and curse, therefore choose life, that both you and your descendents may live (Deut. 30:19). Rabbi Akiva pointed out, "If God did not give humans a freewill, why did He command us to choose?"[28] There is certainly a theme in the Old Testament of choosing God, choosing to serve Him (Josh. 24:15) and choosing "life," which is a metaphor for life in God (Deut. 30:19).

The belief, understanding, and importance of human free will in achieving spiritual goals is not unique to the West or Middle East, nor just in the Judeo-Christian tradition. One other well established tradition also emphasized human choice. It is the

Hindu tradition from south central Asia. The Hindu teaching of choice appears to be most brilliant in the great Indian epic *Maharabata*, of which the famous Bhagavad Gita is a chapter.

Returning to the biblical Scriptures, we go from the choosing God and His instruction in the Old Testament to the New Testament. In this set of Scriptures, we don't find the same emphasis but neither is human free will denied. Because the New Testament emphasizes the good news of what God has done for all of us, that which was impossible for humans to do, it does not emphasize choosing this, but believing the good news. When a discussion of choosing comes up in John's Gospel, it is not a discussion about the disciples choosing God or not, but that Jesus said to His disciples, "You did not chose Me, but I chose you...." (Jn. 15:16). This is not to say that the New Testament writers rejected the doctrine of the freedom of the human will. They were simply pre-occupied with the Gospel which was God's action of saving humankind. But most of them were Jews, and as Jews, they understood the truth of freedom of the human will as a fact of life, and in accepting God's Word, or choosing to turn from it. Jewish piety understood the choice of devoting oneself to God in prayer and study or choosing not to; of choosing to keep the feasts or not to, and choosing to eat Kosher or not to. Earliest Christianity, made up of almost all Jews, did not suddenly reject this commonly held truth. But they looked to the ultimate goal, eternal salvation which is a God-accomplishment. "With man this is impossible but with God, all things are possible," Jesus said (Matt. 19:26). The accepting of salvation by faith can be seen as a human action, but compared to God's work, it is but a response to the divine action and grace. As to whether the accepting is a part of the freedom of the will, Christianity is divided on this. Luther and Erasmus debated about this in the early 16th century. I leave this to you to decide.

The age old human wrestling with the deep theme of good and evil, even to cosmic proportions, have continued to the 21ˢᵗ century. It appears that every generation needs to wrestle with this. If we and others of every generation do not wrestle with this issue, society will most likely slip into darkness where much less light of goodness will be evident. We pray that never happens. The truth of good and evil and the freedom of the human will is very important. They have spiritual consequences. May all the peoples of God receive His goodness, be filled and saturated with it, emanating it out into the world. May we receive His good news, and choose to live with God everyday. May we responsibly exercise our freedom. More importantly, we want to make sure that we are right with God and on the path of destiny of eternal for ourselves and loved ones.

Getting Right with God

O Peoples of God who desire to be right with God, we come to the quintessential teaching of how we get right with God. How is human guilt removed and how does human sin get annihilated?

Throughout the ages, there are universal cries of the human soul that are evident and manifest in most religions. One of those universal cries is "How do I get right with God?" The question itself reveals an underlying feeling that we are not right with God. Human beings from ancient times, before the light of revelation came, tried many things to feel right with the universe and God. It was in the age of sacrifice, so many animal and even occasional human sacrifices were offered. Sacrifices were universal, found in most every ancient culture. Through the universal practice of sacrifice in ancient times peaks the truth of the need and spiritual condition of humanity, before the fuller light of revelation came. The lights of revelation then came, from Zoroaster's Avesta, the Hebrew Scriptures, and the Hindu Vedas, in which sacrifice to

God was articulated as a fundamental truth, and made tangible through cultic rituals whereby souls could propitiate their sins and get right with God or gods.

Modern psychologists came up with their own explanation for what they viewed as the human guilt syndrome, but their theories were misguided, not led by the Spirit of God. Sigmund Freud in his theory on the origin of religion explained that religion was birthed from the guilty feeling that all boys have for the desire to have incestual relations with their mothers, the Oedipus syndrome (Hopfe and Woodward p. 7). Freud's mind was certainly not led by the Spirit of God. But there is the truth that many humans from ancient times to the present have guilty feelings or are capable of feeling guilty over something in life. Consider the positive aspect to this that it may in fact be how God wired us, a part of our conscience, making us special and moral above all the animals in Creation. If we talk about guilt, which is a negative, let us also see the positive aspect. It serves to lead many to turn to God. It leads many to a relationship with Creator God.

Returning to the universal need to sacrifice, ancient peoples felt the need to sacrifice animals for their human sin. It was a human attempt to appease the displeasure of a powerful god or God and get on better terms with the Divine. But through the ancient ages, the light of revelation that no amount of the blood of slaughtered could truly atone for human sin was dawning on many souls.

Christianity provided the world a bright light of remedy to this great problem through the sacrifice of the God-man Jesus Christ who was perfect, as believed, the "spotless Lamb of God to take away the sins of the world" (c.f. Jn. 1:29 and II Cor. 5:21). There were voices before the 1st century CE including prophetic voices in the Hebrew Scriptures which paved then way, such as the following words: from Proverbs, "To do righteousness and justice is more acceptable to YHWH (God) than sacrifice" (Prov. 21:3); Hosea's word: "For I desire mercy and not sacrifice, and the knowledge of God more than burnt offerings" (Hos. 6:6); and Isaiah's word: "To what purpose is the multitude of your sacrifices to Me? Says YHWH (God), I have had enough of burnt offerings of rams and the fat of fed cattle. I do not delight in the blood of bulls, or of lambs or goats" (Is. 1:11). Each of these prophetic words must have been powerful in their day; and they each stand pronounced, even counter to the established Hebraic tradition of the priestly sacrifices. It was Solomon himself who built the first Hebrew and Jewish temple in Jerusalem, which became the central focal point of their religious system dedicated to YHWH God. Animal sacrifices and offerings were the main religious rituals, the center of their religion. The proverb then, being so early, is quite intriguing that God, knowing the end in the beginning, knew that the priestly system, being imperfect, would get off track of the path of true worship, that it is ultimately about the heart of God and the noble principles which He communicates to His peoples, justice, righteousness, mercy, compassion, etc. This pleases God more than the sacrificing of animals. The verses from Hosea and Isaiah seem to proleptically look forward to a day in which animal sacrifices are done away. Despite these prophecies, the tradition of the Jewish sacrificial system, which was re-instituted after coming back from Babylonian exile, continued all the way until the great crisis event of the destruction of the Temple and Jerusalem by the Romans in 70 CE sealed that monumental end.

O learned peoples of faith, while the ancient practice of animal sacrifices have long been ended, there are still lessons from this for us and future generations from which to learn. I discern that human nature really has not changed much since ancient times. That same universal desire to be right with God or the universe is still in the soul of most every human being, if they search their being and clear their minds from the clutter of everyday life.

Religious systems have changed much more in time as they have developed than the nature of human beings changing.

The truth is, religion is good at coming up with rules and obligations to bind the souls of their people to their religion and institutions. People still feel the need for doing something to earn God's forgiveness, for their sins to be propitiated, and for their guilt to be removed. O children of God, how many prayers do we need to say, how many penances, and how many prostrations, how many fasts, how many meditations to make us right before God? Hear the voice of God:

"Not even ten thousand prayers, penances, and prostrations will absolve or atone for your sins. Only my pure Word and my holy fire will purify your souls. I look to repentant and contrite hearts, but this does not save or grant you access. At the great Judgment, all your deeds, thoughts, and intentions will be known before Me at My Throne. My Spirit will have searched your heart and soul and know whether you desire to live in My Paradise. I will turn to My Word-Lawyer, who will know your case perfectly, since the Spirit and My Word are in perfect harmonious thought and communication. If He speaks to Me, 'Grant this soul into eternal glory,' then by My grace, I will grant you in. And my Spirit of fire will cleanse, purify you as the angels carry you through the holy fiery furnace."

And your sweat of bullets on your forehead will become the sweetest drops of honey for the saints to savor in awesome praise of another soul entering glory by God's grace. Only a perfect and powerful miracle worker can take something imperfect and make it perfect. That One is God. This, O peoples of faith is the ultimate answer to how we get right with God, by faith, repentance, fear, trust, love, and obedience, and how God who is perfect will enable human souls, which were saturated in sin, to be purified, made perfect, and brought into the glory of Paradise and Heaven.

The Works of Humankind

O disciples and peoples of faith whom God leads to be productive, we come to the truth of the works of humankind.

Across the profile of humanity, some are industrious and produce abundant amount of work in their lifetimes; some are moderately industrious producing a moderate amount of works. And some are low producers, of which some of them are simply lazy. But oddly, mystics may fall into this latter category because of their usually full-time occupation in intense devotion and prayer with God. The main topic of this teaching, though, is not on the quantity of works each person of faith should produce in their lifetime. There are a variety of souls and a variety of abilities.

But we come to the main topic in this teaching, in conjunction with the prophecy on the Works of Humankind in this Scriptures, namely, the kinds of works, good or bad, light or darkness. There are three kinds of human works: works of darkness, neutral works, and works of light.

Works of darkness includes immoral works, diabolical and evil works, delusional works, and essentially any works that do not glorify God. Sometimes it can be quite subtle, for example, a person who works in a factory that manufactures neutral works (neither innately good or evil), but the company obtains the raw material in a third world country by immoral or dishonest means, or by the careless abuse of natural resources.

Now most of the human works in the world, at work and school, are in the neutral category. They are for earthly affairs. For example, the work done at a clothing factory making T-shirts is of itself neither an immoral or moral work, providing the "goods" of this product, T-shirts, wherein the economics term "goods" is not to be confused with morally good. But then a T-shirt retailer takes some of these plain T-shirts and puts witches, warlocks, and werewolves and other dark images on them, then the retailer is engaged in the works of darkness, although the main product was neutral.

The third category is the works of light which includes works that directly glorify God such as divine ministry professions, and many non-profit organizations that are purposed, motivated by, and operate from the compassion of God to help humanity in various needs: food, housing, health, and medical needs. Some secularists may be engaged in these professions. Even though they themselves may be unbelievers, some are still motivated by compassion, and compassion is a work of light, even though they may not recognize God as the Source of light. Much of life is preoccupied with our human needs which is the fact of human life and not of darkness and not directly in glory to God. But it could be asserted that if God made us, and we are to take care of ourselves and others; therefore when we do these things, we are honoring and glorifying God. In this attitude of the heart, it can be light. Similar mundane jobs, which of themselves are neutral, if they are done unto God, humbly and joyfully, can glorify God by doing them. And indeed God loves our hearts directed to Him through the day and through the years of our lives.

But I would make a distinction of the works themselves. The works that truly shine and will make it through the fire are the intangibles: giving a portion of one's money and time for good purposes of light, caring for family members, having compassion, and acts of kindness. Will there be any other human works that will make it through the fire?

The previous Scriptural basis of this teaching you may already know. John the Baptizer speaks of the fire to come that all works will go through (Lk. 3:9, 16-17). Then the apostle Paul adds more detail of this eschatological prophecy: "Now if anyone builds on this foundation with gold, silver, precious stones, wood, hay, straw, each one's works will become manifest; for the Day will declare it, because it will be revealed by fire; and the fire will test each one's work, of what sort it is" (I Cor. 3:12-13).

Now are not judgments against the dark, ungodly, evil, and diabolical works of people of the Earth spoken against elsewhere in this Scripture, in the Judgments? But divine grace is not a human work.

The Abrahamic Faiths and Grace

O children of God on the journey of a glorious eternal destiny, there have been many books written on each of the Abrahamic faith religions, namely, The ancient Israelite religion, Christianity, Rabbinic Judaism, and Islam. This is a lifetime of study. Let us reflect on these great faith traditions on the theme of grace.

The Hebrew Scriptures, Christian Scriptures, and the Muslim Scriptures all speak of God's grace, with the latter to a lesser extent. The truth of the grace of God has dawned on billions, but that one holy sacrifice brings the full grace of God for salvation through faith makes most sense for Christians. Jews of Judaism do not accept that Jesus was the promised Messiah as Christians interpret the Hebrew Scriptures to indicate. And for Muslims, led by their Scripture, denies that God had any son, and denies that Jesus was crucified, died on the cross (Holy Quran 4:157; 9:30; 19:88-92). The Quran goes further to state that it is blasphemy to believe that Jesus was the Son of God (Holy Quran 19:88-89)29 driving a deep and painful wedge of division between these two noble Abrahamic faiths inflicting irreparable damage. Could the same God sanely and non duplicitously inspire both Scriptures?

These three Abrahamic faith traditions have been at odds over these key issues since Christianity split off of Judaism, 1st cent. CE, and since Islam was birthed in the 7th cent. CE and have not reconciled yet. But there are common points of belief in which these three faiths are united; first and foremost, that God is one; but the Trinity of Christianity has created a problem over the truth of the oneness of God. Second, that the one God of the universe is the Creator who created everything. Third, that God is the sole Sovereign ruler, Supreme one of the universe. Fourth, that God created all things on earth including all people. From here is where differences of tradition arise and understanding of the traditions in their Scriptures, and thus divisions between these Abrahamic bodies of believers. These traditions have spread out to the world.

Faith and the World

O disciples and peoples of faith, we are not surprised that most people are worldly, that is, their lives are occupied with earthly matters. This is not to say they don't think about spiritual matters and the hereafter, but their focus is only earthly things. Energies are put in for earthly success, and seeking to be successful in a careers is not diametrically opposed to being devout toward God, Truth is, God has not given us, even very spiritual humans, the ability to see other people's hearts and spiritual conditions. Therefore, we are inadequate in judging the spiritual state of others. Some will be saints in disguise, and others will be devils in disguise, but most of them will be a mixture of the two, falling in between, with people at all degrees in between.

Broadly, there is the way of the devout and there is the way of the worldly. The devout toward God spend quality time, usually every day and especially for the weekly sacred gatherings and other festivals. People of faith interact with society too.

Faith in Society

O disciples and peoples of faith, we have already reflected upon the previous foundational teachings of faith defined, faith and religious traditions, and faith and reason. We come to one more teaching on faith. We seek real knowledge, practical for real people in this world, not merely to theologize about faith in the abstract. We know that there are billions of people on Earth that identify with at least one faith (religion), and they all, including us, live in human society. The purpose of this teaching, therefore, is to bring the discussion of faith in relevance to human society. This teaching serves as a couplet with the teaching on Tolerance which follows because human societies generally speaking, are diverse in all ways: politically, socio-economically, ethnically, culturally, socially, and religious, which calls for tolerance. It seems like every human society has its pious ones, its pundits, its pagans, and its pessimists, its sacerdotalists, its sacramentalists, its secularists, and its scientists. For a diverse society to be healthy, it seems that everyone should have a voice.

Let us start by asking an obvious question. In what realm does human society exist? It is in Heaven or on Earth? Is it in the state of perfection or in the realm of corruption? We know the truth: human society dwells in the realm of the temporal and corrupted. We do not look to human society to be our inspiration to come closer to God or His Light. In reality, history is full of powerful worldly leaders, conquerors, generals, tyrants, anti-Christ kings, and dictators, all whom made a significant impact on the societies they influenced. And social movements in society change through time, often progressing forward, but sometimes going backwards.

Let us assume that all the prophets, sages, teachers, gurus of the past had intended that at least some of the words to be interpreted as pure spiritual words. One of the systemic problems of humankind is continually interpreting the spiritual words of God in temporal, soulish, and carnal ways. The presumption is that many of the great "spiritual" teachings were meant to be purely spiritual. But as we know in fact that politics has always gotten into religion. And some of the great sages, teachers, gurus of the past may be partly responsible for not expressing clearly enough saying, "People, I intend these words to only be understood spiritually." But perhaps they did in fact see their teaching applied to the temporal and their movement taking on political ramifications.

Society, we know, is fallible, since it is made up of all fallible people, and it can go amiss. We should exercise level one tolerance toward all in society who have different moral standards and customs than we ourselves, and make an effort to lovingly grant them their freedom to live according to the law in society, even laws we may disagree with, for the sake of loving the persons. Perhaps one of the reasons that God allows society to morally go amiss is to test our own love for others who are different than ourselves.

Walls divide and barriers create prejudice.

Walls built by humans fuel prejudice, where there is one people on one side and another kind of people on the other side. This teaches prejudice to the children on both sides against the other. Virtually all peoples on earth are guilty of harboring prejudice or superiority attitudes: Arabs, Jews, Syrians, Turks, Kurds, Armenians, Americans, English, French, Germans, Japanese, Chinese, Koreans, Africans, Canadians, Scandinavians, etc. Multicultural and multi-ethnic villages and cities are the ideal model for human society, because they learn to peacefully interact in society.

Tolerance

Dear disciples and peoples of faith, being reminded of the Golden Rule, we come to this important teaching on tolerance. Many people have perceived an inherent flaw in the talk about tolerance. For example, how do you feel if a loved one or friend says to you, "I tolerate you"? There is an inadequacy with this almost disrespectful use of "tolerance." But there is a valid, essential, and positive use for the term which this teaching highlights, and which distinguishes the levels of acceptance and tolerance in society, therefore clarifying some common misunderstanding.

Every teaching in this Scripture has a spiritual foundation. Some of the teachings apply mostly to the heavenly realm, such as the teaching on Heaven and Hell below, and other teachings apply mostly to the earthly realm, such as the teaching on Faith and Society above. The realm of tolerance is in the realm of human society. In contrast, in Heaven, all living beings are at peace and their loving relationships far exceed mere tolerance of each other. This teaching is also linked to the teaching above on Spiritual and Social Equality.

One need look no further than the definition of the word "tolerance" to find a problem which arises. Many people have a problem with the very word tolerance for a valid reason. It stems from the very definition of the word and common use. To put it into a tangible context, we can hear many peoples' voices say, "Why should I accept them," referring to some new people who moved into the community or neighborhood who are from another culture and religion and perhaps a different race too. The problem arises with actually, perhaps, a misunderstanding of the word "accept" along with the common understanding which tolerance denotes. Webster's Collegiate dictionary states it this way: "a sympathy or indulgence for beliefs or practices differing from or conflicting with one's own" (New Ninth Collegiate Dictionary). No wonder people have a problem with tolerance. It seems to be an odd crucial step that wants to impose upon us an expectation of accepting other peoples religions and cultures. This understanding, whether it was intended to be this way or not, rightly causes people to get upset and offends them, not treating each of us with the respect that we deserve. No one should be expected to accept the beliefs of another person who holds to a different belief. Society would be one huge religious schizophrenia if everyone was continuing accepting other peoples beliefs every time they encountered another person who believes differently. This sense is against common sense and mutual respect. This we can consider to be a corrupted understanding or misunderstanding of tolerance and acceptance. No one, whatever his or her own faith, should expect to accept or "indulge" in other person's faith who has come into society. What does Golden Rule say in this discussion? We don't want to be expected to accept other peoples beliefs which our different than our own, and therefore we should not expect or impose on others the same. Both terms "accept" and "indulge" can and do many different things. It is important to rightly distinguish the valid and positive from the corrupted understanding just highlighted below, by defining three levels of acceptance and tolerance, but dropping the term "indulge" which Webster's uses. We keep in mind that language experts who make dictionaries don't concoct definitions, they merely, expertly, write down the actual uses of words. Fact is, corruption can be found in all places and levels of society and misunderstandings arise because of our corrupted natures, and these corrupted senses of terms gets embedded into the very definitions of words.

The first of three levels of "acceptance" and "tolerance" is simply to accept the fact that there are other people in society and in your community and probably your neighborhood who are different from you, different in culture and religion among other things. This first important and valid step is to simply accept the fact that there are other people in society who are different from you. It is the vital first step of accepting them for who they are, but without any change on your part, and absolutely no engagement with them in society is needed. This is simply the step of awareness and accept the fact of different people. Many countries and large cities today are multicultural. So, this first level of acceptance is to recognize them as people, to know what their culture and religion may be. In the first step, our attitude toward them is not yet formed. But because we know attitude is important, we most move up to the second level. The second level is the harder step of accepting that these people of different culture and religion who are now in your community are a part of your community, members of your community. This directly impacts our outlook of them and our attitude toward them. But it still does not require any conversation or engagement with them. The attitude might begin similar to a sibling thinking of another sibling "I tolerant you." This level is again, within you as awareness and attitude, but it is a vital step to a healthy multicultural multi-religious society. It does not requiring embracing the other peoples, which cannot be imposed, but free and spontaneous. Many religious conflicts and riots in the world have started because the people on either or both sides could not even get to level two, accepting the fact that the other group is a part of the community. Level three, based on level two which was based on level one, is the engaging with others in society who have different religions and cultures, through a number of ways, conversations in markets, interfaith discussions and dialogues, and other places in society, such as community centers, where engagements can take place. This step also does not require accepting the other person's beliefs, but it does require an open mind to learn from them about their beliefs and culture. Here is where mutual respect can shine. And it presents peoples of the faith of God to let the light of God's goodness shine through you to others you engage with. Here, we nurture the outlook and attitude that all people are created by God and are objects as God's love. The Golden Rule, which should be an ongoing motivation for us, empowers our mutual respect. It leads us to listen as much as talk, and refrain from controlling conversations. In this level three, we work to achieve the level of courage to not see the "different people" as strange, or a problem, or a threat to the political power-base. People who immediately feel that the "different people" are a threat to their political ideals are insecure and not yet mature. The fear arises from their base animalistic brain core, not from the higher cortex thinking.

All three of these levels are valid and positive, and the goal of every believer should get to level three by their thirty-third birthday. A forth level would be, after learning other peoples' beliefs, to accept, adopt or adapt or incorporate some or all of them (thus probably changing your own) into your own beliefs. But this gets into proselytizing, which this book is not about.

I have previously blogged about "level one" tolerance and "new tolerance," which is basically now the three levels of acceptance above, stopping short, of course, of the unreasonable sense of expecting to accept other peoples beliefs which are different from one's own. This teaching now expounds more fully with greater distinctions with three levels.

O disciples, eager to learn, say with me as we reflect on a few more thoughts about tolerance and its opposing force, intolerance. The journey is not easy to get to the third level, but abundant blessings are in store for all souls who glean the Spirit-led teachings. Level three presumes we have a good attitude towards those in society who are different in culture and faith. To see the "different ones" as objects of God's love means we surely have a positive attitude. Is not God's will that we live by the Golden Rule and share His love? When others come into the community, are they not opportunities to engage with them in order to show kindness and compassion, thereby let God's light, goodness, and love shine through you!

But we are people, and all people are creatures of custom and habit. When are neighborhood or community was one way, but then it begins to change, we don't like it. We often do not like change. But if we see our purpose on earth spiritually, and not politically, that could change our whole outlook. It could renew our mission in life. God could open doors of opportunity, service, engagements, and maybe even careers that you otherwise did not dream of.

Because people are very social creatures, they keenly feel others out as to the attitudes they hold. People will eventually discover the attitudes that others have regarding themselves, even if the others are discreet. And people get upset and some even incensed when they realize they are made to feel disadvantaged by other people who possess the attitude of being advantaged, which an exclusively held religion can and does often do.

There is a clear distinction between attitudes of intolerance and those who hold to exclusive religions. It is very important to make this distinction. There can be some peoples who hold to inclusive (meaning, truth is found in all religions) faith and yet harbor intolerant attitudes to different people who moved into the community. Conversely, there can be people who hold to an exclusive faith (e.g. Christianity) and yet have a tolerant attitude toward the new different people in the community. Thus, intolerant attitude and those who hold to an exclusive religion are not the same. Regarding ourselves, we must guard against intolerant attitudes, recognizing that they are from our base natures, not from God. Let us lay any intolerant attitudes towards people who are different that arise at the Divine altar. We should be intolerant, however, of great evils. But to be intolerant of a people group identified by race, ethnicity, culture, creed, nation, or gender, works to deny them the human dignity they deserve.

There all a few very significant exclusive religions on Earth. Many who hold to one of the exclusive religions are often viewed as being intolerant by others who don't hold to their own faith. The exclusive religions we are talking about all happen to be the great monotheistic Abrahamic faiths, namely, Judaism, Christianity, and Islam. Exclusive means that each of these belief systems believe their religion is the true religion and all other religions are false. Together, these three faiths represent around 4 billion people on Earth, although not all of them rigidly hold to an exclusivistic view. In light of the three levels of acceptance above, every one of these believers can move through and get up to level three without changing or even compromising their own faith. It is possible to engage with others of different faiths, with mutual respect, and a positive attitude, while seeing their own religion still as the true way. In actuality, many do open up to see that there is some truth to be found in other religions but without going down the slippery slope of universalism.

The very fact that there are some religions on Earth that hold to exclusive view of their faith is a real problem with many others on Earth who don't hold to that particular faith. On this point, there is some conflict between the Abrahamic faiths and those in an inclusive faith and the secularists and atheists. But at the same time, the Judeo-Christian faiths offer so much blessing and comfort to their adherents that they do not feel an unfulfillment to find in another belief system. Judaism, Christianity, and Islam, generally, instill such a strong faith that their belief system is the truth. This in turn leads to viewing all other belief systems as false and inferior. And this creates the "our way only" attitude. And this "our way only" attitude is what gets others upset because it positions others disadvantaged spiritually (which often gets interpreted politically too). The imperfect human attitude of "my religion is true, yours is false," and "my religion is superior to yours" invariably leads to jealousy, strife, and conflicts in society. Perhaps, some ill-intended human beings deliberately corrupted the meaning of "tolerance" to sabotage humanity from getting to level three?

In history, we see the best and worst in humanity. We find a few golden ages of wonderful multicultural engagements in mutual respect and great intellectual growth. Spain in the Middle Ages is a golden example. Jews, Christians, and Moorish Muslims were all living together and exchanging ideas, culture, reading each others sacred Scriptures. But something this good just would not last too long. Two of the greatest thinkers of that age were Maimonides (Jewish rabbi, called the "Second Moses") and Averroes (great Muslim scholar) (Menocal, p. 169).

...My thesis in this discussion is that walls divide people and breed stereotypes and distrust whereas heterogeneous exchanges in society breeds understanding, acceptance, and trust, making for a more healthy society. Throughout history, there has always been cultural and intellectual growth in cosmopolitan cities, from Alexandria, Athens, Rome, Paris, New York, Singapore, etc.

In conclusion, because of the actual senses of the word "tolerance," ideally, we need a better word. But for now, we separated the undesirable aspect of tolerance, adjusted it to fit an acceptable and good application for this teaching and for human society. We have defined and distinguished three valid and positive levels to "acceptance" and "tolerance." Intolerance is unspiritual and immature. God desires to lead His peoples to a more mature mindset, getting to levels two and three, accepting those in society who are different for who they are, seeing their presence as opportunities to let God's light shine through you by engaging them in conversation and dialogue. Human dignity, mutual respect, and the Golden Rule are ongoing operatives and motivations which we should live by every day. Lastly, a healthy society is one that is multicultural and multi-religious, which each group respecting the other, and each having the freedom to practice their own faiths, and to engage with others without fear.

Faith and Freedom

O disciples and all peoples of faith, who in your inmost hearts desire spiritual freedom, partake of these words for the encouragement of your souls and for the souls of your family of God. This teaching is on spiritual freedom and religious freedom. Religious freedom is solidly in the earthly realm of human societies, and spiritual freedom is for us in the life of this realm too, but will continue with us into the blessed eternal heavenly realm. When we taste of freedom, whether it be spiritual or religious freedom, we desire it, and long for its permanence, for you know it to be a good thing. Don't our hearts yearn for it like we yearn to be one with God, reflecting the incompleteness of our souls without God?

Let us address, first, the truth of spiritual freedom. Spiritual freedom is a reality apart from circumstances in earthly temporal realm. Is it not in relation to God, knowing by faith, that His blessings are on us, His love is upon us, and His eternal plan of blessed Paradise will one day be realized? Spiritual freedom is that freedom that one has in their spirit and heart toward God, reflecting a connection, even a relationship with the God of Heaven. When one has this connection, there is no person or power on Earth that can remove this. It is a divinely centered freedom. Is it not a wonder to behold, dear believers, that a believer could be in the deepest darkest prison and yet be completely spiritually free, and another person, ungodly, can be free in society but in complete spiritual bondage to his own sins? There are several models of faith exemplified in great sacred Scriptures of the past and from history who were imprisoned for their faith and their active missionary work but who intimately knew the spiritual freedom they had, that the light of God through them could not be kept bound in the prison cell but shone forth to the world, for the power of God and His light was so strong on them. The apostle Paul is a good example who was imprisoned at least a few times and wrote four of the epistles (letters) in the New Testament from a jail cell. Baha'ullah, the founder of the Baha'i Faith, begun in the 19th century, is another good example. His first imprisonment was in the darkest dungeon, Tehran's "Black Pit" dungeon. According to Faizi, while there, "Baha'ullah became fully aware of the Revelation which was to flow through Him to the rest of mankind" (Faizi, p. 10) and "the revelation of Baha'ullah, which had been born in the dungeon of Tihran and declared on the eve of His departure from Baghdad...(Faizi, p.

13). No matter how bleak the temporal darkness from oppression is from worldly powers, God's Spirit is mightier, who enlightens, comforts, delivers, saves, redeems, restores his precious souls, and brings us to a glorious eternal Paradise. Though by worldly eyes, they are by no means free, in the Spirit, He whom God sets spiritually free is free indeed (c.f. Jn. 8:36). A bright light of the prophecy of spiritual freedom shone through the ancient Hebrew book of Isaiah (dating back to the 7th century BCE). "The Spirit of the LORD God is upon me, because the LORD has anointed me to bring good news to the afflicted…to proclaim liberty to captives and freedom to prisoners (Is. 61:1)

The next truth on spiritual freedom is that it comes to individual souls by faith and it is possessed by faith. Faith latches onto the promises of God. Each soul seeks this in the same way each seeks all good spiritual things from God. It cannot be given to another person. It cannot be purchased from another. It cannot be inherited. It is a spiritual benefit from God to His children, when they latch onto it by faith. In our day to day lives, we often to not feel it. But when the trials of life heat up like a cauldron and we cry out to God, His presence with comfort us and His Spirit will open our spiritual eyes to see our spiritual freedom, like Stephen, who suddenly saw the beatific vision of the glory of God and heaven opened (Acts 7:55-56) at the end of his witnessing the faith, just before they stone him to death. Many, through the years, gave their lives as a holy sacrifice for the cause of faith, and through their life offerings, strengthened the faith of the followers the molten in the blacksmith's making faith more pure.

Let us now turn to religious freedom, which is related to but distinguished from spiritual freedom. This is the freedom in the earthly realm, in our nations and societies, to freely practice our own religion. This we know, sadly, that millions of people in the world live in nations and regions in which their freedom is severely restricted, their religion persecuted, or even illegal.

Our prayer and vision is that people from every nation around the globe, in every society, have complete freedom in the practicing and living out their faiths is all its diverse religious expressions. But the world is far from this. Instead, in this current generation, things are getting worse. Let us not, brothers and sisters, give up on praying. Pray earnestly for brothers and sisters in faith around the world. Pray for their leaders and governments to strongly maintain good laws and to punish murderers and all killers in the name of religion.

Blessed are those who live in countries where they have religious freedoms. And blessed are those who are persecuted for their true faith in God, though in the temporal, the blessings may not be manifested yet. The former Scripture declares, "Call upon Him on the day of trouble, and He will rescue you" (Ps. 50:15).

The fullness of religious freedom covers all areas of their practice and expression: freedom to worship, freedom to study their Scriptures, freedom to fellowship with fellow believers, and freedom to be free to speak and write, text and tweet their faith thoughts, without fear of being harassed, coerced to stop, jailed, or tortured. This world needs more light and much more freedom. But the freedom should not be taken by force. The kingdom of God on Earth comes peacefully (Rom. 14:17). We continue to earnestly pray for those who are oppressed and who do not have the freedom to practice their faith in their country. The fullest religious freedom includes those in religious institutions under holy orders or vows, that they should be allowed to change their order, their vocation, or even renege on a vow, after serving a number of years, without the threat of God's wrath, damnation, or punishment. We have advanced beyond Medieval times, but there is still more steps of progression that religious institutions and organizations can take in this regard. Forcing unnatural vows such as celibacy, while well intended, has also created some painful problems. It seems wise that such a vow as this should be voluntary, not a requirement for all the clergy.

Religious freedom in the 21st century is still not realized for millions of souls. Much work remains to be done. All individuals should be free also in regard to individual vocation.

Vocations: Sacred and Secular

By faith, dear peoples under God, we know that God has a purpose for everyone's life. That purpose to some degree, for some believers, coalesces with a plan for our career lives.

Most broadly, there are two spheres of career-lives: the sacred and the secular. Some sense the Calling to the sacred life, but most are led into secular careers. God can and does use us in both spheres, the sacred and the secular, in whatever profession one is led to pursue, to let the light of goodness and faith in us reflect out to others around us. The sacred Scriptures of the world do not present God, generally speaking, as the Career Counselor for our lives because God is most concerned with our spiritual lives, and He wants each of us to truly live by faith. Very few of us would say that God chose our particular profession for us, communicating it to us by direct revelation. When we are young, we get the general sense of a career, or we may even know exactly want *we* want to do, perhaps nurtured by God-fearing parents, religious leaders, etc. Most of us would admit that we do not have complete assurance that our chosen career path is exactly the path that God wants for us. We make these decisions in faith.

There are three important things God gives us or places in our lives, however, to guide us along the way by faith. The first of these is the set of our aptitudes, skills, abilities, and talents. By the end of our adolescence, we should know our basic gift-set. As we mature through life, we continue to development and sharpen our gift set. In our career life, we should discover what skills we are strongly gifted in and along the way we may also discover new talents. The second thing that should be available to us is the general internal sense of a career, whether it is in the secular or sacred spheres, which comes from our own individual reflection and through prayer. This is the internal voice, not an external voice being imposed on us. The third is the set of guides and resources in our lives, from parents, grandparents, religious leaders, significant others, and career advisers or counselors. All youth before finishing high school should take one or two career assessments, and have it evaluated by a guidance counselor or adviser. Good career assessments are designs to show the set of one's aptitudes, skills, and interests. The whole set most likely is not fully known by their parents, no matter how well they know their children, unless they performed aptitude and skills assessments on their own children. In the broader scope of the two spheres, the sacred and the secular, to those whom God calls for the sacred, God Spirit works this directly to the individual soul, not through the parents because all children belong to God. The Calling may often come before the soul is "of age," that is, an adult according to human society, unbeknownst to parents. When it comes to the Calling to the sacred life, each one has to discern this for him or herself. Parents can support or be an hindrance to a child's Calling, but the cannot be the determiner; it is God who calls, and this conviction comes from the soul of the individual who "feels" the Call. This is based on the premise that God makes every human being including their soul, which we know by faith. We know physically how babies come about, but God knits each of us in our mother's wombs (Jer. 1:5). All parents should give each of their children back to God while they are yet in their youth, as a spiritual offering, and do all they can do to develop their child in every way physically, emotionally, intellectually, and socially, and prepare them for their lives as an adult. They should impart wisdom at every opportunity that arises. When children are turning into an adult, parents should grant the freedom to their child to make important life decisions including career. There are plenty of examples from history of parents, usually the father, who had a career chosen for their son, but this was not God's plan, surmised by faith since we cannot be presumptuous on the will of God. One example is Martin Luther. His father had great ambitions of him being a lawyer (Bainton, pp. 17-18).

God has career-lives for us all except those whom He calls to their eternal homes early, not simply to occupy all this time through our lives, but for the following reasons: God wills that every works and is productive, for all who are able; God want us to have the sense of worthiness through our creative actions and skills; and God wants us to feel a sense of purpose for life; many careers harmonize the fulfillment of a purpose for a higher good and earning a salary to support one's self or family.

Lastly, each adult person should be free to change their career path, in accordance with the Calling or opportunities to use God's given abilities talents that are yet unfulfilled.

The Light of Ethics and Morality

O peoples of faith who strive for goodness, you have been nurtured in divine words, you have been taught right and wrong, and you have had other teachers who were spiritual and moral examples to you. Praise to God for these gifts He sends. May some of you also develop into mentors, guides, teachers, to bring up the next generation in the good and right path.

Religion has been the leader of humanity when it comes to morality and ethics throughout all the ages. Many a civilization was inspired by the religious code of the land for their civil codes, for the moral behavior of every man, woman, and child in society. Every religion, especially the nobles ones, defined, taught, and modeled a moral code. They often went to many places, civilized or remote, to peoples who lacked the light of their moral codes, having a vague sense from the natural law God wrote on peoples' hearts (c.f. Rom. 1:20; 2:14). Even the non-theistic belief system of Confucianism and the religion of Buddhism has had a strong moral code and was the leader of the light of ethics and morality in the lands of the East.

The great monotheistic religions that arose in the Middle East have had particular influence in the Middle East and West. They have been the leaders certainly in these parts of the world, but through the special light of revelation of their sacred texts, they have had a special role of contribution of morality and ethics, and goodness for all humanity, for all who receive. The world should praise the good intents, influence, deeds, and accomplishments of these great religions, helping humanity to stay out of the brink of darkness. The light of religions' ethics and morality has to be taught to every generation, or else fall into the darkness of ignorance, and immorality and spiritually unclean living.

Clean and Unclean

Written into the souls of God-fearers, O noble disciples, is the principle of external purity, that is, cleanliness. Just as there is the knowledge of good and evil, so also is there the knowledge of clean and unclean. Those who seek God and to live a life pleasing to God desire good and right; they also desire pureness and cleanliness. Life is full of ebbs and flows. Some days we feel spiritually down in the dumps, and other days we feel spiritually clean and more pure, closer, approachable to God.

Cleanness before God is in regard to both physical and spiritual cleanness. It is the actual cleanness of our body, clothing, and living environment, namely, our home (but certainly applies to our sacred places too), and in the spiritual sense which includes metaphorical meaning. Both the physical and spiritual meanings are completely connected, directly correlated. The metaphorical spiritual sense is rooted in the physical. In the royal Psalm 24, ascribed to king David, he declares, "Who may ascend into the hill of the LORD? Or who may stand in His holy place? He who has clean hands and a pure heart" (Ps. 24:3-4a). We know from the Hebrew Scriptures that David had gotten a lot of blood on his hands from his many battles, and for this reason God did not allow David to build the house of God (c.f. 1 Chron. 22:8). Yet, David's heart earnestly desired God, to walk before Him. "Clean hands" in Ps. 24 has both a physical meaning and a spiritual meaning. Certainly it included the removal of actual dirt and blood. But because people are spiritual creatures too, it takes on the spiritual meaning, a metaphor for being or desiring to be clean and pure before God, not merely our outward flesh, but our spirit and soul too in which lies the seat of the heart. Another good example of the double-meaning of "clean, both physical and spiritual, from the Biblical Scriptures is when Jesus said, "not all of you are clean," of which John writes concerning Judas Iscariot who betrayed him. The context for the verse is the Last Supper of Jesus with His disciples. At the end of the Passover meal, He washes their feet. Jesus said to Simon Peter, "He who is bathed needs only to wash his feet, but is completely clean, but not all of you. Prof. Kiehl expounds on this passage stating that "all participants of the Passover were to bathe and put on their best clothes. This, Jesus' disciples did in Bethany before setting out to Jerusalem to celebrate the most holy Passover (Kiehl p. 57). So it included a physical bathing, but the meaning of "clean" in the text is certainly spiritual, clean before God, heart and soul, which Judas was deemed certainly not.

The desire to be spiritually clean before God, O fragrant disciples, unveils yet another truth found in human beings, not just for Jews and Christians. The desire to be spiritually clean reveals the deeper insecurity of our feeling of uncleanness. This truth seems to be near universal, found in many lands and cultures from ancient times. The principle of getting spiritual benefit, namely, external purity (cleanliness), forgiveness, and/or spiritual renewal through bathing (a physical activity) is found in many places, not only from the Hebrew and other Semitic cultures but in the Hindu Indian culture, the Japanese culture, and others (Hopfe and Woodward pp. 122, 222). Each culture developed different traditions based on their beliefs about them which may have been determined by unique early sacred texts, that is, revelation, and based on resources available. This symbiotic relationship of the physical bathing and getting spiritual benefit reveals the intimate body-soul relationship. A simple way to depict and apply this truth is this. Wherever your body goes, your soul goes with you. So if you go to a place that is dark and physically and spiritually unclean, your soul is there too and will be affected. Its hard to keep the soul pure in such an environment. The soul can quickly get contaminated.

So why have humans had this universal or near universal human experience, the feeling of lacking spiritual purity and the need for spiritual cleansing? Why have human beings throughout the ages feel the need for bathing for spiritual cleansing? It reveals to some extent, an uncleanness felt in our souls. The Bible calls this sin, and also speaks of corruption in our nature. The concept of sin was not unique to the Hebrews. Even the ancient Egyptians had the concept of sin. Other terms could be used to describe this spiritual condition, felt in the human soul, in naked contrast to the consciousness of a perfect, holy God. The Bible gives its sacred story's answer going back to the fall into sin (c.f. Gen. ch. 3).

The Hebrew tradition in the Bible develops a rich tradition of thought regarding cleanliness before God. It is clearly defined when the people of Israel were with God in the wilderness, and

Moses received the Law of God from Mt. Sinai, giving the holy instructions for the covenantal people, on how to meet God, worship God, and live. Being pure before God at the tabernacle in the wilderness was of utmost importance. No unclean thing can approach God. The wonder of the tabernacle was that God was dwelling in the midst of His peoples. They had to be very careful. Stepping over one boundary in a state of uncleanness could cost a person His life. It is not that God is fickle or angry, unloving, but because His complete holiness and purity demands it. So you see that cleanness is tied directly with purity and holiness (Ex. chs. 19-40).

The Levitical priests were set apart (which is what "holy" actually means), consecrated for the full-time work of God on behalf of the people. So comes many laws from Exodus ch. 20 forward all the way through Leviticus, and then Deuteronomy, laws governing the sacrificial system, the priesthood, and the peoples behavior in the sight of God. Lest you think that the laws of cleanliness and purity pertained only to the priests, be reminded that just before all these laws, in the Preamble to the Law of Moses, God speaks through Moses, "'And you [all] shall be to Me a kingdom of priests and a holy nation.' These are the words you shall speak to the children of Israel" (Ex. 19:6). While indeed the Levitical priests served on behalf of the people, as a whole, all people were to be a kingdom of priests of God. Therefore, all the laws that follow in the Law of Moses applied to them. The principle of clean and unclean applied to them. How they lived their life mattered.

This concept of no unclean thing can approach God becomes magnified up to an eschatological and heavenly level, if indeed Isaiah ch. 35 could be ultimately interpreted to mean, when it prophesies of the holy highway to Zion and to God, adding, "The unclean shall not pass over it…but the redeemed of God will walk" (Is. 35:8c, 9c).

The strong biblical tradition has led to a common expression, held by many in my generation: cleanliness is next to godliness. This high value seems to be waning, not held as a value by as many people today than just the previous generation. If the principle is true, then we need to maintain it, instill it in children and youth to carry it forward to the next generation.

If physical cleanness can be a manifestation of spiritual cleanness before God, so also uncleanness manifests a unclean spiritual condition, whether its simply ignorance of God's principles, or deliberate rebellious living. The filth that some human beings live in is deplorable. We leave it up to God to judge their spiritual condition; for many of them it may be as much a cultural fact of the way they were raised and in which they got accustomed.

So many people on Earth pollute it. God has made this such a beautiful Earth, and some people take their careless and filth and pollute outside their home from little things such as dropping litter, not properly disposing of trash, dumping trash, and pouring out contaminated liquids on earth and in the waters. God's standard of cleanliness applies to all activities of humankind on Earth and in Space. We need to continue to work to maintain and develop a strong ethic of the care of the land, water, and air, all Earth's environment, and Space. We need to work on keeping everything as pollution-free as possible. Deliberately polluting anything is unacceptable for the children of God. Human waste is a fact of life. God has given knowledge and intelligence especially in the modern age to treat waste and mitigate disease.

The secular age has most likely been an influencing factor for more people in modern society leaving behind their monotheistic worldview, returning humans back to a divinely unenlightened way, though they consider it the enlightened way. Scripture-based light of the truth has given a foundation for the ethic of the care of Earth. There are also good people who are humanists, agnostics, and atheists who may have a strong value of or good ethic of the care for the Earth. A spiritual danger is at the very door. Secularism is not merely humanistic, it takes its followers down the path of the worldview of materialism, godless materialism. In this worldview and belief system, there is no spiritual consequence to polluting because God has been taken out of the picture.

Peoples of faith, on the other hand, are God-fearers and God-desirers. The light has dawned on us of a direct spiritual connection between physical cleanliness and spiritual disposition before God. God cleanses us through His Word, Spirit, and our part of the confession of sins, implore His mercy, latch onto God by faith, and have the Word of divine righteousness imputed to us. We should care for each other and for the Earth.

Care of the Earth and Its' Resources

We have just discussed the clean and unclean truths and principles, which is a direct application to everyday life on Earth or Space. We reiterate here briefly these points.

If God made this Earth and all things, then He is really the owner of everything, and we as stewards should take good care of the Earth, all its resources and systems, and the air and Space above.

The cultures that have strongly viewed the Earth and its resources in an exploitive way, whether in the West or in the East, have forgotten the sacred aspect of the Earth. But cultures with religions that were more nature based, and going back to ancient times, whether in Asia or the Native Americans, considered everything in nature sacred. Nothing was taken from the land or water except that which was absolutely necessary. The western European and white American advanced cultures had long forgot that aspect. These resources were viewed as material for capital gain. Spiritually, it could be viewed that they replaced the God of this sacred Earth with the god of money. Ironically, however, the culture that advanced this material exploration, oddly, had Christian roots. I submit the Bible does not espouse or teach the exploiting the land or any of the Earth's resources. But one verse, the first command in the Bible, from God to people says to "be fruitful and multiply, fill the earth and subdue it; have dominion over this fish of the sea, over the birds of the air, and over every living thing that moves on the earth" (Gen. 1:28). First notice the three partite division: the seas, the air, and the land, encompassing all the Earth's inhabitable environment. But notice it only speaks of living creatures. It does not mention or suggest the use of even inanimate objects, materials, or minerals, not even stone for building or paving stones. "Be fruitful and multiply" refers to increasing human population and being productive agriculturally. Then there is that term: "subdue." What does that mean? The proper interpretation is that it grammatically governs that which follows, namely the living creatures in the sea, air, and on land. In other words, this verse should not be applied to any inanimate materials on the planet, because the text simply does not state them. In historical reality, this verse was probably in the back of the minds of Western human beings coming into the modern age, the age of imperialism, colonialism, then the industrial revolution. This would be yet another example where people, who are a people of faith to some degree, corrupt Scripture, if this verse was in their mind when they set out to dominate over nature. In contrast to the possible misinterpretation of the word "subdue," the Hebrew Scriptures in the Torah has a law of the use of agrarian land: it is to be given a Sabbath rest every seven years (c.f. Lev. 25:2-4), if the law in the Torah were followed.

The story of the technology of humankind through the ages is, in large part, the story of a series of discoveries of new elements, mined from the earth, when and where people learned how to make new things from these metals: copper, tin (combined to make bronze), iron, gold, silver, etc. which not only revolutionized technology but the world's economy. And then coal and oil was discovered in the 19th century. And the culture of humankind was further transformed. But all of these are immaterial elements or compounds taken from the earth. In one sense, it may be viewed by peoples of faith to see that God created these elements for humankind's discover and adaptation technologically, and likewise the trillions of gallons of crude oil in earth's deposits for our use of automobiles. This can make some sense, but it also appears to be driven by selfishness, not by the Spirit of God. On the other extreme is the view that God owns this whole Earth and it is a sin for any company or corporation to extract substances, including natural gas, from the earth and sell it for a profit to people. The oil and gas corporations have gotten billions of dollars off something they did not make, they only extract and process it. But I'm sure that some of the people who work for these companies, even in the executive level, may also be people of faith who also tithe or at least give a portion of their wealth to their church, temple, or religious house. But if it is still a sin, then the giving a portion of it for religious purposes does not excuse the sin.

Dear people of faith, as with all of these teachings, the truths are attempted to be grasped, the key points of the topics are highlighted, some key issues discussed, and I leave it up to do you decide the truth for yourself. May we all learn to be good stewards of the Earth's resources, develop the sense of an Earth ethic, feel the sense of the sacred in the Earth, and do what we can to reduce our carbon footprint. And putting it into perspective, if the soil, rocks, plants, water, and air is sacred, how much more sacred are we humans, created to be the crown of creation to have dominion over the whole Earth, and given eternal souls? True care of the Earth leads to peace.

Religious Conflict on Earth

O peoples of faith whose hearts vary as much as black varies from white, as much as the east is from the west. You have come to know the plenty of violence that has come on the Earth, in various lands, in part in regard to religion. Have the peoples of the Earth truly repented of these conflicts and atrocities yet? The truth that has rung out from the hearts of millions of victims of violence and their children and children's children is "We must learn from this lesson. We need to forgive, but we will not forget." It can be good for some to remain blissfully ignorant of the violent nature and acts of humankind on Earth. But once a soul has come to the knowledge, whether through parents, school, news, or friends, we cannot be ignorant. We must wrestle with the issues and take before God in prayer, and channel positive energy to good.

Scriptures exhort believers to "shun evil" and "resist evil", and even "avoid all appearance of evil."

Peoples of faith should not participate in riots, nor should they lead people into conflict unless they are in the charge of military duty to do so.

Religious leaders and spiritual teachers ideally should never steer, incite, or lead their followers or hearers down a path of conflict or violence. There is at least one religious tradition in which religion and politics is and has always been combined together in their one belief system. This does create problems of relationships between the spiritual leaders and the civil leaders. It also confuses the two distinct roles of state and spiritual matters. Is not the purpose of the state to maintain security and order and provide for the general welfare of its citizens? And is not the primary role of the spiritual realm and God's Kingdom to lead people to faith and to keep them in the faith through spiritual care and nurture to eventually make it to eternal bliss? The role of the state and the role of faith/religion/spiritual life are very distinct. In theory, they can be combined into one belief system on Earth, but the reason it does not work is because humans are corrupt, and power corrupts. Political offices are positions of power. And when people get in power positions, what human can keep him or herself from succumbing to corruption? These two roles are almost as distinct as the Earthly realm is from the heavenly realm. We judge not, but we bring light to peoples of faith on Earth toward peace.

If we look closely and are honest, we will find seeds of conflict in our own sacred Scriptures of the past, whether it is the Bible or the Quran. The faithful, having ascented to the truth that God of their own faith tradition is a global God, yet they find some tension with other world religions which hold to a universal belief in one global God.

The peaceful awakening is that the tension is on the surface, but they are all connected in one human family created by the same global God. This does not obliterate the differences of the religious traditions. But they spiritually transcend those differences, fixing their faith on the same fundamental truth that if God is eternal and truly one, and good and sane, that God did not intend to create the conflict and divisiveness between human beings through religion. But God did create diversity. May God's Spirit mold our hearts and minds above the world's impurity, set on the blessed path of unity and peace. Blessed are all souls who strive for peace.

The True Path to Peace

O disciples and peoples of God, these Scriptures through and through contain a spirit of peace, toward a global peace. These Scriptures defines the chief problem as sin, human corruption. How is this malady overcome to usher in a true era of global peace? How many people does it take who desire peace? And how many people does it take to greatly damage or destroy peace?

Blessed are all peoples of faith who both desire peace and are enlightened into the way toward a real path. Blessed is the fact or truth that the way to true peace, and its components, or not hard to understand, but even elementary. The reason why true peace is always sabotaged in the world is because of corruption within human beings.

These Scriptures are not about indoctrinating readers and listeners, but setting Scriptural parameters and shaping the issues and giving you the process by which you can determine what the truth is for you and what the best ways toward achieving religious goals, or in this case, global peace in the earthly realm.

Are these not the seven ways to achieving global peace:

To love fellow human beings and neighbors as you yourself would want to be loved (the Golden Rule);

To truly respect others including those who are different;

To accept, not just tolerate, those in society who are different than you;

To treat all people as equal citizens, that none are treated as second or worse class citizens or oppressed;

Allow all people the freedom of movement for life: work, school, market, and home, and for a flow of goods exchanging for prosperity in society and between nations;

Allow all people to freely believe and practice their religion of choosing;

Allow for multicultural and cross-cultural interchanges.

When speaking of desiring to achieve or working on global peace, we should also highlight the responsible parties. I suggest to you this hierarchy which begins with the state, kingdom or country. For 99.9% of the world could live in peace, but if two kings of different counties decide to go to war with each other, and each lead their armies into war, the world is not at peace. This expresses the truth how important a role that nations, kings, rulers, have in working toward peace.

1. States, Nations, Countries
2. Rulers, heads of states, ministers of government of states
3. Leaders in society, civil, and religious, who have influence over more than just their family
4. All citizens

How many people does it take to gain peace? It takes everyone. But peace can be greatly damaged by just one person committing a grave mistake.

I end with the beatitude by Jesus Christ: "Blessed are the peacemakers, for they shall be called sons of God" (Matt. 5:9). These truths are good in every age.

The Ages and The New Age

O disciples and peoples of faith who are spiritual descendents of peoples of faith through the ages, we come to another teaching with yet another broad perspective, no less than the whole sweep of humanity throughout history.

The sacred Scriptures of past origins speak and prophesy of the ages past and ages perhaps to come, looking to the most glorious age of full Transformation, the heavens and Earth made new, Heaven and Paradise full of all people that God has brought in, in addition to the myriads of angels. All prophecies of the past and present are still but mysteries from our human perspective, though we have already been partially enlightened, because its still so imaginably grand, unfathomable, almost unbelievable and too good to be true, where we will be glorified and holy, basically perfect, and there will be no pain, sorrow, grief, or cries.

The spiritual ages of humanity in the great Scriptures of past origins have been defined in a few key ways. The first key is faith. Through this key, we see the two major ages of mankind as the age of pre-faith, unenlightenment, and ignorance then the age of faith, enlightenment, and spiritual life and ascent. The second key is in regard to sacrifice, this universal need within human's souls to give something up in order to appease the displeasure of spirits, gods, or God and gain their favor. Throughout the ancient ages, all kinds of sacrifices, from the bloody ones of animals slain to cereal and drink offerings were common place. The two major ages then from the key of sacrifice is *the age of the bloody to the age of the non-bloody.*

With both of these keys, we see the two main sweeps of human ages on Earth. There is yet the third, and greatest Age of all, the all-glorious Age from the Transformation of souls into Paradise and Heaven.

So which of these is the "New Age"? Christianity would say that Christ's first coming, death, and resurrection ushered in the age of God's grace for humanity. This certainly qualifies for being a "New Age." But the eternal age after the heavens and Earth made anew still to come is yet more glorious still. Then Baha'ullah steps into the scene about 1,834 years after Christ's sacrifice, and he claims that he has ushered in the New Age for humanity, fulfilling all previous Scriptures and prophecies (Hopfe and Woodward, p. W14-3), which Baha'is believe. Baha'is understand Baha'ullah's declaration to be both a spiritual reality for which all past prophetic ages moved ahead to see, and an earthly reality, in the similar sense that in Islam, religion and politics are not separated-they are mixed up together. All these meanings of the "New Age" above are spiritual, and are not determined, defined by, or tie to political or social events upon the Earth.

Then, starting in the 1960's, comes the "New Age" movement. The modern religious "New Age" movement is mostly out of modern Hinduism, marked by a few Hindu gurus coming to America. Their core belief of searching to find the "God within you" instead of paying tribute to and worshipping the God in Heaven not only seems very distinct and different but even fundamentally different from the monotheistic systems. The concept of finding the "God within you," has its origins in the Upanishads in the Vedas (Hopfe and Woodward pp. 87-88). Representatives of the "New Age" movement in recent years speak of the Transformation of humanity, but they do not define what this is, how it happens, and who is the causing agent. They seem to have no clear answer on what this is or will be. In contrast, sacred Scriptures accepted by millions even billions, for the most part, have clear messages to His peoples. Several observers of the times with a monotheistic perspective have discerned at least a subtle deception in this movement as a whole. Let the Spirit guide you, not to be quick to judge, but be God's light, marked by love. From the monotheistic, there is no question that God is a definite Being apart from us, not inside us in all His glory, and perfect, who expects our worship of Him. Can human souls earnestly seek, pray, and worship the God of Heaven and Earth who reigns above in all glory at and the same time seek to find the same God inside their souls? I will leave this to you according to the Spirit guiding you and your piety.

There are plenty of religious visionaries or leaders who have tried to syncretize at least two different religions into one.30 We could even find someone who has tried to marry the "New Age" movement with Christianity or more generally the monotheistic view of God. Shri Mataji Nirmala Devi is one such person. The "Age of Aquarius" was associated with the New Age movement and popularized in the song by the same title. Starting first from its meaning as an astrological age of the 11th zodiac sign, it came to take on religious, divine, and eschatological meaning. Shri Mataji Nirmala Devi, raised a Christian but married a Hindu, defined it this way: "The Aquarian Age is pre-eminently a spiritual age, and the spiritual side of the great lessons that Jesus gave to the world may now be comprehended by multitudes of people, for the many are now coming into an advanced stage of spiritual consciousness...." (Mataji Nirmala). This is indeed an interesting blend of the Hindu-based New Age and Christianity, at least viewing Jesus as a great guru.

We have thus surveyed the religious meaning of the ages of humankind and the New Age.

Most religions are other-worldly, spiritual and heavenly minded. They spend most of the time focused on a plane higher, with little attention to the earthly realm of worldly politics. But for Islam, politics and religion is one package deal. God is the Sovereign of the universe above all earthly kingdoms and politics, but the religion on earth is understood to dominate all earth and its kingdoms. The spiritual disposition is ever mindful of God's judgment of all souls on Judgment Day, which many have little comfort and assurance of God's forgiveness. They have more assurance of entering glory by being a martyr by dying by fighting, even if they are fighting a fellow Muslim. Paradise is essentially the New Age for Muslims.

The world defines things and terms its own way, sometimes even adopting religious terms, but changing the meaning to fit their agenda which is most often not reflecting the mind of sacred Scriptures.

But O peoples of faith renewed each day by God's grace, we look forward to the blessed eternal New Age to come.

History of Humanity: Cyclical or Linear

O dedicated disciples, we come to this advanced teaching on the history of humanity. A part of all learning is asking questions, and learning how to ask the right questions. Some questions beg an answer, that is, the answer is implied in the question or steers it in a certain way.

The question, "Is human history cyclical or linear," is one of those questions that forces the answer. It presumes an either/ or answer, one or the other. But they both can't be right, the question leads on to think. But in fact, we can see aspects to both linear and cyclical aspects in human history. Both are right, which means the question should be re-phrased, which itself is part of the learning process. But to illustrate first: is light in the physical universe a wave or a particle? One scientific experiment shows it to be a wave, and another experiment shows it to be a particle. So, we'll say, they both are right. Light is both a wave and a particle, but how you see it depends on which lens you are looking through.

Regarding human history, and even natural history, the standard accepted truth is that all has been moving forward on the framework of time. As peoples of faith enlightened by revelation, our worldview includes the truth that God created all things in this universe, of which invisible time is an aspect. It is defined by the beginning, and time continues to move forward at a steady rate all the way to the end of time, the consummation of the heavens and the Earth, of which that specific day remains a mystery to us.

Now upon this overall time, human history has been playing out since the first generation of humans on Earth. And humans built civilizations. And throughout history, civilizations have come and gone, they have risen and fallen. If one were to study this, one would find out that knowledge, information, ideas, artwork, and even some Scriptures from previous civilizations were passed on to new civilizations that rose after. And so we certainly do find cycles of cultures, like the Olympic torch passed on to the next culture and civilization through transference on knowledge and ideas. But overall, all events and lives on the Earth are moving on the linear framework of time. There is both the linear and cyclical aspects to the history of humanity.

Having established this general view, even natural and secular, now let us focus on religious history and the view of religious history. In my study of world religions, I discovered a fascinating pattern. It is a belief by a peoples of faith that their ancient religion was started purely, but it later got corrupted by its own people. And God sends prophets and reformers along throughout history to get the religion back on the pure path. It is fascinating the peoples even in ancient times, specifically, in the 6th cent. BCE had this view. One of the religions that arose in this century was Jainism, an extreme ascetic path within the Hindu worldview. Hopfe and Woodward, in beginning to write about the life of Mahavira, the founder of Jainism, writes that Jains [afterwards] believed in this view of "time and religion... that over enormously long periods of time the truth is discovered, fades, and is lost, and is found again" (Hopfe and Woodward p. 123). Even in more ancient times, perhaps as much as a thousand years before Mahavira, "the pre-Zoroastrian Aryans also believed that whenever religious practices stray from the truth, prophets or reformers called Saoshyants...would restore the purity of the religion (Hopfe and Woodward p. 236).

Now let us try to put this overall picture together joined with the truth to some degree of human corruption. Upon the overall framework of time all history moves forward, lineal. Civilizations rise and fall throughout human history evidencing to some extent a cyclical nature. Then we have religious movements that started and rose, similar to civilizations, or movements within civilizations. They presumably were all started with pure ideals and intentions. But each one of them, in time, becomes impure and to various degrees, corrupt. They then need to figuratively return to their pure roots. They can't reverse time. They live in each of their moments of history. They attempt to restore their faith on the more pure ground upon which they believe it was established. Now add one more and final piece to this now complex picture: progressive revelation! Most people today have been taught the idea of progressive revelation, that throughout history, God has continued to reveal more and more truth and light to humanity. Now how do you fit the idea of progressive revelation in with the picture of time and religious history just described? I will leave you to ponder these intellectually and spiritually stimulating concepts.

Detachment

O disciples, your teaching would not be complete without the knowledge of the path and purpose of detachment, and its spiritual reality. This is a part of the spiritual path of every soul on their way to eternal bliss.

In my studies on this topic in various traditions, I discovered that virtually all of them have this concept and goal to eventually be detached from the life in the body. Herein, O keen disciples, we discover the truth of detachment. It is based on the universal truth and experience of humanity that life in the human body of flesh and bone is not Heaven. Here in the earthen body, we have pain and suffering as well as some pleasures. But the pains in the body, in part, along with the spiritual yearning of the soul, have birthed the universal quest of detachment. Each of the religious traditions speak of this universal truth in their own terms. You may not find the term "detachment" in each of their doctrines. But they have the same general or similar concept. Virtually all religions' ultimate goal is out of the body, either in

Heaven/Paradise or Nirvana. "Salvation" is an integral aspect of detachment. The term "detachment" itself is a negative term with positive meaning. To detach ourselves from this world and the body is to attach ourselves to God.

Now in regard to the human experience of working toward detachment, there are various degrees which corresponds to how rigorous each chooses their path, and may vary with the ebbs and flows of life. Some days we feel real attached to things. Other days we feel so spiritually free. But when the day of the ultimate detachment comes, then we are permanently detached, except if one reincarnates only to have to repeat the cycle of life again.

O disciples, how much we can still learn about the things of faith! The term "detachment" itself is really a metaphor for a spiritual reality. You may consider it a mental reality in your life, the degree to which you feel attached or detached to things in life. But know the truth that ultimate detachment is an objective reality, when you will actually be permanently detached from your body. It will not just be a state of mind. As sure as you know you exist, that day will surely come to you and all humans, since we are mortal. There is a higher reality in the invisible spiritual realm which we never see.

Those without faith dismiss all these realities. Do not condemn them, but love them, and help them to see the author of the universe, the Creator of all souls, and our destiny in glory, not the god of their own destiny. If it be true that we all stop existing when we physically die, that we have no souls that continue to live, just plan "annihilation" as philosophers and theologians call it, then religion cannot help us in the afterlife since there would be no afterlife. But religion is still good in this life. If greatly helps to tame the beast in human nature. Religion serves this very purpose, for which it is devoted to. Law enforcement of the state can drive the fear of consequences for those who break the law, but religion inspires the goodness to arise out of the beast of human nature better than any other agency in human society. We should grant people the freedom to hold to this view of human non-existence after death. Every human deserves common human dignity all through life, to the very end, even to their last moment.

But this worldview and belief system of mere physical human existence has not explained nor has it ever made sense to those who have faith in the "beyond." The other view fails to explain how this world and universe came about; and it fails to explain the purpose of life, that is, one that satisfies the longing of the human heart and soul. So many human beings have felt this longing so deeply, that it has led them to a degree of faith, even if they have been a functional agnostic.

Returning to detachment, we find strong traditions of practices of detachment going back to ancient times in various places, from Hindu ascetics and mystics through the ages, Jain ascetics monks, and Buddhist ascetic monks, Christian ascetic monks of the early Middle Ages, and Muslim mystics. The teaching of Detachment gets carried forward all the way up to the 19th century in Persia, as was also taught by the founder of the Baha'i Faith, Baha'ullah. Simpler disciples would simply accept revelation from God as the source of texts written by inspired writers. But scholars seek further to other sources as well. So in considering the possible influence on Baha'ullah's exposure of the teaching of detachment, the first place one should turn is the Muslim mystics and dervishes. But I highly suspect that as a young man, Husayn Ali (Baha'ullah) was taught well in the royal family in which he was raised, and in his royal education, it included the reading of the famous Indian Bhagavad-Gita, a classic sacred text of Hinduism. In this famous Gita, it teaches of detachment perhaps more so that any other sacred text in the world. "For when a man loses attachment to sense-objects and to action, when he renounces lustful anxiety and anxious lust, then he is said to have climbed to the height of union with Brahman" (The Song, p. 63). If Brahman is synonymous with God as understood by the monotheistic traditions, oh how we would love for this to be true, to be in full union with God! Is this not our ultimate goal? But seconds after our minds and souls have hoped this to be really true now, we are reminded of our earthen bodies with beating heart, clinging flesh, still in the glove of sin. Our natures are not yet transformed. Mystics believe they achieve this height while still in their earthly body. But is their nature really transformed? Do they ever lose patience? Do they understand their wives and children perfectly? Do they love God perfectly and do they love all people perfectly? May we all be transformed but may none of us deceive ourselves to think we are what we are not.

In returning again briefly to the Indian Hindu tradition of detachment, we should find it very intriguing in light of their firm belief in reincarnation. Is it that the practitioners are so eager to get out of this life only to reincarnate into the next life, go through this cycle in a new body, only to seek out of that one, in order to get into yet another body and repeat it over and over? This not only does not make sense but it approaches insanity. The better way to see it, as they do from their worldview, it is an accepted fact of life that they will repeat many life cycles because of karma. But it is believed that through the extreme ascetic practices, including long hours of meditation and yoga, that they will be released (moksha, Hopfe and Woodward p. 89) from the karmic cycle, achieve permanent detachment when the soul returns to Brahman.

But most peoples of faith live normal lives of work and raising families. Then at the end of their life, they too know they will have to be detached from all earthly things.

O disciples, learn from the teachings of sages through the ages. Learn their wisdom, learn the validity and goodness of the paths which they teach. And accept the love they give, and be the light of love to others. If you choose the ascetic or mystic path, chose it for the right reasons, not shirking responsibility. Virtually all the sages and teachers through the ages allowed their disciples to freely chose the path to follow them. They may have asked for a time commitment, say of two, three, or five years. But be cautious of a teacher who takes away freedom from you and imposes unreasonable restrictions. Blessed are those who are free to come and stay awhile, and then free to return home or get back to work. The love commitment that brothers of an order have for each other and for God is very commendable. Love should be the ultimate motivation in every order, love of God, love for the teacher, the teacher's love for the disciples, and the brothers love for each other. What all of them reveal and hold in common is the truth that none of us can be permanently attached to anything in earthly life as it is. We must pass from it to the better more enduring glorious state. Devout religious ones who have gotten the love of God, the strong sense of the other-world in their soul, the Spirit-wrought holiness, know that nothing on this Earth can match the beauty and glory that await us, not even a scene of beautiful flowers, the sound of a harmonious orchestra, the tastes of delicious food, nor even sexual ecstasy.

In conclusion, the essence of detachment is being heavenly-minded, not earthly minded. It is the awareness of and the lifestyle of not being attached to the things of this world. It prepares the soul for the permanent detachment on that step into eternal bliss of which salvation is a metaphor or important step in the ultimate goal.

Salvation and Ascent of People of Faith

Fundamental to understanding what "salvation" means, O disciples and peoples of faith, is to know what one is saved *from*. Scholars are good at using abstract words such as "salvation" without defining their meaning and use of the term. If there is nothing from which a person is saved *from*, then the word "salvation" has very little meaning, like a well without water. The biblical tradition is clear from the contexts of each of its books what salvation is and from what the people of faith will be saved from.

Firstly, the Bible with clear prophetic voice declares that the people of faith in God will be saved from persecutions and tribulations on Earth. This does not mean that God snatches people up from the Earth without allowing them to go through any tribulation. John's Gospel is clear when Jesus Christ says, "In this world you will have tribulation, but be of good cheer, I have overcome the world" (John 16:33 NKJV). The Greek word for "tribulation" is *thlipsis* which simply means stress, distress, hard circumstances, trouble, and suffering (CGEDNT pg. 83). What the biblical message is here, in essence, though we will experience stress, distress, hard times in life and from events on the Earth, they will have no lasting consequence to us. They will not determine our destiny. For our destiny is with and in God, and in His time, whether by our own natural death, or accidental death, or the rapture to come, God will bring us to Himself in glory, at which time we are completely saved from all human and earthly stress and troubles.

Secondly, in biblical theology, the number one problem of humanity on Earth is sin, brought on by the spiritual fall of Adam and Eve in the Garden of Eden. Therefore, in essence, salvation is being saved from sin and sin's consequences and results. One of the consequences of sin, according to the apostle Paul, is that death came to all people as a result of Adam's sin, which spread through all people through the seed. (c.f. Rom. 5:12).

Thirdly, as mentioned in the second point above, salvation is being saved from death. The biblical understanding is not physical death, but spiritual and everlasting death apart from God. The biblical understanding is this is what all people deserve as a result of sin, but God in His grace redeemed us, desires us to live forever with Him in Heaven. After our sins are annihilated at that great step of our journey is taken, when God purifies and glorifies us, taking us up to Heaven, not judging us to be dammed in hell, is the time when this ultimate salvation comes to us.

In summary, there are two spheres or levels of salvation which parallels the two main realms: salvation from earthly trouble, trials, distresses, and salvation from eternal death apart from God in the spiritual realm.

O blessed ones, God's desire is for us to complete the path of ascent to blessed eternity: salvation to glory in Heaven and Paradise. The ascent is another facet of the diamond of these truths. The accent of humanity focuses on human achievement and development in character, nobility, civility, and spiritually. The ascent of the people of faith does consider the human side: our thoughts, attitudes, deeds/actions and our spiritual relationship with God. The term "accent" normally implies human actions, that we are the ones who walk on two legs up the hill to, for example, a sacred place. But the psalms of Ascent in the Hebrew Scriptures, book of Psalms (Psalms 120-130) should be understood in their context collectively, and in context of their antecedent, Ps. 24:3-4 which reads, "Who may ascend into the hill of the LORD? Or who may stand in His holy place? He who has clean hands and a pure heart.... (NKJV). Together, they express a balance that there is something on our part to do but more importantly, what God does. If God does not forgive us our sins, the number one spiritual problem of humanity, it does not matter how much we do, we will not achieve ascent. Do not be deluded to think as millions of religious people throughout the ages have so thought, that "if only I do this, this, and this, I am safe and will be on good terms with God for good or that I will get to Heaven." Do not be deceived to think that you can lift yourself to Heaven. I say, O blessed ones, that it is good for us to desire the pure goal of ascent to live in glory with God in Paradise and Heaven for ourselves and for others. But how will it be achieved and actualized? Only by God's mercy and grace. Only by His mercy and grace He allowed the saints before us to enter in, and He will allow us to enter in. It does not rest on the number of penances, although God loves a contrite heart, or the number of prayers or rosaries we do, or by any pilgrimages to sacred places we make, or by any special vows, pacts, or covenants we make with God. It is by his mercy and grace and power that He will purify us of sin, transform our corruptible nature into the incorruptible, and bring us into the glory that awaits.

New Age teachers speak of a spiritual transformation of humanity, which seems akin to the ascent of humanity. But they often speak in unclear terms. Salvation would not be complete or realized if God turns away the seeking soul at the Great Judgment.

The Great Judgment of Souls

As we have highlighted, O conscientious peoples of faith, the truth of God's judgment of all souls has been held by billions through the ages even now into the 21st century. We need not hammer this point, especially for precious souls that already feel the weight of sin. No human soul, no matter how spiritual they think they are, should race to this Day. It will be the Day of full sobriety upon all souls, as we stand before the Judge of all souls, and the books of our lives are open and known completely. We will be utterly naked. None can hide or cover themselves. This is a necessary step, the beginning step of our purgation which leads to transformation and glorification. Detachment takes place upon giving up the earthen body before appearing before God's awesome Throne.

Blessed are the souls to whom God imputes His righteousness, the righteousness of Abraham by faith to whom God brings into glorious Heaven. Unfortunate are the souls God's sends away to the darkness.

The peoples of faith have been divided on whether a soul's state is sealed upon death, or whether their state is affected by the prayers and rituals of living believers on Earth on their behalf after death. I commend this to your own study and seeking the truth on this matter by the aid of the Spirit. I will not indoctrinate you into any one position. But as you go to search, consider the natural religious nature of human beings, the desire to perform rituals in belief of achieving merit before God. Not all of it is based on revelation and truth, but on mankind's soulishness. God will guide you by His Spirit, O seeker of truth. The key to this truth is the mystery of when God judges the souls after physical death. Biblical Scripture (and perhaps also the Avesta and Quran) have left open a huge gap of time and interpretation as to the state of souls who have already died to the time of the Great Judgment. No prophecy of Scripture is clear on the chronologically of the state of the souls who have already died. The peoples of faith have been living in the "in-between" time of the prophecies and the Great Judgment where all souls will get their blessing or sentence of their eternal destination, either to Heaven or to Hell.

Heaven and Hell

Much has been said and taught about Heaven and Hell through the ages, O disciples and peoples of faith. Through the ages, the belief in Heaven and Hell as real places were inspired by sacred texts and enlivened by vivid sermons. Add to this fact, fanciful artistic images by artists with great and sometimes wild imaginations producing graphic imagery that have been carried forward into the 21st century. Many educated people in modern times have dropped the belief in the reality of such portrayals, especially on Hell, some considering a superstitious concoction.

But we find from ancient times, the concept of a hell appearing in many places among various peoples in the Zoroastrian-Hebrew traditions and outside them. Was this concept a part of spiritual-natural revelation that dawn on many human beings from ancient times, not by indoctrination by Zoroastrian or Jewish priests? If this place is real, we don't want to go there at all let alone spend any time there. It is much safer to live this life in fear, faith, and trust in God, confessing our sins to God, receiving His forgiveness to escape the darkness and fires of hell, than to disregard it in this life thinking its just a concoction of human imagination, only to find oneself in reality of hell when its too late.

There are some enlightened one who have come to the realization that it would be unjust for a just God to condemn souls to eternal hell who have finitely committed bad or evil deeds during the short span of their lives compared to eternity. It seems grossly unfair to condemn a person to a torturous eternal hell for wrong choices of a finite life on earth. This is a rational view, but truth is greater than our fallible rationalism.

Some have come to understand hell as a myth, a concept developed within the imaginative mind of man, and then developed into a theological system. In this view, Zoroaster of ancient Persia in the 2nd or early 1st millennium BCE, is probably the first one who imaginatively created this myth and developed a theological and ethical system which included a hellish hell for the unrighteous. In time, Zoroastrians passed this onto Judaism, it is supposed (but which hard historical facts are lacking), through the Babylonian portal. This view does not consider divine revelation, and therefore lacks faith.

Whether only man-made myth or divine revelation, the belief in Heaven and Hell gets carried forward and funneled through blessed teacher Jesus Christ who clearly articulates the imagery of hell as a permanent place of "weeping and gnashing of teeth." This belief gets codified in the New Testament canon and Christianity thus has carried this belief solidly into the 21st century. Muhammad of Islam also believed in Hell. It was his main concern with his unbelieving Arab peoples, and so it also in a foundational belief that is found in the Quran."

Some individuals have come to believe, based on their own hellish experiences, that there is plenty of hell on earth, they thus find in hard to believe that God is that cruel or harsh to sentence people to an eternal hell. Some have experienced excruciating physical or emotional pain, that their reasoning seems justified. In the moments of great pain, we cry out, "Why?!!! Why God, do you allow so much pain to come to us?" So indeed have experienced a "hell" on earth. But this is a rationalism based on the fallible mind which cannot override truth. We must seek the Spirit of God's truth on all matters including this matter of eternal consequence, since as creatures, we do not create truth nor is objective truth subjective to us.

Turning then to the leaven of Heaven, we ponder its wonder, glory, and eternity. If there is any doctrine that seems to truly inspire and satisfy the soul with eternal bliss and blessing, it is the doctrine of Heaven.

That better place that many hope to obtain is Heaven. "Heaven," most glorious and splendid and inspiring of perhaps all thoughts to have come to human minds, have been most clearly articulated by the sacred texts of the monotheistic faith traditions. But they all have only given us glimpses of this glory, leaving it to Medieval and modern religious traditionalists and novelists to depict their imaginations of human journeys from hell to heaven.[31]

The truth that has dawned on the hearts and souls of millions is that Heaven is a place of eternal blessedness in God's presence. The second truth is that God desires people to dwell in Heaven after the Great Judgment in the hereafter. There remains the mystery of which souls get to go straight into Heaven and which ones remain in the ground until Resurrection Day, which inaugurates Judgment Day. The pure teaching of Heaven could led us to meditate, praise, sing, and dance for days and days in this life, in unity with the community of faith.

But there comes moments to sit again, and be fed on more learning, O blessed disciples. The truth of one glorious Heaven is good enough for me. I do not fathom the tradition of multiple levels of Heaven. There was a Jewish tradition of seven levels of Heaven in the first century CE The apostle Paul refers to a man "caught up to third heaven..." (2 Cor. 12:2). Centuries later, we find also a tradition of seven Heavens (or levels of Heaven) in Islam in connection with the prophet Muhammad's vision taken up to all the levels guided by Gabriel (Calder, Mojaddedi, and Rippin p. 21-24). The sacred Scriptures themselves except for Paul's reference speak of Heaven. When we speak of Heaven, we speak of the highest level. The reservation I have with teaching on the levels of heaven is it smacks of human teaching, setting up intrinsic esoteric and Gnostic meanings which seems to control which humans beings determine passes through or not. Let us not open the door to corrupting God's truth of grace. God grants us into Heaven not by our deeds but by His mercy and grace.

How can we talk about Heaven without mentioning depictions of it? The few depictions of Heaven in the sacred Scriptures and then in the traditions that follow evidence the cultural eyes through which these people saw, and usually described in tangible terms. In the Hebrew tradition, it was sitting underneath a fig tree. In the Christian tradition, there are several images with several Old Testament allusions like "eating from the "Tree of Life" (Rev. 2:7). In the Arab Islamic tradition, it is like eating dates under palm trees of an oasis. There are additional traditions such as feasting, dancing virgins, and idyllic scenes. Are we to understand this literally or figuratively, actually on a new Earth made into Paradise or spiritual metaphors? God has not yet revealed all the mysteries of Heaven. He has given us just enough to wet our appetite. Let each one consider these according to their piety and how the Spirit may lead them.

Because we yet remain in the body, be encouraged and exhorted in these final words on this blessed doctrine.

Believe and trust in God for your eternal salvation and transformation into eternal glory. Do not trust in human beings, including those you love, even devoted spiritual teachers, to guarantee your way to Heaven. Trust in them up to their human ability but no further. Only God can grant you the Way eternally. The Spirit of God is a guide for all souls that earnestly seek God and His Spirit. A truth that many "Spirit-filled" believers have been enlightened with is that the Spirit does not force itself on anyone. The Spirit of God does not lead anyone astray.

Rest in the assurance of God's eternal love for us, that He does not turn anyone away who humbly comes to Him repentantly. He is a loving father, like a grandfather so happy to see his grandchildren. When we are in Heaven, God will be the happiest grandfather of all.

The Consummation of "Heavens" and Earth

Finally, dear faithful disciples, we come to the topic of the Consummation of the heavens and Earth. So what is meant by "consummation of the heavens and Earth" or the "final consummation? Zarathrustra, the prophet of ancient Persia taught it (Hopfe and Woodward p. 242). The Hebrews, pre-Rabbinic Jews taught this too. And Jesus Christ taught this, re-confirming the previous prophecies. In the words of Isaiah's prophecy: "Fix your eyes on this: I [God] create new heavens and a new earth (Is. 65: 17 MT). The final consummation in essence means God bringing to completion human history, the end of things as we know it in the earthly sense. Isaiah speaks of a new heavens and new Earth but does not describe what will happen to the current Earth. But it has popularly been understood as the "end of the world." This is one of the final events in all the eschatological (end-times) prophecies. The word "consume" is a strong word. In human experience, fire is one of those powerful forces in nature which can consume things very quickly. So when the apostle Peter prophesies that on "the day of the Lord…the elements will melt with fervent heat and the heavens…elements will melt with fervent heat" (2 Pet. 3:10, 12) seem to be joined with Isaiah's prophecy of the new heavens and new earth. What we have been told is sufficient for faith. God has not considered it necessary to reveal details. But rest assured, God is in the details.

The teaching of the consummation of the heavens and Earth has served a few purposes. First, it teaches us that God is in control of all history. He is also in control of this whole universe. We know not all have a belief in the global God, the God of the universe. But we should maintain our faith. Secondly, it warns souls. Thirdly, it prepares souls for eternity. Blessed are those who trust in God, and come to the blessed glory.

Concluding Words

O friends, there is no end to our learning and growing in the things of God, faith, and religion in our earthly life. Blessed has been this time together with you. Sacred are the hours in the words of Scripture. Through the many hours in the word, take breaks to rest your mind. Follow my instruction to continue to study. Remember, God does not lead anyone astray. But various traditions between each other can cause some confusion as to what is true and correct. Seek the Spirit of God to lead you to all truth (c.f. Jn. 16:13).

Among peoples of faith around the globe, some are optimistic in these 21st century days, such as for seeing the continued spiritual awakening of humanity, seeing bright days ahead in this new age. And there are some who are more pessimistic, focusing on the End Times prophecies of tribulation, of which the current global economic troubles is seen as a sign these days have come. Whether you are more optimistic or pessimistic, be strengthened in your faith which has been nurtured. Believe in your blessed eternal life with God in heavenly glory, whatever happens on this temporal world. O human soul, if you are discouraged with what you see when you look around in this world, be not ultimately discouraged. Hope in a better tomorrow, if not in this world, in the blessed hereafter. And instill this hope in your children, grandchildren, and great-grandchildren. If the corruption in this world makes you sickened, be reminded that it has been actively around since before the days of Noah. But when you stand for goodness, rightness, and divinely inspired righteousness, you do make a difference. Stand firm but with humility, and lead others on this righteous path, and God has promised many studded jewels like shimmering stars in your crown. Look beyond this world, look above to your God, Savior, and Hope of eternal glory. Be wise, guided by the Spirit of God, keeping your eyes ultimately on God.

Part V
Exhortations and

Moral Guidelines Exhortations
To Individual Souls

"Fear, love, and trust in God above all things"[32] and worship and adore Him.

Give offerings or "sacrifices" to God, preferably non-bloody, and certainly not human sacrifices is this age.

Gather together on a regular basis with others of your faith tradition, for the sacred gatherings and fellowship and social times.

Love yourself.

Love and care for your family members, even if you don't like every one of them.

"Love one another" (Jn. 15:12, 17)

Love and have compassion on strangers, the poor, and destitute.

Give the same respect and dignity to all other humans as you would want them to give to you.

Live by the Golden Rule. Do not just give it lip service. Put your heart, soul, and mind to live by this wisdom and light that dawned around the world.

Open foremost your spiritual ears to hear God. And actively listen to others.

Be trustworthy. Do what you say you will do, unless it was foolish. Work to build trusting relationships with family members, friends, and co-workers.

Set your mind on God, yet be responsible for all your earthly responsibilities.

Lead a life before God, family, and community with upright behavior, blameless, and an example to others.

Have wholesome speech through day and night, home and out, constructive speech, exuding with peace, care, and love in your relationships with family and friends and strive for peaceful speech even in business dealings and work affairs.

Seek good. Pursue it like a great treasure. Go after it like a lost lover. Dedicate your life to good, perpetually seeking goodness for self, for others around you, and for making a difference in the world. Seek to continually live with the ethic of "good thoughts, good words, and good deeds" (Zoroastrian ethic, quite similar to the Hebrew-Jewish and Christian ethics).

Shun evil. Run from it. Do not open your door to it. Do not keep company with those who want to steer your life down a bad path.

Respect and honor those who are in authority: your parents, religious and civil leaders, police and military officers. Do not speak bad of others including those in authority unless they have done something surely wrong and you feel it is your moral and/or social/political duty so to do.

Do not injure another human being in body or in person through words, nor take the life of a human being except and only in case of self-defense in a mortal threat situation.

Buy and possess the things you need to for yourself and family, and add in some reasonable wants for richness of life according to available funds, but don't let them possess you. (This is based on the modern word of wisdom, "Possess things but don't let them possess you." My apology for my ignorance of not knowing the originator of this and whether it has been published by someone."

Do not take anything that does not belong to you.

Do not have a serious relationship or sexual relationship with another person committed to someone else, even when they consent, out of pure love and consideration of the other committed person, even if it is a non-marriage boyfriend-girlfriend relationship.

Take care of yourself including your body, mind, and soul. All three are very important. When one aspect declines or fails, the other aspects are directly impacted. While ultimately, the spirit/soul is greater, since it will go on to eternity, in this life, the body is so important. It is your one body you have through this life. Balance the nurturing of the spiritual soul and the physical body. Eat healthy and exercise and study to feed the intellect and soul, and worship/meditate.

Keep yourself from places or situations in which you know you will be tempted to go down a path of sin or wrong, or non-pleasing behavior before God.

Do not covet other peoples possessions, property, or positions, nor be envious or jealous.

Live a moral life first and foremost before God, for your own sake, and also before family, neighborhood, community, and world. Take the Ten Commandments seriously, and other basic moral codes which essentially say the same thing. Keep the Commandments not to get merit before God or think it you earn your way into Heaven, but out of love of God and integrity of your character.

Follow God first and foremost, the sole perfect and faithful one. Second, follow the leaders God places in your life, but not with complete dependence, knowing that they are of the same fallible nature as yourself. Third, follow your heart but with caution, because some times our own hearts, laden with desire, pull us in directions away from God's commandments, and our hearts our also touched by corruption. But our hearts, sometimes led by God's Spirit, steers us into the path of our destiny.

Take care of the Earth and all its resources. Not only did God create and place all these resources here, He really owns everything. The is impacted by humans, and life systems are all connected together. They should not be taken for granted.

Conquer your demons, whatever they may be, fear, chemical dependency, etc.

Do not waste your life. Strive to reach your full potential.

Do not fret over unbelievers, scoffers, skeptics, or critics, but remain centered in your faith in God, rising above in a tranquil state. God just may have sent some of them to test and strengthen you. Pray for them and love them. It may be that some of them one day will become a beautiful believer.

Live peaceably with all people in as much as is possible and depends on you (c.f. Rom. 12:18).

Men, treat women as gifts of God to be cherished.

Women, dress decently, respectively, modestly in public, not exposing skin that welcomes the eyes of strangers. Reserve your body for your spouse. Do not invite or entice others into sin of lust.

God has made everyone unique. He has given a special gift-mix of intellectual ability, various aptitudes, skills, creativity, and other talents. Place your life on a beautiful journey of discovering this whole gift-mix. It does not matter if your body or face is not attractive by the eye. The inner, and yet hidden gifts of God in you are waiting to be discovered, and they can only be discovered by you!

God has a purpose for you, a specific purpose, not merely a generic cookie-cutter purpose. One size does not fit all. Discover your specific mission and purpose in this life. It could manifest in so many different ways. Do not get worried if you do not have this figured out by the age of 25.

Young people, make plans for your future, for career and life. Chose an honorable profession. Lift them in prayer before God. Commit your way(s) to His care and guidance. Do not fret if you are not completely sure, as is the case for many people. It is not just the decision of a particular career path, but it is your faith that is just as important. This is what God seeks in all His children. Believe that God will bless your life within the bounds of right living, and He will.

EXHORTATIONS TO COMMUNITIES OF FAITH IN CONGREGATIONS OR GROUPS

Strive for unity and peace within your own community of faith and between your community of faith and other communities of faith.

In times of discussions, arguments, or debates, listen to the other's views. But have courage to speak the word that is in the spirit of God's word, will, and peace. On Occasion, it may even mean to express opposition to another's statements or views that seem unwise or not in alignment with the spirit of grace, love, sound teaching, fellowship, and unity or mission for the religious community. Spiritual leaders, exhort your members to right living and good works.

Strengthen each other in faith. Encourage one another. Care for one another, especially the weak, orphaned, sick, shut-in, and widowed. Advocate for those who are too weak or unable to speak up legally for themselves. Comfort each other in times of losses. Keep declaring messages of hope to peoples in this world. Eagerly expect God's daily blessings unending!

POSTSCRIPTS AND APPENDICES

ABBREVIATIONS TABLE

B.C.E.	Before the Common Era
C.E.	The Common Era

Biblical Books in the Order in which they appear:

Gen.	Book of Genesis
Ex.	Book of Exodus
Lev.	Book of Leviticus
Deut.	Book of Deuteronomy

1 Sam.	1st Book of Samuel
Kgs.	Book of Kings
1 Chron.	1st Book of Chronicles
Ps.	Book of Psalms
Eccl.	Book of Ecclesiastes
Is.	Book of Isaiah
Ps.	Book of Psalms
Prov.	Book of Proverbs
Is.	Book of Isaiah
Jer.	Book of Jeremiah

Ezek.	Book of Ezekiel
Dan.	Book of Daniel
Hos.	Book of Hosea
Mic.	Book of Micah
Hab.	Book of Habakkuk
Hag.	Book of Haggai
Matt.	The Gospel of Matthew
Lk.	The Gospel of Luke
Jn.	The Gospel of John
Acts	The Book of Acts
Rom.	Epistle to the Romans
I Cor.	First Book of Corinthians
Gal.	Epistle to the Galatians
Eph.	Epistle to the Ephesians
Heb.	Book of Hebrews
1 Jn.	1st Epistle of John
Rev.	Revelation of John

Other Books and Abbreviations:

BHS	*Biblia Hebraica Stuttgartensia*
CGEDNT	*Concise Greek-English Dictionary of the New Testament*
LSCE	Luther's Small Catechism with Explanation
MT	Author Mark's translation of the Masoretic Text of the Hebrew Scriptures

ATTESTING TO THE SPIRIT OF GOD

This book is by no means perfect, especially as a first edition. To capture the essence of the great monotheistic faiths and bring them into the 21st century sounds like a monumental task, worthy of perhaps a life-long project. It did not fall down from heaven nor did an angel, that I am aware of, bring the words to me. By faith, however, I believe the Spirit of God guided me in the process, guiding many of my thoughts as I by intention engaged in this spiritual process. But I do not go so far as to claim inspiration as the "word of God" in the biblical prophetic sense, although I attempt to capture that prophetic voice in that section of the book. My human voice is allowed to slip into many places of the text in the Didactic/Wisdom section. This first edition will have plenty of room for improvement. This could be a lifetime project. But I wanted to get this book published in 2012.

In connection to attesting to the Spirit of God, I share this aspect of my life that ironically I consider aids in the Spirit working. I was diagnosed with dyslexia in the third grade by a private tutor. I struggled academically through the years, most pronounced in my elementary and middle school years. But by diligence, I succeeded in college, then some years later seminary but not with a "scholar's" grade point average since the day of extended test taking time based on the American Disabilities Act had not yet come. This is mentioned for the interested reader to realize scholarship did not come natural to the author, but through years of hard work. And being a slow reader, I scarcely have time to read one-fourth of all the books I wish I could read, time permitted, due to my dyslexia. Of all the sacred Scriptures of the world, I have only begun to delve into the texts outside of the Bible and the Quran. Most of the reflections that got worked into this book were from the Bible and Quran.

I attest that God worked amazingly through me in the compiling of the text in about four months (May-Aug. 2012), and how God guided me in the process. For example, I would pick up a book from one of my book shelves in which I wanted to cite a passage I remembered, and flipping through the pages and somehow in seconds finding exactly the reference I was looking to cite. This happened on more than one occasion. I knew God's Spirit was helping me in this process.

Without mentioning my dyslexia, one might assume from the nature of this book and the sources consulted (see below) that I am one whom scholarship comes naturally and who absorbs book information easily. This is not the case. It has come through years of hard study-kind-of-work... Interestingly, Muslims make the claim of the Prophet Muhammad's illiteracy to support the claim of their Scriptures were from God. Whether you find this a parallel or not, you decide. God be glorified in our weaknesses. God be glorified in this book. And may God be glorified forever and ever by all His children on Earth.

OVERVIEW OF THE BELIEFS EXPRESSED IN THESE SCRIPTURES

Below, is an overview of the beliefs expressed in this Scripture. It is convenient for the student and other interested readers. Perhaps it is even thumbed through by some before reading the main portions of this book to decide whether you want to read or buy this book. Even if you do not believe a significant portion of the statements below, you still may find several passages in this book that expresses universals that you may hold to, and perhaps your heart will be touched by. So you too are invited in.

After the decision was made to expressly write this book from a monotheistic perspective, the perspective most comfortable to the author, it colored the approach of every topic essentially in this book. Its purpose is to try to bridge understanding among the peoples of faith around the world, but it maintains its footing from monotheistic viewpoint. The author then strove for consistency in this approach and assist in presenting a cohesive book. Worldviews and beliefs go hand-in-hand. The worldview then it operates with is a theistic one, specifically, monotheistic, with God as the Creator, Sovereign of the universe. At the same time, it articulates the commonly held dualism of a heavenly immaterial world and a material universe, spirit and material, spirit and flesh. Various dualistic beliefs have been held by more than a few influential belief systems from ancient times. The dualistic view of the universe held in this book does not compete with the monotheistic worldview because it believes that God created both of these two main dimensions: immaterial and material, with the material inferior. Some form of dualistic belief of the universe has been found in so many belief systems, it is accepted as universal truth by so many. It is found in Platonism, Neo-Platonism, Zoroastrianism, Manichaeism, Christianity, Judaism, Islam, Hinduism, Jainism to name the mostly recognized ones.

Not everyone believes the monotheistic way. But all are invited to find universal truths, spiritual aspirations and spiritual nobility in this text. May all be inspired and work toward peace on Earth, one of the main purposes of this book.

The following list is now the overview of beliefs presented:

God is One and All-Supreme and Eternal.

God is the Creator and Source of all things (although not believe He created evil)

There is a heavenly immaterial realm where the angels live, and a material

Universe and its parallel dualism: spirit and body, spirit and flesh.

God created a beautiful Earth.

God created human beings, beautiful creatures and made them as the crown of Creation on Earth.

God created all people (while humans do reproduction like animals.

God is the Designer and Power behind all life and creates every human soul).

Life is sacred.

Every human being contains a part of the "image of God," and deserves Dignity and respect.

God created both male and female, and both genders have spiritual equality before God.

God assigned to humans the role of being the chief caretakers, stewards of the Earth, to protect life and minimalize pollution.

All humans are corrupt in relation to God's perfect holiness, while also possessing

The aspect of the "image of God," and all the human positive qualities.

Humans are capable of both much goodness and horrible evil.

God is loving, merciful, gracious, compassionate, and just. His justice means

That He has to deal with human sin, remedy this great problem.

God's desired destiny of all human souls is heavenly Paradise where there is no sin, pain, sorrow, or grief.

In order for human souls to enter God's perfectly holy heavenly Paradise, each human soul needs to be purified from sin and sin annihilated.

God judges all human souls. Judgment Day is still to come.

God makes the salvation of souls possible through His grace.

The Day of Transformation is when our corruptible takes on the incorruptible and the mortal takes on the immortality.

God's living Word transcends earthly temporal reality, yet comes tangibly to people through the spoken and written word in human languages by chosen vessels moved, inspired by God's Spirit.

God's living Word is very important for the nurturing and sustaining faith in human souls, for inspiring hope, and comforting.

Faith is essential for human beings to think, feel, experience their Faith, hope, and salvation.

Pious human beings created and create religions, often arising out of a core of originally-divinely or semi-divinely inspired messages, but all messages are received corruptedly because all the recipients are corrupted.

There are many spiritual/religious works: prayer, fasting, penance, temple offerings, charity, etc. all of which may be of religious and spiritual benefit but none nor all to the point of effecting salvation or even guaranteeing God's favor, only a contrite repentant heart crying out to God, opens God's grace.

Faith in one's salvation should not be based on any religious, spiritual, human Works, but only by reliance on the grace of God.

AN INTERPRETATION GUIDE
FOR THESE SCRIPTURES

To discover the interpretations of the world's sacred Scriptures is to discover a dynamic living history, living in the communities of faith long after they first were written. Interpretation has always been more of an art than a science.[33]

Texts and their interpretations have adapted to the needs of contemporary communities of faith as their Scriptures get passed from one generation to the next. No matter how loud and clear an ancient prophet was, he was a mortal who passed on, and so who can authoritatively speak for any of the prophets after they are gone? This is to say, "Prophet_____, what did you mean when you said or wrote this_____?" This is will also be an interpretation issue.

So it will be with this text, if it becomes received as a sacred text and outlives myself. Readers may ask, "What was in his thoughts or mind when he wrote _____?" Interpreters will have to do their best in studying all things in context and use sound judgment.

All the established sacred Scriptures of the world have taken on a life of their own, way beyond the original writers. These original writers or authors, once they gave up the earthly body, had no control over the texts of their books, how carefully they were handled or how much editorial work a later scribe or monk may decide to insert or rearrange. This author, having studied these issues is not naïve to this possibility after he is gone from earthly life. By faith and trust, he releases these Scriptures freely to peoples of faith in the contemporary time and for the future. He trusts the Spirit of God will guide its transmission and sound interpretation. At the same time, there is openness to them being alive in the communities of faith, speaking in fresh and sometimes "creative" ways, applying them to their time and culture.

Sound interpretation begins in the mind. In one's mind is unsound, it matters not how clear and simple a passage is. If they are asked to explain it, they will take the simple and clear and make it sound hard and unclear. "God is not the author of confusion," one scripture verse says (I Cor. 14:33). If God desires "all to be saved," as another scripture says (I Tim 2:4), and faith is important for salvation, and understanding is an important aspect to faith, then it stands that God's desire is to make His messages clear, with the exception of perhaps some of His prophetic oracle that deals with deep prophetic words and mysteries. But woe to the person who deliberately takes clear words of Scripture, perverts their clarity, darkens or confuses them, and leads people astray. God will have severe judgment for those souls-God is the Judge.

The following principles presented are guidelines, not laws or rules, but they do flow from plain sense of words and metaphorical and spiritual meaning that spiritually minded people will be able to grasp. They also express the writer's thoughts so that contemporary readers as well as those in the future will have a good grasp of how the writer intended the passages to be understood, whether they agree or not. In interpreting, we should always keep in mind the intended meaning by the revelator, the Spirit of God. The Spirit's work of inspiration, without force or bodily possession, could have moved thoughts upon the writer to write, conveying meaning beyond what the writer was consciously aware of or had knowledge about.

As you probably know, interpretation is even more of an art than a science. But it has a valid "scientific" process too, that is, the careful study of the meanings of words in their various contexts and through the grammatical contexts, and then panning out to the linguistic, cultural, historical, and geo-political contexts.

What are the linguistic, cultural, historical, and geo-political contexts for these Scriptures? There were written in the English language, initially over the period from 2004 to 2012 and compiled in 2012 into a book, in Florida, USA, by an American. 2012 is eleven years after the fateful date of September 11, 2001. The writer spent almost a year studying as a graduate student in Israel and has been deeply impacted by Middle Eastern culture on top of his American cultural roots. And in geo-political economic context, it is an age of the "Global Village" with international commerce happening all over the globe. And this age in technology is (back to cultural context) is the most sophisticated the world has even seen in history so far, in the electronic and digital age not only with personal computers by hand held computer, Internet, texting, and cell phone communication devices. But faith and religion is still quite alive on planet Earth, as the writer tells his college religion students, although there are a gradually growing number of people who do not identify with any one religion or may not have a faith (we could call functional atheism or agnosticism).

The first principle is that the words are intended to make grammatical sense in its original language: English. The rules of English grammar are literal guides to understanding the meaning of the words, since context is so important to meaning. But the reader should not assume that a specific word used more than once will always be used in the same sense or with the same meaning. Let the context always guide you.

Keep in mind the ultimate spiritual intent of these messages, which are at a higher level of understanding than mundane earthly things. Some words may be loaded with rich theological meaning which leaves the reader to try to unpack and understand.

The words are intended with good intention for the impact of the readers. Put positive construction on them.

....By faith, people believe that God's Spirit is an active force even in this world, as well as in guiding human vessels past and present in bringing messages to humankind. Pray and seek God's guidance in understanding and interpreting the texts.

These Scriptures take a universal perspective, or attempts to in all things, imperfectly. This is not intended to force absolutism upon no one. It may be another way of thinking than you are used to where in this age, relativism is commonly held. Distinguish between a universal perspective, like looking down upon the Earth from outer orbit, and imaginatively viewing all of humanity, all the cultures and nations, etc. This is the attempted perspective. This is related to absolutism in that if a person, seeing from this perspective, believes that their particular faith/religion is the absolute truth-this is indeed possible. The book suggests a couple basic beliefs as an absolute, namely: the one God created all things, and He made all people. But the reader will discover from this book that its tone is not top-down upon you, arrogant or superior, but in the trenches of life with you wanting to lovingly lift your mind, heart, and soul to see and believe that the God who created this whole awesome universe actually individually knows and loves you!

THE AUTHOR'S BIOGRAPHICAL

The author chose the name Mark Ahavel as the pen name for this book. The reasons and meaning behind this pen name are as follows. The author had started to blog as markforgood and markforever in 2008, where "mark" was meant as a verb, not a noun, meaning "mark these words as being very enduring." And "Ahavel," which in Hebrew means "the love of God," was chosen for this book which is very fitting, emphasizing the love of God. The author submits also the following specific thoughts. 1) Sacred Scriptures reach out to many souls, pointing souls to universals; the author's names are not important in terms of the message, since they are messengers (but more important to scholars). These words may live on for many years after the author's name is forgotten on Earth. 2) Considering the reason behind the absence of many author names in previous Scriptures, their names could detract from the attempt to communicate the pure word of God and its noble universal goal. But humans, as social creatures, want to know; they are interested in "who's who." 3) The human penman is not to be worshiped, glorified, or praised by other humans; using a pen name helps to mitigate this. 4) Lastly, the pen name serves to spiritually protect the readers from lifting the author up higher than he should be and helps to protect the author from pride and arrogance. This last reason is a good-enough reason alone.

The author was born in St. Louis, Missouri in 1963 in a Roman Catholic hospital during the middle of Vatican II (1962-'64). And his exact birthday coincides with a significant event in the life of the Prophet for Muslims. And In his birth year,

1963, the Baha'i Faith celebrated their 100th anniversary and they established their International House of Justice on Mt. Carmel, Haifa, Israel. These coincides combine for some perhaps to find significance, portent perhaps of an ecumenical and interfaith destiny.

The author was baptized as an infant in a Roman Catholic parish, and was raised in a Protestant congregation and its parochial school for his elementary years. These were faith-formative years for the author, raised in a Christian tradition.

He felt the Call to the Ministry during his first two years of college. He completed his Bachelor of Arts Degree in Elementary Education at a private Christian liberal arts college in the mid 1980's.

After working a few years after college, with the sense of the Call to serve God full-time intensifying, he entered seminary, earning a Masters of Divinity degree in 1994.

He took an early sabbatical to study in Jerusalem, Israel, where he worked for a year toward earning an MA in Ancient History of Israel-Palestine. He returned to the U.S. to continue to serve in the pastoral ministry in the States.

His sense of the ministry continued to expand out ecumenically beyond the smaller conservative body

In which he was serving. In time, the Spirit placed in him a global vision. At the same time, the Spirit set him on a quest for studying universals with the goal of writing them in books for various audiences.

His ecumenical ministry began as a global online prayer ministry. After launching his first basic global prayer website in 2008, it was replaced in 2009 with a new dynamic one, www.globalprayingservants.com, complete with an online temple page and prayer forum.

In 2009, the same year, he got the opportunity to begin teaching the World Religions course for the first time at the community college as an Adjunct Instructor. This did not seem coincidental. The teaching of this broad course stretched his own understanding tremendously and he intensified his research in the world's religions, beyond the Judeo-Christian foundation of which he was most acquainted.

He is a member in the American Academy of Religion and the Society for Biblical Literature.

AUTHOR'S STORY OF THIS BOOK

It is not traditionalist background that led me to write this book. From the beginning, I realized my thoughts were leading me to write a book not merely on religion or a religious book, but a sacred Scriptures, which I realized was unusual since few undertake their hand so to do. Traditionalists don't set out to write new Scriptures. They are quite content with the Scriptures they already have. There were two impetus' that took place that propelled me to actually set out to write new Scriptures. The first was the basic realization, from an historical perspective, that every sacred text of past origin, for example, the Bible, gets locked culturally in the time of which they were written, and they therefore do need to be updated. This does not deny the universal truths which they so beautifully express. But the cultural aspects, such as male dominance, ignorance of what mold and mildew is (in the Torah, priests were called into peoples homes to examine mold on the wall in someone's house, because they did not know what that white stuff or black stuff was. All they needed was some bleach, but humans did not have that knowledge yet. Humanity has advanced so much in knowledge. A new text was needed to reflect this. The second impetus was actually getting fresh material, insights, thoughts, and messages I received from the period of 2004 to 2012.

All the developed religions already have their own Scriptures. The majority of the practitioners are satisfied with them. Many of them believe their Scriptures are the voice and word of God to humanity on Earth. Therefore, what need of any other Scriptures? The thought of writing a new Scripture would not only be far from their minds, but unthinkable, perhaps even taboo. What possesses a person to write a sacred Scripture in the 21st century? Why would a clergyman from one established faith tradition set out to write a new set of Scriptures? From a clergyman's perspective, his work may be considered heretical or viewed as sacrilegious by his colleagues. "Is he out of his mind?" And would not a clergyman who sets out to write a new Scripture face the prospect of being defrocked from his clergy status? All these thoughts did occur to me, but they never weighed heavy on me, because I believed that God was leading me on this path, His Spirit giving me insights to lead to a text that is faithful to God, glorifies Him in the biblical tradition, but leaving the archaic cultural things behind. I knew it was an uncommon path, beyond mere conformity of traditionalism to a broad, ecumenical, even global outreach. Instead of fear, I had to trust God. If the consequences were losing my clergy status on the fellowship of my upbringing, I accepted that believing God was leading me on to a larger pasture in the world. What seemed closer to home was the fear of possibly losing some friends from my faith-tradition, even a close friend. But the holy Scriptures of the Bible says there is a friend who is closer than a brother. I proceeded forward to complete and publish the book, considering these costs, realizing that all servants and prophets of God have a cost to pay, a sacrifice of their normal lives, valuing the obedience to God more than the praise of man. For the sheer joy of God's Holy Spirit, I poured my mind, heart, soul, and life into this project. I allowed my mind to be gripped by the power of creative thought that came, even positive visions of the potential peace that this work could touch in the lives and hearts of millions of people. This was the main motivation for me to write this book. Therefore, believing I have been led by the Holy Spirit, I put my life on this "God assignment," as I have called it, while also running forward toward the finish line, in sobriety, and in humility, combating arrogance and conceit all along the way. It is also possible that these words were not guided directly by the Spirit of God, the same Spirit who spoke through the prophets, but arose from my own years of study, from collective thoughts, from my own soul, from human will blended with altruistic desire.

The idea to write a book such as this one first came to me in 2004, as my hand-written notes in a binder for this project reminds me. The title of the first piece of writing for a future book such as this evidences a clear thought of the nature of this work as a sacred text: "A Bible for a New Age of Humanity (an introduction to)." Easily detectible appears to be a Baha'i Faith influence; only I don't believe I started attending occasionally (and just for a season) the local Baha'i house until 2005 again a couple times in 2006.

When I was first conscious of this prospective book project, writing a new sacred Scriptures, I was humorously cognizant advice of a seminary professor I remembered regarding if we ever get the idea of writing a new liturgy (which in turn would certainly apply to Scripture too). In his traditional view, even writing a liturgy was a taboo. He said, "If you get the idea to write a liturgy, drink two Scotch (strong alcohol), then repeat until you forget the idea." He made is point, but years later, as you can discern from the sound text of this book, I did not take his advice. I started in 2004 simply hand-writing my own thoughts and reflections that came to me. The vision in those first few years was still fuzzy as to what shape this book was going to take. In October 2010, after I had already laid down to bed at night, as my notes remind me, I got such a clear message, the Divine Spirit leading me to "write and compile all that has been given to me." From that time till and through 2012, I kept getting this message. I picked up the pace and started to type on the computer (since all were hand-written notes), word processing and compiling my notes in the spring of 2012, with my goal of finishing by the summer. I had accumulated around 200 hand-written pages of notes that would be source material for the texts of this book. And the thoughts that came to me greatly accelerated in the last two years, and I knew it was time to actually compile all my notes on my computer, plan a structure for the book, and bring it to completion.

What started as the first set of thoughts on a given day in 2004 became a series of blessed thoughts from 2004 all the way to 2012. I wrote down each piece of writing as soon as I could get a pen and paper, and I dated each piece. Some of the thoughts came like gleaming flashes of insight (Buddhist term *satori*). Outside of myself was the world of stress, the noise from the street, thoughts of needs and responsibilities. But deep inside me, I experienced a serenity, and the assurance of the Divine guidance. It seemed as if many of the thoughts flowed out of this calm deep within like an effortless transmission from the spiritual Source to my finite being in this frail vessel.

The places I was at as these thoughts came ranged from home to religious houses (church or temple) to the outdoors to market places. Some thoughts came while laying down to sleep, and some came the instant I awoke. Some thoughts came while studying at home, whether before leaving to teach my religions course, or on Sunday morning before going to church, reading the biblical Scriptures. Some thoughts came while worshipping in church. Some thoughts came while meditating in a beautiful garden or reflecting in the forest I or while walking in my neighborhood or in a park. And some thoughts came while out in other places, in the grocery store, post office, bookstore, or mall, or even while doing mundane chores like laundry. The most vivid thoughts came like a revelation of words at the end of a dream-state when waking up in the morning but flowing out of the dream-state. These in particularly more than the conscious-state thoughts was what led me to believe that the Spirit was guiding me in this book. When I committed my mind to this special effort, the thoughts would come to me while I happened to be at various places, when I returned my mind to contemplate on thoughts worthy of a Scripture for today.

The author's story of writing this book would not be complete without acknowledging mentors, those who have influenced my thinking, and those who have assisted me on this project. (See Acknowledgments).

Author's Additional Comments On This Book

Initially, the vision I had for this book was so broad as to encompass universal expression of the whole of faith in humanity globally. But I soon realized that would be near impossible, and knew I had a decision to make. I decided to squarely anchor this book from a monotheistic perspective, which is my own perspective, while striving for universal truths held common by peoples of faith around the world, not limited to monotheists.

The sacred scriptures of the ancient and modern past, especially from the Middle East, have been sources of inspiration and foundation for this work, in particular, the Jewish biblical Scriptures, the Christian Scriptures, Muslim Scriptures, and Baha'i Scriptures. They are the starting point in general to the whole of these Scriptures. This book is not a compilation of this sacred Scriptures of the past and brought into the 21st cent. A deliberate effort was made to bridge key concepts and thought patterns of the world religions. In the diligent search for universal truths, concepts, and principles, I no doubt unconsciously have written texts that make many allusions that could be found in Scriptures elsewhere well beyond my conscious awareness, due to the nature of this work, but a very limited number of sources were actually used. Human beings have been exchanging thoughts and ideas since the stone age, and parallel thoughts can occur also independently on different continents. Allusions in these texts to other texts can be explained for these reasons: the same Light in other revealed Scriptures are assimilated is subconsciously produced, or the internalized knowledge and thought patterns are consciously re-written in fresh way for today's audience, or merely coincidental or the same revealing Spirit leading. But in no wise did the author consciously copy, as in plagiarize, by not citing a source used. I have cited all the sources I actually consulted for this book, referenced them, and provided amble footnotes. That is in academic terms. In spiritual terms, I consider myself the penman in this transference of lore, prophetic word, wisdom, psalm, and sacred teachings. This book builds upon the Scriptures of the past and brings to the present fresh thoughts.

This work is a result of a major realization and a dynamic. The dynamic, namely, is a creative force which produced such a quantity and quality of beautiful thought that both surprised me and Both were necessary to create this work.

The major realization was the awareness that this world, I sensed, was ready for new scriptures. So as not to be misunderstood, myself a lover of books, especially old books, I do not mean by this that any previous scriptures should be thrown out, discarded. The realization of the need of new sacred scriptures is itself a conclusion based on a few thoughts I will summarize here. First is the fact that all sacred scriptures of ancient origin have gone through an evolution of meaning and re-interpretation. In some cases, as would be valid to hold to, each generation applying them to their time and life. But in many cases or several passages, I assert, the original context was totally different, than say, today, and the meaning has totally changed thus that generations after may in fact be in danger of misinterpreting the author's intended meaning and coming to conclusions that are way off base from the original meaning. On the other hand, there is the general rubric of interpreting sacred texts that they do take on a life of their own, and God's Spirit has Its hand in the texts and in guiding their interpretation by true seekers and devotees of God in every generation. This too is a valid thought, which demonstrates a complexity before us. But more clearly, there are some passages, I submit, that are descriptive of past historical contexts not applicable today but they still present a problem, like the extermination texts where God commands the ancient Israelites to utterly destroy the peoples of the land Canaan when they enter. I wrestled with this in both seminary and as a young pastor. Why would God command the Israelites to kill every man, woman, and child in Canaan when they enter in? Third, the realization is that the religious conflicts particularly from the 7th cent. CE to the present among Jews, Christians, Muslims, Sikhs, and Baha'is' are in part based on their sacred scriptures. The conflict, and in some cases fighting continues, because issues from their own sacred texts themselves, along with their theologies, traditions, cultural differences, are still unresolved. One could argue that it is not really the texts themselves that have caused the conflicts, but the religious peoples' *interpretations* of them. I would argue that there are a few passages in the Quran that sets Islam on a clear path of conflict with the "people of the book" (Jews and Christians), though other passages speaks peacefully of them. The number one motivation and goal of this work, therefore, is global peace, peace through a new scripture that attempts to peacefully build bridges of understanding and coalesce these universal faiths. This work articulates a unity and commonality in the spirit of a blessed peace and spirituality with a truly global perspective.

We, in the early 21st century, are poised much better today in producing a sacred text than the ancients. Other books have already been written about the issues and problems in the scripts and the transmission of the texts through the ages. I will leave the reader to research other books on these issues.

This book launches from the foundation of monotheistic sacred Scriptures. It then attempts to synthesize their voices, even the prophetic voice of the Scriptures of the past and to speak them to today's world. It attempts to weave knowledge and modern science into a sacred text. Humanity has learned so much more since the 1800's when the last of world religion's sacred Scriptures were written. This book aspiring to be a sacred Scripture, is written with much of the new knowledge of the world including science and genetics would thus make it the most modern sacred scriptures in existence in the world today.

In one of the opening versicles to this book, I highlight the fact of peoples on Earth impurely and imperfectly receiving God's pure messages to humanity. I expound on it here. Not necessarily every verse of every Scripture is from the Spirit of God. But let us assume that we are talking about messages that came from God. They begin as pure thought through God's Spirit into the mind, soul, and heart of the prophet. The prophet has to process those thoughts in human language. The message has already arrived in the impure realm of humanity. The prophet himself never has perfect understanding of God's messages, no matter how pure they begin. And then the step three, when the message is communicated to other people orally or by reading, it becomes more impure because people can only imperfectly understand God's messages. Not all of this is by fault of sin in humanity; part of it is the messages getting filtered down to us through language and human culture. As soon as the messages are conveyed to people by human default, the messages come through each of their cultural lens of the languages, and in their historical-political-geographic contexts. In addition to the cultural lens through which the message is conveyed, the message is received impurely because all people are impure (the "sin" state). Even if an angel of God is conveying a pure message directly through a prophet to people standing only one meter away, the message received would still be impure because the recipients are impure. Even though pure words of God be spoken from lips of a prophet, they are received impurely by the human listeners. The main point of this is that human beings, through their culture and pride in their culture, considered their cities better that foreigners' cities, thus Mecca and Jerusalem got pitted against one another although Muhammad's Night Vision account in which he was transported to heaven, demonstrates that God is the God of the Jews and Arabs, the God of Israel and Arabia. A secondary point from this understanding of the conveying of God's messages to humans is that it really helps us to understand why many people initially rejected the messages of prophets (whether the Hebrew prophets or the Arab people of the Quraysh tribe rejecting Muhammad's messages). Ultimately of course, both the Bible and the Quran would lead us to conclude that people not receiving the message (unbelievers) is a grave spiritual problem. But before we are quick to judge, consider ourselves, and next, consider the truth that God made us human and understands our weaknesses including the cultural lenses through which we hear and see, and that God is gracious, merciful, and patient. We need to give people time to accept the messages of God. How much time? How about a lifetime, and let God determine their destiny.

So how then can anyone receive God's pure word and or know His unadulterated truth? "Search the Scriptures," people are exhorted to do, and earnestly seek God, and you will find God, and you will find truth.

SPEAKING ON BEHALF OF GOD?

Precedence has been set in the Scriptures of the past of them claiming God is speaking in the first person. On occasion, this book speaks using this convention, of which the author was conscious, but always intended for nothing but purity and goodness of thought, Divinity focused. By definition, prophets do speak on behalf of God or gods. Let the Prophecy section of this book. Speak. Using this "convention," if you will, such as "God says…" is not intended to put words in God's mouth by any corrupt or false intention. In one human sense, it seems absurd, presumptuous, and preposterous for a human writer to write any "God says…" or "Thus says the Lord God…" statements. But that view is not from the view of faith. From the view of faith, the prophets of the past, such as the Hebrew prophets, often wrote, "Thus says God…" Certain pious ones of past ages have so penned which became sacred Scriptures, fully believing that God's Spirit was moving through them. The author of this book personally does not consider himself worthy to be among the ranks of these prophets of the past, but he has set to task using skills that God has given him which produced this text for the glory of God and for the blessing of millions of people.

Some people of faith, I humbly propose, may hear the voice of God's voice in these words to various degrees. Others may simply find the texts herein as creative human imagination through theological and global lenses. Let each be free in their will and mind so decide for themselves, uncoerced. From my perspective, I did not think I was capable of producing such a text as this. This too led me to believe that the Source, or rather, God's Spirit, was aiding me. I leave it up to the reader to decide whether the words contained in this book are pure imagination or perhaps divinely inspired or somewhere in between.

May this book coming on the scene, stand as a beacon of light of faith, from the monotheistic view and sow peace, not discord, among the peoples of global faiths in the 21st century and beyond.

AUTHOR'S CHRONOLOGY OF SOME SOURCES VIEWED OR READ

I also here document a chronology of the specific sources I consulted or viewed during the period of this book project (2004-2012) which expanded my knowledge and spiritual horizons, influenced my views, and impacted my writing of this book. The list is not comprehensive. I have viewed several documentaries and YouTube video clips for the World Religions course I teach, and none of them I used specifically for this book. They do directly relate, however, and some may have impacted my perspective, but did not consult them specifically for this book.

2004:

I discovered book: The Global God: Multicultural Evangelical Views of God, A. Spencer and W. Spencer, eds. while in Reformed Theological Seminary library, Orlando, Florida, and perused through it and took some notes.

JUNE 2005

I discovered the following two books in the local public library and perused through a portion of them, taking down some notes:

Pal Clasper's *Eastern Paths and the Christian Way*

Wayne Teasdale's *The Mystic Heart: Discovering a Universal Spirituality in the World's Religion*

MARCH 2008

I viewed "The Celestine Prophecy" DVD.

JULY 2008

I viewed the History Channel's DVD, "The History of God", based on Karen Armstrong's book by the same title, and took some notes

SEPTEMBER 2008

I viewed disc 1 of Bill Moyer's DVD documentary on "Joseph Campbell and the Power of Myth," and took some notes

OCTOBER 2008

I viewed Depak Chopra's "Seven Spiritual Laws" DVD.

Sometime in 2008 I viewed a VHS episode of great Indian epic *Maharabata*, and noted the clear emphasis of choice and free will in this classic.

AUGUST 2009

I discovered Wayne Dyer through PBS. I viewed his television seminar, "Excuses Be Gone," PBS, on August 8, 2009.

I begin to teach the World Religions course at a local college utilizing Hopfe and Woodward's book, *Religions of the World.* Eleventh Edition, Upper Saddle River, New Jersey: Prentice Hall, Inc., 2009.

2009 OR 2010

In 2009 or 2010, I happened upon Manly Hall's book, *An Encyclopedic Outline of Masonic, Hermetic, Qabbalistic and Rosicrucian Symbolic Philosophy*, while in a private library. It is not the kind of book I read, and I did not read this book, but I scanned its table of contents, and it sharpened my view of the two main spheres, the heavenly/spiritual/metaphysical and the earthly/temporal realms, which is a basic theme in my book *Light from Above.*

SPRING 2012

I viewed National Geographic's "Birth of Civilization" on DVD

SOURCES CONSULTED

Sources with no are sources I actually cite or reference in the text or footnotes of this book, but sources with the * are sources I consulted during the compiling of this book, but did not use any of its source material either by quoting or referencing.

Armstrong, Karen. *The History of God*. The History Channel. DVD. 2005

Baha'ullah. *Gleanings from the Writings of Baha'ullah*. trans. Shoghi Effendi. Willmette, IL: Baha'i Publishing Trust. 1976

Baha'ullah. *Tablets of Baha'ullah: Revealed after the Kitab-I-Aqdas*. Willmette, IL: Baha'i Publishing Trust. 1988

Bainton, Roland H. *Here I Stand: A Life of Martin Luther*. Nashville: Abingdon Press. 1978

Biblia Hebraica Stuttgartensia, 2nd ed., Deutsche Bibelgesellschaft, Stuggart, 1983

"Birth of Civilization." Washington D.C.:National Geographic. 2008. DVD

Boorstin, Daniel J. *The Discoverers: A History of Man's Search to Know the World and Know Himself*. New York: Random House. 1985.

Bright, John. *The Kingdom of God*. Nashville: Abingdon Press. 1983

Brown, Daniel W. *A New Introduction to Islam*, 2nd ed., Sussex, England: Wiley-Blackwell. 2009

Calder, N., J. Mojaddedi, and A. Rippin (eds. and trans.). *Classical Islam: A Sourcebook of Religious Literature*. New York: Routledge. 2003

Chopra, Depak. "Seven Spiritual Laws" DVD

Clasper, Paul. *Eastern Paths and the Christian Way*. Maryknoll, NY: Orbis Books, 1980

*Dyer, Wayne. "Excuses Be Gone." Television Seminar. Public Broadcasting Service. August 2, 2009

Eliade, Mircea. *The Sacred and the Profane: The Nature of Religion*. trans. Willard Trask. New York: Harper and Row. 1959

Eller, Cynthia. "Revealing World Religions". Thinking Strings. CD. 2010

English Translation of the Message of the Quran, trans. Prof. Syed V. Ahmed, Book of Signs Foundation, Lombard, IL, 2006

Faizi, Gloria. *The Bahai Faith: An Introduction*. New Delhi, India: Bahai Publishing Trust. 2003

Fletcher, Joann. *Ancient Egypt: Life, Myth, and Art*. New York: Barnes and Nobles. 2004

Frazier, George. *The Golden Bough: A Study in Magic and Religion* (9 vols). New York: St. Martins Press, 1990

*Freke, Timothy. *The Illustrated Book of Sacred Scriptures*. Wheaton, IL: Theosophical Publishing House. 1998

Goldschmidt, Authur Jr. and Lawrence Davidson. *A Concise History of the Middle East*. Philadelphia, PA: Westview Press, 2010.

Hall, Manly P. *An Encyclopedic Outline of Masonic, Hermetic, Qabbalistic and Rosicrucian Symbolic Philosophy: Being an Interpretation of the Secret Teachings Concealed within the Rituals, Allegories, and Mysteries of all Ages.* Los Angeles: Philosophical Research Society. 1977

Holy Bible: The Open Bible Expanded Edition, NKJV, Thomas Nelson, Nashville, TN, 1983

Hopfe, Lewis M. and Woodward, Mark R. *Religions of the World.* Eleventh Edition. Upper Saddle River, New Jersey: Prentice Hall, Inc., 2009.

Interfaith Resources: Book of Comfort and Healing…from Many Faiths, Interfaith Resources, div. of Special Ideas, Inc., Heltonville, IN, 2010

Kiehl, Erich H. *The Passion of Our Lord.* Grand Rapids: Baker Books. 1990

Lewis, C.S. *The Great Divorce.* New York:Collier Books, Macmillan. 1946

Lings, Martin. *Muhammad: His Life Based on the Earliest Sources.* Rochester Vermont: Inner Traditions. 2006

Luther's Small Catechism with Explanation. St. Louis: Concordia Publishing House. 1986

Mazar, Amihai. *Archaeology of the Land of the Bible: 10,000-586* BCE New York: Double Day. 1990

Menocal, Maria Rosa. *Ornament of the World: How Muslims, Jews, and Christians Created a Culture of Tolerance in Medieval Spain.* New York: Little, Brown, & Co. 2002

Moyer, Bill. "Joseph Campbell and the Power of Myth," PBS Television. DVD. 1988

Murray, Joseph. *The Amazing Laws of Cosmic Mind Power.* West Nyack, NY: Parker Publishing. 1970

Nestle-Aland. *Novum Testamentum Graece*, 26 ed., Stuggart: Deutsche Bibelgesellschaft, 1979

Newman, Jr., Barclay M. *A Concise Greek-English Dictionary of the New Testament*, Stuttgart, Germ: United Bible Society. 1971

Oppenheim, A. Leo. *Ancient Mesopotamia: Portrait of a Dead Civilization*. Chicago: University of Chicago. 1977

Osman, Ahmed. *Moses and Akhenaten: The Secret History of Egypt at the Time of the Exodus*. Rochester, Vermont: Bear and Co. 2002

English Translation of the Message of the Quran, trans. Prof. Syed Ahamed, 2nd ed. Lombard, IL: Book of Signs Foundation. 2006

The Holy Quran: English Translation and its Meaning, ed. The Presidency of Islamic Researchers, IFTA. King Fahd Holy Quran Printing Complex

Redfield, James. *Celestine Prophecy*. New York: Warner Books. 1993

Runes, Dagobert D., ed. *Dictionary of Philosophy*. Totowa, NJ: Littlefield, Adams. 1980

Shri Mataji Nirmala Devi. Website: Madishakti.org/age_of_aquarius.htm. Aug. 4, 2012

Simon, Scott. The Scott Simon Show, National Public Radio. Aired Dec. 11, 2010

Smart, Ninian. *Worldviews: Cross-cultural Explorations of Human Beliefs*. New York: Charles Scribner's Sons. 1983

Spencer, Aida B. and William D. Spencer, eds. *The Global God: Multicultural Evangelical Views of God*. BridgePoint Books. 1998

Steinberg, Milton. *Basic Judaism*. New York: Harvest/Harcourt Brace. 1975

Strong, James. The New Strong's Exhaustive Concordance of the Bible. Nashville: Thomas Nelson. 1984

Stumpf, Samuel E. *Philosophy: History and Problems*, 2nd ed. New York: McGraw Hill. 1977

Teasdale, Wayne. *The Mystic Heart: Discovering a Universal Spirituality in the World's Religion*. Novato, CA: New World Library. 1999

The Rig Veda: An Anthology. Middlesex, England: Penguin Books. 1983

The Song of God: Bhagavad-Gita, trans. Swami Prabhavandanda and C. Isherwood, New York: Mentor Books. 1972

Unger, Merrill. *The New Unger's Bible Dictionary*, ed. R. K. Harrison. Chicago: Moody Press. 1988

Wiesel, Elie. *Messengers of God: Biblical Portraits and Legends*. New York: Simon and Schuster. 1994

World Scripture: A Comparative Anthology of Sacred Texts. Project of the International Religious Foundation. St. Paul, Minn: Paragon House. 1991

Zacharias, Ravi. "Absolutism in a Relativistic Culture," Ravi Zacharias International Ministries. audio cassette

ENDNOTES

1. Gobekli-Tepe is now considered to be the oldest sacred site discovered on earth, dating back to about 9000 BCE, not long after the last ice age according to the article in *National Geographic Magazine*, June 2011, "The Birth of Religion: The World's First Temple."

2. Gen. 12:3c

3. Of all the world religions today, only two of them at the most along with their Scriptures were birthed in the modern era: Sikhism of the 16th cent. and the Baha'i Faith of the 19th cent.

4. Ninian Smart expresses it this way: "For most of human history, people have had rather rudimentary ideas about their own and other peoples' beliefs. Often imprisoned within a culture or credo, they have had no desire or the chance to venture on a more detached and sensitive exploration of religion. Too much tied up with their own concerns, they have often found it easier to dismiss the faiths and feelings of others as heretical, devilish, ignorant, or antisocial…" Smart, p. 2

5. The Hindu Vedas, Zoroaster's *Avesta*, and the Hebrew Scriptures were all likely being penned during the same

centuries in the late 2nd millennium and early first millennium BCE) (Hopfe and Woodward pp. 77, 234, 253).

6. Gautama Buddha referred to himself as "Talhagata" which means "truth-gatherer," Hopfe-Woodward, p. 140. 7.
An acquaintance of author, Herve Decordey speaks of this phrase "snippets of eternity" and I received permission from him to quote him, placing it into this book.

8. The word "office" is a better fit than "position." The office of prophet is not a position in the sense of a worldly career. Prophets often received rejections, ridicules, scoffing, mocking, persecution, imprisonment, and maybe even being killed for their message. But they go forward obediently, propelled by the Spirit of God, trusting God, knowing the eternal reward that awaits them.

9. The ancient and current capital city of Yemen, Saba, preserves this place where Sheba came from, c.f. Unger p. 1172.

10. Holy Quran, 2:225 p. 50-51).

11. A BBC radio listener will frequently hear the word "corruption" mentioned by its reporters going on somewhere in the world. As this book was being compiled, Dr. Ravi Zacharias reported on his radio program, "Just Thinking," a new global poll reported by BBC on the number one concern of people. It "is no longer poverty and the environment. It is corruption."

12. There are many ministers and messenger-lights in our age broadcasting their messages for the betterment of humanity, lifting human beings to greater goodness through sages, prophets, priests, and teachers.

13. Baha'ullah, Abdul-Baha, and Rumi to note a few.

14. The author wrote this in 2002 and had remained unpublished until this book. It was one of the last pieces added, after the

manuscript was complete, in the proofreading stage, but is technically the very first piece of writing in this book.

15. Many scholars, observers, and commentators of these times often speak of the clashing of ideologies including among the two main camps of the absolutists and the relativists.

16. There are ample examples of magic incantation in ancient sacred writings, too many to cite here, but one text example is the Egyptian Book of the Dead.

17. Quran speaks of this using the Arabic term is Jahiliyya, Brown, p. 302.

18. John Bright's book *The Kingdom of God* is a history of the biblical view of the kingdom of God on earth, spiritually understood, through the Old Testament and the New Testament and the Church age to the end of the Age.

19. A day or two after "the author penned, that is, typed these words, he pulled the following book from his shelf, not having read it but intending to sell online: *The Amazing Laws of Cosmic Mind Power*. He first scrolled through the table of contents and saw that it has a chapter on "The Secret Law of faith." The opening paragraph defines faith in a remarkably similar way: "Faith is the fusion of your thought and feeling, or your mind and heart, which is so complete, inflexible, and impregnable...."

20. Christianity does also have one or two at the most, required rituals to enter Heaven: baptism and communion. Sikhism also has two main rituals, baptism and a communion meal, which no doubt is borrowed from or at least influenced by Christianity).

21. This thought is based on the Magic theory of the origin of religion as espoused by James George Frazier in *The Golden Bough: A Study in Magic and Religion*.

22. Matthew quotes Zechariah 11:12 but ascribes it to the prophet Jeremiah, Matt. 27:9.

23. Mahavira, the founder of Jainism, was called Jina by his disciples which means "conqueror," Hopfe and Woodward p.124).

24. Quran uses the term jihad, which means "struggle," is used in a more general sense of "striving for the cause of Allah," not just in a fighting or military context, c.f. Quran 29:69).

25. See Rabbi Steinberg's discussion on this, pp. 61-63 but on p. 112, he explicitly states Judaism has expressly rejected the Christian doctrine of original sin since its founding in the 1st cent.).

26. "The heart is deceitful above all things, and desperately wicked; who can know it?" Jer. 17:9 NKJV, and "all have sinned and fallen short of the glory of God" Rom. 3:23 NKJV).

27. Sigmund Freud's theory that the original of religion was from the Oedipus syndrome, all boys natural sexual desire for their mothers, creating a tremendous guilt which produced religion seems to be a ludicrous and very unenlightened theory, Hopfe and Woodward, p. 7)

28. quoted by Rabbi J. Romberg in a sermon August 17, 2012.

29. This translation does not use the word "blasphemy" but "most monstrous," but in the subject index, it is listed under topic of "blasphemy," p. 2039)

30. Religion scholar Cynthia Eller believes all religions are a syncretism of various ideas, beliefs and practices picked up from various sources and packaged into one unified system, Eller, *Thinking Strings*, Introduction, CD.

31. C.S. Lewis may not have been the first one to have written of an imaginary journey of a soul from hell to heaven, but also

an account is found in Islamic tradition, Calder, Mojaddedi, and Rippin)

32. Luther's explanation to the first commandment of the Ten Commandments, LSCE, p. 9)

33. This idea of living history of the interpretation of sacred text I was certainly exposed to in seminary. I have checked the few hermeneutics books in my library and do not find a reference to this thought pattern. It may have been a synthesis from my hermeneutics and homiletics studies that produced this thought.

34. The word "ecumenical" broadly means "world" but is often used in the more strict sense of applied Christian inter-denominational circles (CGEDNT p. 124).

SUBJECT INDEX

Due to the formatting of this book, the locations on the pages of the subjects below were modestly altered. Use this table to locate the subjects:

Pages 0 - 74	No Changes
Pages 75 - 99	Subtract 1 page
Pages 100 - 160	Subtract 2 pages
Pages 161 - 199	Subtract 3 pages
Pages 200 - 299	Subtract 4 pages
Pages 300 - 359	Subtract 5 pages
Pages 360 -371	No Changes